Slade Cutter

Slade Cutter

SUBMARINE WARRIOR

Carl LaVO

NAVAL INSTITUTE PRESS

Annapolis, Maryland

Naval Institute Press
291 Wood Road
Annapolis, MD 21402

Library of Congress Cataloging-in-Publication Data
LaVO, Carl, 1944–
    Slade Cutter, submarine warrior / Carl LaVO.
        p. cm.
Includes bibliographical references and index.
    ISBN 1-55750-505-5
    1. Cutter, Slade Deville, 1911– 2. United States. Navy—Officers—Biography.
3. World War, 1939-1945—Naval operations, American. 4. World War, 1939-1945—
Naval operations—Submarine. 5. World War, 1939-1945—Campaigns—Pacific Area.
I. Title.
    V63.C88L39 2003
    940.54'51'092—dc21

                                                            2003005262

Printed in the United States of America on acid-free paper ⊚
10 09 08 07 06 05 04 03   9 8 7 6 5 4 3 2
First printing

For all the heroes who went before—and for all
the heroes yet to come

For my father-in-law, Albert Ferber Sr.,
who served on the destroyer USS *Picking*
during World War II. He lost his last battle on
7 February 2002, but won the ultimate war.

And for my personal hero, my father, Carl Sr.,
who served in World War II aboard the destroyer
USS *Halford*—from Guadalcanal to Japan.

CONTENTS

ACKNOWLEDGMENTS

In 1994, Paul Stillwell of the U.S. Naval Institute approached me about writing a biography of Slade Deville Cutter, former heavyweight boxer, All-American football player, and one of the most decorated Navy officers of World War II, winner of four Navy Crosses.

Paul, as director of Oral History at the Institute, became fascinated with Cutter's incredible life story while completing a series of taped interviews with the retired captain in 1985. After reading my book, *Back from the Deep*, published by the Naval Institute Press in 1994, he contacted me in the belief I might condense the oral history, add to it, and produce a biography of the storied submarine captain. Flattered, I said I would attempt the biography as long as Captain Cutter was willing. Slade is a humble, self-deprecating man who eschews publicity. He only agreed to the project after being approached by Paul, reading my book, and then reviewing a proposed outline for the project.

There are many people to whom I owe a debt of gratitude during the time it took me to research and write this book, not the least of whom is Paul Stillwell. Among others are Tom Cutler, senior acquisitions editor at Naval Institute Press, and my good friend, Tom Taylor, a resident of Bucks County and retired U.S. Navy captain who served for thirty years as an intelligence officer in the Special Operations community with an emphasis on counterterrorism. Tom, who is an admirer of Slade, reviewed my manuscript in its various stages, giving me an understanding of the fine points of the Navy's hierarchy, how its career track works and how Slade fit into it. Tom also accompanied me to Annapolis where he met Slade for the first time in 1999.

I also am grateful to Gary A. LaValley, archivist at the Nimitz Library, United States Naval Academy, and archives technician Beverly Lyall for their help in my research of Slade Cutter's Academy years. Many thanks to the folks at Levittown Regional Library in Bucks County who assisted me in viewing microfilm and microfiche, as well as securing interlibrary loans of archival material. Also a nod to dear friends at Café Ferraro where the morning-after edit of the night before's work took place over well-supplied coffee.

A tip of the hat to Dave Bouslog. As the author of *Maru Killer: The War Patrols of the USS Seahorse* published in 1996, his interviews with *Seahorse* veterans gave me greater understanding of their first five war patrols during which Slade Cutter was initially executive officer, then commanding officer. A note of appreciation to Bill Budding, who served under Captain Cutter as fire control officer, and shipmates Sheldon Stubbs, Charles Kovach, Phillip Wilson, Jim McGettigan, and Roland Lehman. They attended a *Seahorse* reunion in 1999 on Tilghman Island, Maryland, where my wife Mary Anne and I had the opportunity to retrace the story of the submarine through their eyes. Also thanks to James O'Meara, *Seahorse* lookout, who provided additional help from his home in Grants Pass, Oregon.

The several years it took to complete this work required Mary Anne's able assistance in condensing and crystallizing the narrative. We often discussed the many episodes of Slade Cutter's life, and she accompanied me on trips to Annapolis to visit the Cutters, where she not only got to know them but filmed them for this book.

My thanks also to David J. Estrin, who carefully copyedited the manuscript of this book and suggested many changes that strengthened and streamlined the text.

Finally, my deepest thanks to Slade and Ruth Cutter for their warm hospitality on Tilghman Island, at their home in Annapolis, and at the Army-Navy game in Philadelphia in December 2001 where Slade, incidentally, met and sat next to President George W. Bush. During our visits, the Cutters were very patient through all the questions and the audio tape sessions. Early this year they gave us a guided tour of their retirement center's recreational facilities. To ward off the debilitating effects of Parkinson's Disease, Slade daily swims laps in a swimming pool and works out on a stationary bicycle. During our visit, we wandered into a room containing a pool table. Mary Anne suggested I challenge Slade to a game. It was a spirited match. He won. As usual.

At age ninety-one, Slade is an amazing person. While driving home from Annapolis, Mary Anne and I caught an old Paul Simon ballad on the radio. The song, "The Boxer," is about overcoming great obstacles in life. To me it captures the essence of this man I have grown to know and admire. Slade Cutter is that boxer who persevered in battle and overcame great obstacles to bring his men back home alive. I hope you enjoy his story.

Slade Cutter

1

Test of Valor

SLADE CUTTER gripped the tubular steel handles of the search periscope and leaned into the rubber padding of the bifocals. Slowly, he rotated the eyepiece 360 degrees, walking it around in a circle in the conning tower of the USS *Pompano,* the submarine that had been his home for nearly four years. Cutter wanted a complete view of the ocean surface ninety feet above. Despite the fact it was an hour before sunset, darkness had apparently descended over Sagami Bay. Perhaps a heavy overcast or fog was responsible. Lt. Cdr. Willis Thomas, in command of the *Pompano,* had Cutter, his executive officer, take a look to confirm what he had seen: a dark, glassy sea with no apparent surface traffic. Both men agreed it was safe for the submarine to surface. The nearby coast of Japan's Honshu province bristled with artillery and watch posts, all in regular radio contact with reconnaissance aircraft, patrol boats, destroyers, and cruisers searching the bay for any sign of a submarine. For Cutter and his shipmates, surfacing near a warship could well be catastrophic. Every man aboard knew the probable consequences: the submarine's thin steel hull, little more than a half-inch thick and made of welded plates, could not withstand the impact of shelling from the big guns of a destroyer or cruiser. The *Pompano* also was operating in the shallow part of the bay, where it was often no deeper than the submarine was long. Escaping depth charge attack would be difficult, if not impossible, in such shallow water.

Still, the submarine high command (Commander Submarines, U.S. Pacific Fleet [ComSubPac]) in Hawaii had good reasons to position the *Pompano* in the bay. The submarine had been lurking there for six days, waiting for troop transports and cargo haulers transiting the ten-mile-wide passage between the Izu-Hanot Peninsula of Honshu and O-shima Island to the east. The bay, within view of snow-capped Mount Fuji, was a nautical highway between Tokyo Bay thirty miles north and newly conquered territories in the South Pacific. In the summer of 1942, the pace of shipping had increased, much of it to reinforce Japanese control of the Solomon Islands and the air base on Guadalcanal Island at the eastern outer ring of Japan's southern defenses. Tokyo expected the United States to take aim at the Solomons. In fact, that was just what was planned.

The Navy was about to mount its first major counteroffensive of the Pacific War—the amphibious invasion of Guadalcanal. To support that strategy, the Navy had deployed seventeen undersea boats to the central Pacific to blockade Truk Atoll, a heavily fortified naval base supplying the Solomons. Another half-dozen older boats were dispatched northwest from Hawaii to interdict enemy supplies and troops being shipped from Japan. The *Pompano,* with an unsurpassed reputation for skill and daring, took the most forward position.

On the evening of 9 August 1942, intelligence from U.S. codebreakers indicated a large warship, perhaps a battleship or aircraft carrier en route to the front, was expected to pass through Sagami-Wan Bay that night. If a submarine could slip in and sink the vessel, it would be a tremendous morale boost in a Pacific war that had steadily gone against the United States since the surprise attack on Pearl Harbor and the Philippines nine months earlier. To those in the *Pompano,* it was imperative to surface as soon as possible to allow the boat to use its high surface speed to locate its assigned target and sink it. No one was more anxious to begin the hunt than Cutter. He was a dominating presence at well over six feet tall and more than two hundred pounds, a bear of a man with a square jaw and determined countenance, "one big ball of fire," as a crewman put it. His eyes mirrored the crew's determination to carry the war to Japan, and he often told confidants, "I hate to lose."

At 1915, the skipper gave the order to surface.

Cutter and four lookouts scrambled up the ladder of the conning tower to the bridge as the black, unmarked submarine bore upward with the release of air into the water-filled ballast tanks that girded the 310-foot-long vessel, and it broke the surface in a frothy upheaval. Simultaneously, the boat's powerful diesels roared to life. Electricity generated by the diesels began recharging the 126 battery cells in the keel, each the size of a crewman and weighing nearly a ton.

Cutter and the lookouts had expected to emerge under the cover of darkness, and they were aghast to discover there was no darkness. "My God, we thought we were naked. It was daylight!" Cutter later remarked. "Well, nobody was around so we decided to wait it out, because it was going to be dark in a little while." However, at twilight disaster struck the *Pompano.*

On the starboard quarter searchlights illuminated the boat and fire belched from a distant warship. It was a Japanese cruiser, firing a broadside from turrets forward, amidships and aft from half a mile away.

Cutter sounded the alarm on the bridge intercom. "Clear the bridge! Dive! Dive! Two hundred feet! Cruiser firing at us! Rig for depth charge!"

The lookouts vaulted through the hatch, Cutter close behind as the officer of the deck dogged the watertight hatch cover behind him. The exec landed with a heavy thud as the deafening *ah-oo-gah* of the diving alarm reverberated throughout the submarine. Crewmen raced to their stations. Diesels went silent. The *Pompano* plunged in a steep descent into the ocean depths. It still took almost a full minute to clear the surface, an eternity to the crew—long enough for the first shells to scream past and splash loudly into the ocean. "We heard them hit the water as we went down," said Cutter.

The boat's sonar operator reported that the cruiser was operating with as many as five other vessels. Crewmen stood at their posts in stony silence, some staring at the overhead. In each of the submarine's seven watertight compartments, talkers listened on battle telephones for reports from the tracking team in the conning tower monitoring the approach of a destroyer.

"He's turned toward us. . . . He's coming in. . . ."

The men froze. Was the submarine deep enough?

The sound of propellers was faint at first, a slight throbbing outside the hull—but it grew in intensity as the destroyer drew closer. The sound of screws cleaving the ocean rose to a shriek—like a freight train racing through a tunnel. It seemed the destroyer would carve its way right through the *Pompano's* hull. Crewmen, their hearts in their throats, turned an ear to the pressure hull around them. Cutter's mouth was dry: "I thought school was out. I didn't know how we were going to get out of there."

The splash of depth-charge canisters could be heard. The *Pompano* dropped below two hundred feet as the first depth charge exploded with an audible "click" followed by a hammer-like concussion. Seawater smashed against the boat, rushing through its superstructure—some believed momentarily that the vessel had been holed. More than a dozen explosions ripped the ocean at thirty-second intervals. Heavy objects intermittently hit the hull and deck and bounced off. Shock waves battered the boat, shaking it violently, knocking crewmen to their knees. Broken glass from shattered instruments showered compartments. Chunks of insulating cork fell from the overhead. In the stern, an exhaust valve ruptured, spewing a fountain of seawater into the engine room. Crewmen fought to control the flooding: nothing could be done. Bilges began to fill, but the sump pumps could not be started because the noise would give away the submarine's location.

Cutter, passing orders to his men, cursed the situation. They had been sighted on the surface; a cruiser had shelled them; a destroyer was dropping depth charges on them; and multiple vessels were triangulating on the location of the *Pompano*. The situation was dire.

The boat slid deeper.

At 403 feet, the pressure caused more cork insulation to buckle and fall from the overhead. The superstructure crackled ominously, threatening to rip apart. Skipper Thomas demanded more speed from the electric motors, despite the drain on weakened batteries. He had no choice but to start the bilge pumps in the engine room to begin expelling seawater threatening to sink the boat. Predictably, the cranky equipment and the high-pitched squeal of the boat's rotating propeller shafts betrayed the *Pompano* to hydrophone operators on the warships above. The destroyer charged again, ready with a fresh barrage of depth charges. All it would take was one to detonate below the submarine to break its back and finish it.

Thomas secured the pumps for silent running as the sonar operator counted down the approach. "He's at 180 . . . 170 . . . 160 . . . 150 . . . he's coming in." The sound of the approaching warship rent the thick air. Would this be the end?

Depth charges fell fast as the submarine veered off its track, trying to escape to the west. Detonations whipped the boat wildly. Its steel frame groaned and creaked under the strain. Ventilation pipes vibrated dangerously, threatening to break loose and fall from the overhead. The leak in the engine room became more pronounced. The boat took a sharp upward angle.

The *Pompano* was still alive but barely. Officers moved through the compartments, whispering encouragement and gathering status reports. The silence was nerve-racking. Even the squeak of sandals or a crewman accidentally dropping something caused others to bristle, fearful the destroyer would relocate the boat. In utter silence the submarine drifted as search vessels crisscrossed astern. Soon the sound of a heavy ship with a four-ship escort could be heard approaching. The convoy thrummed past on the port side of the pinned-down submarine—no doubt the *Pompano*'s intended target.

As the convoy sailed away, the submarine was at the limit of its endurance. The buildup of carbon dioxide and heat had worn down the crew after being submerged for more than sixteen hours. Some were nauseous from the tension and stale air. Lead-acid batteries in the boat's keel were nearly spent; the struggle to maintain position against the great current that flows north through the bay toward Tokyo had drained them. The batteries needed to be recharged, but that could only be accomplished if the submarine surfaced so the diesels could power the generators. But seawater in the engine room had reached the deck plates, swamping the two aft engines and short-circuiting the generators. The motors subsequently shut down. Suddenly, at a depth of 294 feet, the nose of the submarine hit the bottom of the bay with a jolt, and the sonar pod was crushed beneath the boat. Without sonar and with no motors to power an escape, the *Pompano* seemed to have lost its last chance. The boat was helpless.

Thomas summoned Cutter to his quarters and told him and another officer to get all the ship's records together, that the *Pompano* would have to be scuttled after surfacing to allow crewmen a chance to get off. Cutter pleaded with Thomas to give the boat a fighting chance, to stay submerged for as long as humanly possible. "And he went into his room and stayed in there for a while. I guess he had given up," said Cutter. With no power to propel the *Pompano,* it could only lift off the ocean floor by blowing its ballast tanks. It would then be at the whim of the sea and the stiff current. Yet, if the boat could remain submerged long enough, if the flooding in the engine room could be slowed, the *Pompano* might still lose the hunter-killers.

The skipper, having thought it over, agreed to the plan. But everything hinged on Cutter, as the navigator, in steering a westerly course in the northbound current. If he could reach the coast away from the shipping channel, he reasoned, it might be safe for the *Pompano* to surface, start the engines, and slip away before daybreak. The trouble was the exec had no idea of where the submarine was after the pursuit. All he knew for certain was that the five-knot current in the bay was strong enough to keep the boat moving. But that current swept toward Tokyo where capture and death waited. Everything depended on using the submarine's hand-operated rudder to buck the current slightly to the west. It was a slim chance. But at least it was a chance.

The fate of the boat and its crew was in Cutter's hands. He had little time to contemplate how a hardworking boy from a Depression-era farm in Illinois who had hoped to one day become a flutist for the Chicago Symphony Orchestra now found himself trapped on the bottom of a bay off the coast of Japan with an enemy above intent on destroying him.

2

The Man from Fox River

WHEN SLADE CUTTER was a child the furthest thing from his mind was becoming a submarine sailor. In fact, the idea repulsed him. Radio broadcasts of a disaster aboard the U.S. submersible S-4 in December 1927 reinforced that feeling. For two weeks that month, the fifteen-year-old eldest son of a an Illinois grain farmer lay in bed with diphtheria, diagnosed during a visit to his grandmother's house in the farming hamlet of Oswego, Illinois. The contagious bacterial infection required a complete quarantine of the house. A big red sign warned visitors to stay away. From his sick bed, Cutter tuned in to hour-by-hour radio accounts of the unfolding undersea tragedy.

The S-4 had been on a submerged periscope training run in a designated safe zone near where the U.S. Coast Guard cutter *Paulding* was on patrol in the Atlantic Ocean off the tip of Cape Cod. The ship had been busy all month, trying to stop Canadian and Cuban rumrunners from rendezvousing with bootleggers off the Massachusetts coast. Making eighteen knots on the afternoon of 17 December, the *Paulding* veered off course to avoid a fishing boat and crossed the feathery wake of the S-4's periscope. The ship's bow rammed the submarine's starboard hull and conning tower, ripping them open and sending the S-4 plunging like a stone to the ocean floor. Though lifeboats were lowered from the *Paulding*, no survivors surfaced—only oil and air bubbles. One hundred feet below, the skipper, Lt. Cdr. Roy K. Jones, and thirty-three crewmen managed to escape flooding in the control room by sealing themselves in the engine and motor rooms in the stern. Six others took refuge in the forward torpedo room. There, they prayed for a miracle to save them. By the afternoon of the following day, Navy divers were able to reach the wreckage but could not get inside. They heard Morse code tapped out by survivors wielding sledgehammers against the hull in the forward torpedo room. However, there was no sign of life in the stern compartments. In the days that followed, a combination of bad weather and inability to refloat the submarine foiled rescue attempts.

"And for ten days or two weeks," said Cutter, "they'd hear tapping on the hull, and they finally died; the tapping stopped. And here I am locked up in my grandma's house with diphtheria, and the radio the only thing I had for diversion. I can remember saying, 'How can anybody be so stupid as to get into one of those damn things?' I guess I sort of used that to soften the blow of those poor devils down there in that thing."

The horrific drama convinced Cutter that duty in the "iron coffin" service was something to be avoided. Yet forces were already at work around the world that would eventually set his course. It was a world heading toward the cataclysm of a greater war than the Great War. In 1927, three men who would alter history came to prominence. In Japan, twenty-seven-year-old Prince Hirohito was about to be crowned emperor. In Italy, Benito Mussolini had consolidated control of a fascist government. And in Germany, Adolf Hitler was attracting populist appeal with a book he wrote in prison. *Mein Kampf* sanctified war for its "cleansing" effect, blamed Jews and communists for Germany's defeat in the Great War, and glorified the country's ancient military tradition.

For boys like Slade growing up in the pastoral, hard-work environment of the Fox River Valley, fifty miles west of Chicago, war and service to the country was the stuff of distant fantasy. Born in Chicago on 1 November 1911, Cutter grew up on his family's 250-acre farm on the Fox River, a mile from Oswego and seven miles downstream from industrial Aurora. A railroad trolley passed through the farm, giving the family easy access to the outside world. The homestead consisted of fifty acres of sloping, dense woodlands along the river and another two hundred acres of cleared, level ground of extraordinary fertility. Storms sweeping off nearby Lake Michigan produced moisture like clockwork, ensuring a good harvest even when other areas of Illinois suffered from drought. The farm dated back nearly a century and was the fruit of an amazing odyssey by Slade's great-grandfather, which in turn inspired Slade's own adventure in years to come.

In 1849, young Henry Clay Cutter hoped to cash in on the gold that had been discovered in California. Cutter left his home near Boston with his brother-in-law, his uncle, and a trusted hired hand, boarding a ship for Panama via Havana. At the Isthmus, they hired natives to take them up the Chagres River in canoes, then hiked over the mountains to the Pacific where they joined eighty prospectors, who had purchased an old Spanish ship and set sail for San Francisco. The ship was caught in a dead zone six hundred miles off the coast of Mexico where no winds blew. It took two months for the ship finally to reach Acapulco, where Cutter buried his brother-in-law, who was killed in the explosion of a ship's cannon (during a ceremonial salute to the city for its kindness to the sailors). Cutter decided to walk the rest of the way, a trek of more than one thousand miles. Reunited with his uncle and their hired hand in San Francisco, he went to the site of the initial gold strike at Sutter's Creek in the Sierra Mountains, and in eighteen months worked a rich vein in an abandoned mine shaft. With his earnings, Cutter sailed back to Boston, then journeyed west by train to Illinois in search of a place to settle down. Reaching the Fox River, he was impressed by the lush beauty of the valley and the slow moving river, once navigated in colonial times by French-Canadian fur trappers. He bought the land, built a sturdy, three-story home, married, and had four sons and a daughter, naming his boys after friends back in Massachusetts—Scott, Cyrus, Watts, Slade, and Blanche. (Watts and Slade were last names.) Cutter also chose their future occupations—doctor, pharmacist, veterinarian, and farmer. Watts D. Cutter became the farmer. His son, Watts C., eventually inherited the farm. Slade Deville Cutter was born to Watts C. and his young wife, Esther Sundeen, the daughter of Swedish immigrants who founded a department store in Moline on the Mississippi River. The couple met at the University of Illinois where Esther was a freshman and Watts, president of the senior class of 1910, was completing an agricultural degree. At the time, Watts's mother wanted to be more involved with her Methodist friends by moving to Oswego. Thus she made a deal with her son: If she paid for him to go to college to get a degree, he would return home to take over the farm so she and her husband could move to town. "That was the deal, and he kept the deal," Slade said of his father. "But he was never happy."

Not that his father could not make a go of the farm. On the contrary, through good management skills, the farm made the family self-sufficient with a narrow profit. The third-generation Cutters reared three boys and a girl while cultivating oats, corn, and wheat with teams of horses and a Fordson tractor. The Cutters also employed a field hand whom they paid forty dollars a month. They gave him the use of a house, garden, and a cow to induce him to live on the farm year-round. As soon as the Cutter boys were old enough, they helped too. "You worked. You worked. You worked hard," recalled eldest son Slade. "When I was twelve years old, I went out in the fields and did a man's work as soon as school was out." That meant in the summer time getting up at 5:30 A.M. to feed the horses and hitch them to the plows, then working the fields until 5:30 P.M., six days a week with only a half-hour break for lunch. The family expected the kids to carry their fair share of the chores, and punishment for misdeeds was doled out equally through tough discipline. The three boys, fifteen months apart, often got into trouble and the expectation was that if one was punished for a prank, they all were punished.

"I spent a lot of weekends with my grandparents," recalled Cutter. "I spent this one weekend, and my brothers were in real serious trouble. My mother had collected twelve dozen fertile eggs for a neighbor to put in an incubator to hatch. My two brothers, who had collected these eggs, went out into the yard and had thrown all of them away." The boys used them for target practice against the rafters of the barn. "Of course, they were going to get a spanking, and my father was there to give them the spanking, and I said, 'Grandma, take me back.' Because every time any one of us got a spanking, we all did, because we were always into things together." This time, however, he was spared.

The Cutters wanted their kids to make a better life for themselves— off the farm. "And my mother was the motivating factor there," recalled her son. "She would never let any of us be farmers. Not that she would prevent us from doing it, but she kept harping on it: 'You've got to do better than that; you can't be here.'"

Slade often was reminded of his great-grandfather's adventure getting to the gold rush fields of California. Though he never knew him, a photograph of him taken the day before he died hung prominently in the Cutter household. The photo showed two-year-old Slade sitting on his great-grandfather's lap.

There was no perceptible gold rush on the horizon for kids growing up on the farms of Fox River. Moreover, educational opportunities were slim in the valley. When the Cutters enrolled Slade in the farm community's public school at age five, there weren't any students in the first grade. "So they put me in the second grade. When I got to the fifth grade, there wasn't anybody in the fifth grade, so they put me in the sixth grade." Slade, whom classmates nicknamed "Devil" after his French middle name, excelled at English but was deficient in mathematics because he had skipped two grades. "It was a little country, one-room school. The most we ever had was eighteen students total in seven grades," he said. Graduating from eighth grade at age eleven in Aurora, school officials would not allow him to enter high school because of his youth. So he repeated eighth grade.

Cutter was unusually large and he naturally was attracted to school athletics. His parents, however, were determined to keep him out of competitive sports, especially his father, who had suffered an eye injury playing football for the University of Illinois. At age thirty-nine, he developed a malignancy in that eye and it was removed. Physicians blamed the disease on his earlier injury. "This is why I couldn't play in athletics," said Cutter. Nevertheless, his father whetted his son's appetite by taking him to football games at his alma mater in Champaign. One such clash was between the University of Michigan and the Illini in 1925. Legendary halfback Harold "Red" Grange on the Illinois team made quite an impression. "I remember that fellow, when the opponents punted—he was a safety man—and he would wait back from the ball, and he would catch the ball on a dead run," recalled Cutter. "He wouldn't stand to get under the ball and then catch it. He would stay back of it so he could catch it full bore with no fair catch business at all."

Slade's father was a good singer and belonged to a barbershop quartet that practiced regularly at the Cutter home. His mother played the piano. Slade and one of his younger brothers followed her example by taking piano lessons. However, Slade suffered a fractured knuckle in an apple fight in the farm orchard. The knuckle never healed properly, hampering Slade's ability to play. Slade sought some other musical outlet, and found the flute, which he practiced by the hour. So great was his passion that his mother frequently chased him from the house and he would go into the woods by the river to practice.

Cutter joined the junior high school band at Aurora. To belong, students were required to take private lessons. "Well, I couldn't afford private lessons. What we would do would be to get one teacher, and maybe four of five of us would take lessons at the same time. I remember my share of the cost was twenty-five cents for a half hour." By the time Slade reached high school, he was a budding talent who arranged to take professional lessons every Sunday morning for a year from Arthur Kitt, first flute in the Chicago Symphony Orchestra. To recover the five-dollar cost of each lesson, Cutter taught nine students back home. "I got a dollar a lesson, and I had enough pupils to pay for my own music lessons and the train fare to Chicago."

As a high school junior, Slade entered competition, and won the Aurora city championship at age sixteen with an astonishing performance of a classical work that he arranged. "Technique is everything; the faster you can play, the better," he recalled. "If you can triple tongue and things like that, which I could—that's the criteria for that. I played the 'Carnival of Venice.' That's a trumpet solo, a famous trumpet solo with all the variations. The flute doesn't go below middle C, so the score had to be changed. I had taken music appreciation and a little bit of composition, so I rewrote the thing. I did it with black India ink and did a real good job. I wrote it as I played it."

Cutter not only took the city championship, he won the district and state competitions, and then took aim at the national title. The U.S.

Interscholastic Band Contest was staged in Joliet in 1928, just seven miles from the family farm. The judge was famed conductor and composer John Philip Sousa, whose band was in Chicago at the time. The competition was held in a large auditorium with a balcony in the back where Sousa was seated. "Wasn't that something? John Philip Sousa," recalled Cutter. "I didn't know he was in the Navy then. I didn't know who he was." Impressing the bandleader with his arrangement as well as his ability to play, Cutter captured the national trophy.

Sousa was in Joliet to recruit young musicians for his band, which was planning a series of farewell performances throughout the country that summer. One of the musicians with him was a young clarinet player from Chicago by the name of Benny Goodman, who invited Cutter to join the band for the tour. Though the invitation was an honor, Cutter turned it down because of his intense ambition to join the Chicago Symphony Orchestra. The shortest route to that was through attending the Sherwood School of Music in Chicago where symphony musicians were teachers. Though he enrolled in classes that summer, he soon came to a bitter self-discovery.

"I began to realize that I didn't have it," he said. "You've got to have everything. If you want to be a top musician, you've got to have rhythm. I had the ear, and I had the technique, but I didn't have the rhythm." So abruptly he turned his back on the ambition that had inspired him for so many years. "I just said, 'I can't do it. I've got to do something else.' When you are seventeen years old, you don't worry too much about those things."

For a summer job between his junior and senior years, Cutter took a job at the All-Steel-Equip Company in Aurora where he got a rough awakening to business practices in his valley. "In those days, it was open shop in Aurora, and anybody that tried to organize a union in the plant got fired. And if you got fired, you couldn't get another job anywhere in the Aurora area because you were blacklisted by the Fox River Valley Manufacturing Association." It was a practice that appalled young Slade. Though the effort was a closely guarded secret, he knew about it because his father worked for the association following his bout with cancer.

After Cutter's high school graduation the following year, the equipment company rehired him at twenty-six cents an hour. He had no money for college, nor could his family afford it. Therefore, it appeared in the summer of 1929 that he would have to make his way in Aurora's factories. Then one warm Sunday, an attractive older woman drove up to the Cutters' Fox River farm in a gleaming Cadillac LaSalle luxury sedan. What happened next was to change Slade Cutter's life forever.

3

The Six-Hundred-Dollar Tryout

M RS. SAM LOOMIS stepped from the sedan and completely surprised the Cutters. The big shock for Slade was that she was his father's high school girlfriend. Slade overheard bits and pieces of the animated conversation that followed. Apparently one of Mrs. Loomis's sons was sick. And there was something about Annapolis on the Chesapeake Bay. "Hell, I didn't know where Annapolis was. They were talking about Annapolis. I thought it was in Indiana—Indianapolis. I had no idea where. The biggest body of water I had ever seen was Lake Michigan, and that was only a couple of times."

Mrs. Loomis was in need of a favor. Sam Jr., who was about Slade's age, had contracted tropical undulant fever in the Philippines, then a U.S. territory. The disease, contracted through contaminated milk or meat, caused aches, pains, loss of appetite, and weakness. The family had been stationed in the Philippines because Sam's father was commander of Destroyer Division 38 of the Asiatic Fleet and commanding officer of the destroyer *Tracy*, based at Cavite, the big naval base guarding Manila Bay. At Cavite, a doctor advised Mrs. Loomis to take Sam Jr. back to the United States where he could get plenty of fresh air and sunshine. She and her two sons subsequently returned to Aurora where her parents lived. She thought of the Cutter farm; it would be ideal to speed her son's recuperation. So, she drove out there "cold turkey," as Slade put it, to ask if Sam could stay on the farm until late summer when he was due to enroll in the Severn School back East. The school in Maryland was a preparatory institution for students entering the U.S. Naval Academy in nearby Annapolis.

Just as Mrs. Loomis had imagined, the farm proved to be the perfect antidote to Sam's illness, and he and Slade became best of friends. Both the Cutters and Mrs. Loomis marveled at the close bond between the two. By late summer, Sam had fully recovered and left for Severn School.

For Slade, the future was still in flux.

Although he continued to work his summer job at All-Steel-Equip, the practice of blacklisting gnawed at him, especially after witnessing the harrowing mistreatment of one of All-Steel's employees. "Harry Hardwick was his name. He had six children, didn't have any teeth; I guess he was forty-five years old. They had a paint shop and these pieces of all-steel equipment—we made lockers—the doors, the sides, and the backs were all in sheets before they got assembled. They would bring them on a conveyor belt that would carry the parts down into this tank of paint, come up, and then go into the baking oven. The tank was about ten feet deep, five feet long, and maybe two feet wide. After a while the paint would get skins in it, and they had to strain it and clean the tank out. They would pump the paint out, and lower Harry down there on the hoist. He'd start cleaning the tank with rags until he would pass out. They would haul him up, take him outside, and lean him up against the building until he came to, and then put him down again. "That is what they did to people in those days. You go up, as I have done, to Newport, Rhode Island, and see those homes on the waterfront up there, where the Morgans and the Vanderbilts and whoever they were—they all came out of the blood of the immigrants that they put into the coal mines and railways. I'm not what you would call a liberal exactly, but I am sympathetic to those people who suffered that way in the time when they were terribly exploited. I saw it in this factory that I was in."

Disillusioned, Cutter considered college, eyeing the University of Illinois, his father's alma mater. However, neither he nor his family could afford it. So he applied for and received a music scholarship to Elmhurst College, a religious school with an enrollment of three hundred students in suburban Chicago. "I was just there," said Cutter. "I didn't learn anything to help me at all in the courses I took. The English was good, but I was always good in English. That was about all I took. I just killed the year is what it amounted to." As a diversion, he joined the Blackhawk Symphony Orchestra, a community orchestra based in Aurora, where he played the flute and piccolo. In addition, he became interested in campus football, went out for the team despite his family's wishes but never got a chance to play.

By the spring of 1930, with his year at Elmhurst behind him, eighteen-year-old Slade was in a predicament. Though agriculture provided a measure of security for the Cutter family, times were getting decidedly tougher. The stock market crash of the previous year and a prolonged drought had created the greatest economic and natural disaster the country had ever faced. Life savings evaporated in successive bank failures, ushering in the Great Depression that soon put 1.5 million Illinois workers on unemployment lines. One out of every four Americans would lose their jobs. Mountains of debt and failed crops demoralized the nation. In the Fox River Valley, many farmers went under. "Things were pretty rough," said Cutter. "The Northwestern Life Insurance Company got a lot of farms in our area, but Dad was able to hang onto ours." However, the shaky local economy left Slade with few choices. He either had to acclimate to life as a farmer, or perhaps return to work in the manufacturing sector that was limping along in the valley. Both prospects were unappealing. Then, just as suddenly as she had come the previous year, Mrs. Loomis returned to the farm.

She was upset. Her son had not done well at Severn. He had failed the academy entrance examination and would have to repeat the year at Severn. Mrs. Loomis was fearful he lacked the discipline to succeed. "For some reason known only to her, she thought that I was a good influence on him," said Cutter. "So she thought that if I went to Severn the next year, her son Sam would study more and get in the Naval Academy."

The Cutters listened with great interest to her plan. The prospect of Slade following a naval career was appealing to them because it was the only practical way for him to receive a quality education. An appointment to the academy would ensure free tuition and board for all four years. Nevertheless, there were major obstacles. How was the family to pay for a year at Severn? And even more critical, how was Slade to get an appointment to the academy? The Cutters had no political connections of any consequence. For Slade to attend the academy, he had to be sponsored by someone in Congress.

Fortunately, the family's barber in Oswego happened to be the Republican Party chairman in rural Kendall County. "He heard of my problem," said Slade, "and volunteered to help. He said he would go to Congressman [John T.] Buckbee in Rockford and see if he could get an appointment."

Thus, on a Sunday, the barber, Slade, and his father drove to Rockford to see Congressman Buckbee. The barber pleaded with the congressman, noting that no one from Kendall County had ever been appointed to the Naval Academy or to West Point, and that the county deserved an appointment. The congressman agreed to a tentative appointment—"to see how this boy makes out."

There was still the matter of paying for Severn. "I didn't have any money to go there," Slade explained. "It was during the days of the Depression, and a friend of my father's, named Dudley Edwards, lived in Chicago. He was in the construction business there. He came out to the farm one day after hearing about my situation, and he had six hundred dollars. I'll never forget it—six one-hundred-dollar bills—and he loaned me those. I gave him a note. My father said, 'I'll sign it, Dud.' And Dud says, 'No, I will take Slade's signature.'"

Now it was up to the younger Cutter to make the plan succeed. Doing well at Severn was paramount. Not only for Slade, but for Sam Loomis Jr. as well.

4

Severn

THE REASON Congressman Buckbee took a wait-and-see approach to Slade's nomination to the Naval Academy was because he knew the road ahead was daunting. Being appointed locally was no cinch to admission. Every U.S. congressman and every senator could nominate five young men each year. However, of that number, only a select few became midshipmen. Annapolis was very selective and applicants were weeded out through notoriously difficult competitive exams. Under the supervision of the federal Civil Service Commission, the tests were administered every third Wednesday in February and April in cities all over the United States. They covered English spelling, grammar, and punctuation; geography; American history; arithmetic, algebra through quadratic equations, and plane geometry. If you failed the examinations, you could take them again the following year, as long as you were no older than twenty on 1 April of the testing period. This window of opportunity gave the eighteen-year-old Slade plenty of time as he packed his bags to leave for Severn School.

The school, located on the mile-wide Severn River nine miles upstream from Annapolis, was founded in 1914 by Rolland M. Teel at a time when many candidates for the academy were not sufficiently educated to pass the entrance tests. Severn was one of several preparatory schools in and around Annapolis that offered rigorous courses to round out the nominees. Classes began in late September and continued through May. The school consisted of a large classroom building, a dining facility, and a few neighboring homes that the school purchased for additional space. Students typically lived at the school and studied until they took the entrance tests. If they passed, they took physical examinations and reported to the academy beginning in June.

By the time of Slade's arrival, Mrs. Loomis had used her influence with the headmaster to get him a job waiting on tables in the dining room to help defray the cost of tuition. Obsessed with becoming a midshipman, he attacked his courses with the same enthusiasm and determination that had marked his childhood. That ability to apply himself rubbed off on Sam whose academic standing improved—just as his mother had anticipated. Cutter did well but faltered in algebra. After the first month, he had scored no higher than a D (1.5) in all his algebra tests. One night he sought out Wilmot T. Debell, one of his teachers. "He didn't know me at all. I went to his room and asked for help, and he said, 'Mr. Cutter, you don't know how to do fractions.' Mind you, eighteen years old and didn't know how to do fractions." It was due to Slade's skipping two grades in grammar school. "Well," Debell told Cutter, "we'll have to do something about that." That evening the teacher explained how to add and subtract fractions, how to multiply and divide them, how to get a common denominator and get the numerators lined up so they could be added. It took no time at all—just that one night—for Cutter to grasp the concept and bring up his grades.

In the meantime, Slade's interest in sports became more acute. Debell, an amateur boxer, was impressed with Slade's powerful build and size, and persuaded him to take boxing lessons at Severn, which had an active athletic program in line with the academy's requirements. Cutter proved to be a formidable heavyweight boxer, fostered by his habit of hitchhiking with Loomis on weekends to the academy to observe boxing matches. Unbeknownst to Slade, Loomis had gotten to know the Navy boxing coach, Hamilton "Spike" Webb, who had trained all U.S. Olympic boxing teams since 1920 and had coached heavyweight boxing champion Gene Tunney. "I don't know why or how Loomis got to know

Spike, but he did. We were walking on the grounds of the academy during one of those hitchhiking trips from Severn School and we came upon Spike Webb walking there, and he gave me a left hook in the belly—Spike did. I didn't know him; I had never seen him before, and I thought, 'What the hell's going on?' That started my association with Spike."

However, it was the influence of Severn's dynamic young football coach that really inspired him. Paul Brown, the future National Football League (NFL) prodigy, was just twenty-two years old: an intense, wiry man who in many ways was just like Cutter. Brown spent summers as a kid on his grandfather's farm in Norwalk, Ohio, and grew to appreciate the healthy, wholesome lifestyle of a rural upbringing. "We led a very ordered existence, and both parents were even-handed and fair in their discipline, convincing me that everyone's life needs the same," Brown recalled. Like Slade, Brown's parents had hoped he would become a musician. "At least I was given weekly piano lessons, and my teacher, Mrs. Oberlin, probably spent her time hoping that I wouldn't show up," Brown said. By the time he entered Miami University in Ohio, the family thought he would become a lawyer. However, his focus shifted to teaching and coaching athletics. After graduation, he accepted his first teaching job at Severn School, which was also looking for someone to assist the head coach, who had contracted cancer.

Among the duties inherited by Brown was running the school's underachieving football program. Right away, he noticed Cutter, whose size made him stand out from the other students. At the time Slade was on the soccer team and was not happy about it. "Well, here I was, weighing two hundred pounds, and they had a football team. The school had only 135 students and they had a 125-pound team, 135-pound team, a junior varsity team, and a varsity team. Then they had those who were not physically able to engage in football, and they played soccer or just ran around. I was relegated to that outfit because my father said, 'You cannot play football, because it will interfere with your academics.'" Slade was so embarrassed that the school wrote to his father, pleading with him to allow his son to play football. He finally relented.

Brown immediately invited Slade to try out for the team and was impressed by this "bubbling, exuberant young man," as he later described

Cutter. "When Slade came to us from Elmhurst College in Illinois, he was supposed to have preferred playing the flute to playing football, but we made him a tackle and, on some goal line plays, even our fullback because he was so strong."

That fall the coach installed his first successful football system (albeit in an eight-game season), one that he would build on in the future in the NFL. One of the things he preached was obsessive devotion to the task at hand. "I was strong-willed and single-minded and possessed a fierce sense of independence. I believed strongly in the things that were necessary for us to win," he said, adding, "My basic philosophy, the one I have stressed with every team I have ever coached is simple: everything we do must be in terms of our team and of doing our best." To bolster that spirit, Brown discouraged cliques. He insisted that players eat at different tables with different people during the football season. "I was sensitive to everything that went on in our locker room, and anytime I felt there might be some sort of confrontation brewing, I'd step in and try to make a joke about it." He also was honest with his players. "I talked to our players: sometimes about football; often about matters which touched on their lives as a whole."

Brown recruited the fastest players for his Severn varsity and that included Cutter who, though huge, was fleet afoot. "I placed great emphasis on my belief that players at all positions should be fast and quick," Brown said, calling himself a "speed freak." He witnessed first-hand in Annapolis what speed could do. "I had watched Jimmy DeHart's Duke [University] team mesmerize Navy with a version of the close double wingback formation, which used deceptive ball handling and quick movement of the backs to hide the ball from the defense. I found a coaching clinic where it was being taught, learned it and [became] convinced of its merits."

Brown was a stickler for precision. "If a lineman was told to split six inches from the player next to him," he said, "it had to be six inches, not a quarter of an inch more or less. If an end had to run eleven yards down field, then cut six yards to the sideline, everything was measured, timed and worked out to that precise distance." Virtually overnight, Brown transformed Severn into a state powerhouse. "He was tough," recalled Cutter. "It was a big transition from high school football to college ball, because they hit so much harder in college. The high school kids weren't taught to hit like that. He did. He was always fair, always clean, never took advantage of any of the rules or anything like that."

One of the nuances that Brown brought to the game was scouting opposing teams on weekends. "We had this old Packard touring car," said Cutter, "and he would put about six of his players in there. And we would go scout the team we were going to play the next week or two weeks from then."

As a guard on the offensive line, Cutter pulled out in the double-wing formation to lead the blocking on an end run. Occasionally, if the offense struggled, he moved to fullback. "I was the biggest guy on the team, and I would lumber in there and try to pick up a couple of yards." Cutter also saw duty as linebacker on defense because of his speed.

Severn went undefeated that year. In the Maryland Division A state championship title game, underdog Severn toppled perennial power-house Baltimore Polytechnic Institute, a school much larger than Severn. The Baltimore *Sun* subsequently named Cutter to the all-state team.

That Christmas, as the school emptied out for the holidays, Slade was too poor to afford a trip home. "I was the only student at Severn who didn't go home." However, that was not so bad because he was dating a local girl of stunning beauty. She asked Cutter to go with her to a holiday party in the exclusive Round Bay community on the Severn River near school. "We got there and there was a guy by the name of [Joseph] Burt Davis, who was second classman at the Naval Academy, intercollegiate middleweight boxing champ, first-string football player, a handsome guy. You knew he was a catch that night, and you'd wonder what this gal was doing with a candidate whose clothes were kind of seedy. So, very early in the evening, it didn't take very long for my date and Davis to make connections. They went outside twice during the night, and I knew what for. So I commenced looking around for somebody else, and my future wife was there, unattached." Her name was Frances Leffler, an only child. She was a friend of the hostess. Cutter and Franny hit it off immediately and frequently dated afterwards.

After the holidays, the first round of academy entrance examinations was fast approaching. Slade still struggled with algebra. "Geometry was real easy, because that's really not mathematics. But algebra, forget it. I blundered through, because, you know, they just pass you." Cutter went into the examinations with trepidation on April 22, 1931, in Annapolis. He scored highly in all subjects but one. "You had to get 2.5 in everything, and I got 2.6 in algebra—just barely made it," he said, adding, "At least I went into the Naval Academy knowing how to do fractions."

With his admission assured, as well as that of his friend, Loomis, Cutter decided to go home for the summer. Unable to afford the cost of a bus or train ticket, he decided to hitchhike—a decision that nearly cost his life.

Annapolis

EARLY ON a May morning of 1931, Slade Cutter left the campus at Severn, thumbing a ride on U.S. Route 2, the old Annapolis-Baltimore highway. He headed north to Baltimore, then northwest on Route 30 through Pittsburgh. It was not unusual for young men to be hitchhiking during the Depression because money was so tight. Cutter got as far as Youngstown, Ohio, by the end of the first day, and he paid a few dollars to stay overnight at a YMCA. In the morning, he rose early and made his way to a two-lane brick highway leading west. On the outskirts of town, a sleek Cord convertible with its top down purred to a halt. The driver motioned Cutter to jump in, telling him he was going to Joliet, which was only twenty-five miles from Slade's Fox River farm. The low-slung luxury sports car, known for its speed and radical front-wheel drive, raced ahead. Broad, sloping front fenders and a vertical chrome grill gave it the appearance of a highway carnivore. Young Slade was impressed by its power. "I was looking at my watch and was timing us with my second hand. We were going a mile every sixty seconds."

Roaring along, the amiable driver engaged Slade in conversation while passing slower moving traffic. On an open stretch in western Ohio, the driver veered around another vehicle, thinking the road ahead was clear. However, a dip in the highway masked the presence of an oncoming car. "As he was passing this car, all of a sudden this other car was there in front of us," said Cutter. There was no time to drop back or pull ahead. A head-on crash seemed imminent. Instinctively, the driver of the Cord turned sharply left off the highway, heading for a ditch. "And the other guy—normally, you would expect him to go that way too, but the other fellow did the right thing. He stayed on his side of the road, and we just went across him in front of him."

A fatal collision was averted by inches. The driver of the Cord wrestled with the brakes as the racing vehicle plunged into the roadside ravine where it sank to its floorboards in mud. Neither Cutter nor the driver was injured. A farmer hauling a wagon of hay with horses in a nearby field saw what happened. "He unhitched and brought the whiffle tree over and had a rope or chain or something and hooked it on and pulled us out, and on we went," said Cutter. "We got back to Illinois safely, but that's about as close as I ever came to getting knocked off."

Cutter got a warm homecoming. His family viewed his impending enrollment in the Naval Academy with enthusiasm. Cornell University and Western Maryland College (now known as McDaniel College) had offered football scholarships. "But I didn't know what college life would be like at either school," said Slade. "And at the time, I thought the Naval Academy was the greatest." Which was good news to his parents, particularly his father who was gratified his son would not devote his life to football.

In June 1931 Cutter eased into his first, or "plebe," year with no difficulty. All those weekend visits with Loomis made him familiar with the campus. He often marveled at the massive gray granite classroom buildings and dormitory perched on a spit of land on the Chesapeake Bay between the Severn River and Annapolis. The academy's cathedral, an ornate domed chapel housing the crypt of naval hero John Paul Jones, rose majestically over the school, visible from all approaches to the campus. The academy, founded in 1845, grew out of an attempted mutiny by a midshipman aboard the U.S. brig *Somers*. On a return voyage from the west coast of Africa in 1842, Philip Spencer, nineteen-year-old son of Secretary of War John Canfield Spencer, planned to seize control of the ship, murder Commander Alexander Slidell Mackenzie and loyal crewmen, then with fellow mutineers become pirates in the West

Indies. The captain discovered the plot beforehand, and moving quickly, arrested the leaders. After a court-martial at sea, Spencer and two coconspirators were hanged from the brig's yardarm. The ghastly episode called into question the selection and training of Navy officers, and emphasized the need for a naval training facility. Secretary of the Navy George Bancroft persuaded the Army to relinquish obsolete Fort Severn commanding the harbor at Annapolis. Thus, the academy sprang up at that site, thirty miles east of Washington, D.C.

Upon arrival, Cutter signed his name, hometown, address, birth date, religion, and father's occupation in the school's ledger:

Slade D. Cutter Oswego, Illinois 1 November 1911 Oswego, Illinois Methodist Farmer

For rural youths like Slade, the academy's daily routine was natural —up at 0630 and lights out at 2200 in Bancroft Hall, the largest dormitory in the world, housing all twenty-four hundred midshipmen ("middies"). Plebes roomed together in fours, whereas upperclassmen were in pairs. Every minute of every day was covered by a precise schedule. After awakening, the students would wash, shave, and eat breakfast by 0800, at which time they would march from the hall, upperclassmen in formation and plebes in double time. The students were organized into battalions and traveled from class to class with their group. First-year courses included marine engineering, naval construction, mathematics, English, and Spanish or French. Morning classes ended at 1215 for lunch; afternoon sessions began at 1320 and continued until 1520. Classes were followed by military drills until 1730, when the students broke for dinner. Afterwards, midshipmen were expected to remain in their rooms studying until 2130. For plebes, custom demanded they keep their eyes fixed straight ahead in the presence of upperclassmen in the dorm, to turn corners squarely, and to eat sitting rigidly on the leading two inches of their chairs. Each midshipman was paid six hundred dollars a year. To cover the cost of a uniform and other clothes, the academy reserved $350. For the remainder, a plebe could withdraw one dollar per month in cash. Second-year men received more than twice that. As at Severn, middies were graded on a 0-to-4 scholastic scale. To pass, they had to earn at least a 2.5. Anyone with a grade of less than 2.6 could not go on Christmas leave, the thinking being he needed to remain on campus studying through the holidays to bring up his grades.

Officially, the academy was an all-male, classless society. But in some ways it had social divisions similar to any college. Many midshipmen belonged to fraternities and dated debutantes, referred to as "Four-o debs." Many middies came from upper-crust naval families and called themselves "Our Set" and "blood." Nevertheless, the typical midshipman came from a small town or farm or from the fleet as an enlisted man. Because they were allowed to choose their own roommates, middies tended to bunk according to similar backgrounds or friendships. Thus, Loomis and Cutter were roommates.

The students inherited a slang vocabulary unique to the academy. Among the descriptive nouns: a "grind" (a student who studies too much), "savoirs" (especially brilliant students), "bilgers" (midshipmen expelled for academic reasons), "greasers" (those that curry favor with higher-ups), "spooning" (the practice of upperclassmen befriending a plebe, initiated by a handshake), "crabs" (local girls), "snakes" (midshipmen who were heavy daters), and "drags" (young ladies on dates with midshipmen). Every student was expected to play on a class team. Organized sports, part of the afternoon curriculum, consisted of baseball, basketball, boxing, crew, fencing, football, gym, lacrosse, marksmanship, soccer, swimming, tennis, track, water polo, and wrestling. Cutter went out for boxing, football, rifle marksmanship, and lacrosse. Middies were forbidden to drive cars on campus or anywhere in Annapolis. Smoking was prohibited except in a designated recreation room at Bancroft Hall known as Smoke Hall, where a large brass bowl containing loose tobacco and cigarette papers was kept under constant guard. Smokers were held for the purpose of debating a posted topic of current interest, such as "The Submarine on Trial before Humanity. Is it justified as a weapon? Should it be abolished? Limited in application? How?"

For all middies except plebes, the highlight each summer was an annual cruise on Fleet battleships to distant ports in England, France, Spain, Italy, and Hawaii. These cruises were rites of passage, teaching midshipmen practical seamanship and emphasizing naval traditions as nothing else could. Duty stations ranged from standing watch to shoveling coal in the fireroom.

Classes at the academy were in two-month segments, normally taught by line officers. Students were expected to study texts carefully, solve problems in class, and answer questions on the blackboard. However, the most important rule, according to Admiral James L. Holloway Jr., was not to appear to be too bright or eager. "I'll never forget when the instructor asked a question," said Holloway of his plebe year in 1915. "I put my hand up as one did in high school and quickly had it hauled down by a bilger, a friend of mine, who said, 'Don't do that!' So we learned never to volunteer any information, but to force the instructor to dig it out. The savoirs, the brilliant boys, oftentimes slowed down their work, so they would not have too many problems checked off on the blackboard for purposes of invidious comparison with us poor dummies from Arkansas and Alabama who had only been wearing shoes for ten years and just got in the Naval Academy by the skin of our teeth. This all added to human dignity, to my way of thinking. A greaser, someone who took advantage of his contemporaries, was looked upon with contempt. It was all for the service and not for the person."

Indeed, said Cutter. "The main thing they taught at the academy goes back to Admiral Holloway's philosophy, 'We are teaching you discipline and tradition here.' You can laugh at it in a way, but that's what your country expects you to do in time of war, and that's what they train you for. You become more scared of not doing your job than you are scared of what's going to happen to you." Part of that grooming was to emphasize the consequences of making a mistake, he added. "Any time a ship went aground, the captain got a court-martial, and, of course, everybody in the watch that had anything to do with it got hurt. Careers were ruined on something for which you weren't responsible. Of course, they were responsible, because they are in charge of the training. So the Navy isn't wrong, but the system promotes a hesitancy to do something without proper authority."

Adherence to the rules became more pronounced with the arrival of junior Rear Admiral Thomas C. Hart as the new academy superintendent in 1931. "Tommy Hart was not beloved by the midshipmen. He was cold," said Slade of his early encounters with the admiral who would become commander-in-chief of the U.S. Asiatic Fleet prior to World War II. Hart was a stickler for tough discipline and decorum. "For instance," said Cutter, "we all had one-eighth of an inch of our collar showing, and he insisted on that. It never happened before—on a full dress parade, one-eighth of an inch, exactly one-eighth of an inch. I think it was a half or a quarter on your cuffs. So what we did was cut off our shirt sleeves and sewed the buttons inside the sleeves to hold the cuffs onto the sleeves of our shirts and put a button inside the collar in back and the two buttons in the front of the collar, to hold our full-dress collar in place. But we sure looked good out on parade. He had these standards that were very, very high, and he didn't go along with relaxing the rules. We took pride in being deprived."

Most of the academy's professors had little formal scholastic training other than that received previously as midshipmen. Because of this deficiency, the school was not accredited until 1933, the year it awarded its first academic degree in science. "The thought at that time was that your education was continuing, and you would have to get it yourself after you got out into the fleet," said Cutter. "There was no lecturing; you'd get into class, and the instructor would say, 'Any questions, gentlemen? Man the boards.' You didn't dare ask any questions, because they couldn't answer most of them. So you manned the boards and the slips were made out by some Ph.D. assistant head of the department. And you would draw a slip, and if it covered material you knew, you would do all right that day."

Cutter was a moderately successful student. "You didn't have to think. You just had to memorize. Little things that you were interested in—for instance, the torpedo—we had to diagram it, draw a diagram of a torpedo, very complicated thing. That I got very interested in. I always got 4.0 on that one, because I liked torpedoes. A good thing, because later on I got very familiar with them." Math continued to be a stumbling block, and Cutter's Spanish was rudimentary at best. "We had a Spanish teacher who was a naval officer; he couldn't speak Spanish any more than I could. I'll never forget the only thing I ever learned from him: 'No tengo tobacco, no tengo papel, no tengo dinero, Goddamnit to hell.' That was funny. Still you picked up enough so that you could go to Spain and get along. They would all laugh at you but you could make yourself known."

Slade's success depended in large part on one of his roommates, David Wooster Taylor Jr., an avid cribbage player who was to graduate 34th of 442 graduates in the class of 1935. "Anybody who spent the whole night studying was absolutely a dullard to Wooster," said Cutter who became Taylor's nightly opponent at cribbage. Loomis, because he needed to study to survive, moved across the hall to another room. "Wooster would go through the lessons with me. He would brief me, but I didn't study them. He was so good he could always tell what the slips were going to be. He could pick out the key things in the lessons and then would say, 'You'd better know this, Slade.' And I would say, 'Okay, fine.' And I did all right in my daily lesson as a result. But when you got to an examination, that was something else. You had a little trouble."

Hazing was an academy tradition, though the administration officially frowned on it after two attempted suicides in 1919 prompted a congressional investigation. The feeling among middies was that "real" men could take verbal and physical harassment. To them, faculty members, and alumni, it was good preparation for military life in which absolute subservience to commanding officers was critical. Despite the fallout from the 1919 scandal, hazing continued in minor ways in the dorm, such as upperclassmen making derogatory remarks about a plebe's accent or his physique, or ordering him to recite poorly worded verse or comic doggerel, and whacking him with the bristle end of a broom. Cutter could not recall anybody griping about such treatment. "It was a little different then," he noted. "This was during the Depression, and everybody was so doggone happy to be there." Cutter did recall one upperclassman who harassed him constantly during plebe summer. "He gave me an awful time. Well, Hundredth Night came along where you reverse roles and plebes become upperclassmen for a day. Well, I went to work on that guy, and, do you know what he did when I got done? He spooned on me. We shook hands, and we were friends forever."

For the most part, Cutter viewed his four years as fulfilling. "It's funny. I can remember going to the head at night. It was quiet, nobody was up. And I can remember thinking how lucky I was to be at the Naval

Academy. That just about says it all, you know. In those days, there weren't many options."

Almost from the time of his arrival, Cutter was involved in boxing. Spike Webb, who was training the national Olympic team at the academy during Slade's first summer, needed a temporary sparing partner for Ensign Francis D. Crinkley, a former heavyweight intercollegiate champion. "So I was his sparring partner and got a deviated septum," said Cutter. "Of course, it was good training but he was experienced, and he was a big man, but I stuck in there. So I got interested in boxing, and I went through plebe year and wasn't defeated." Cutter also excelled as a rifle marksman, a skill he developed as a youth shooting rabbits and squirrels on his boyhood farm. He played third-string fullback and linebacker on the Navy football team as well.

Cutter's first training cruise, in the summer of 1932, was to Texas. "That was during the era of lack of funds in the Navy, so they just made the cruise down to Galveston," he said. "We were scrubbing decks, and we were just acting like seamen. We did the job of seamen. We also were able to have liberty like the ship's company did. We just had a good time." The cruise emphasized the relationship between officers and enlisted men—with a touch of irony: The midshipmen took orders from petty officers although, in actuality, the midshipmen were senior to the petty officers. In successive years, summer cruises on the battleships *Wyoming* and *Arkansas* brought increased responsibility. "We got up at the crack of dawn to take star sights, took them at evening twilight and got practical experience in communication and engineering. It made more meaningful the things we studied when we got back to the academy," said Cutter.

In his second and third years, Cutter moved up to the varsity boxing and football squads. By the end of his third boxing season, he still was undefeated. He won successive heavyweight bouts against Penn State, West Virginia, Western Maryland, Washington and Lee, North Carolina, and Virginia with a record of three knockouts, two forfeits, and one decision. Tall, lanky, quick on his feet, weighing 210 pounds, with broad shoulders, well-developed musculature, and a chiseled countenance, Cutter possessed a fierce determination backed up by a thunderous left hook. He often won by knockout or forfeit, and became a feared competitor throughout the intercollegiate circuit. His coach viewed him as a future world heavyweight champion. Webb was in a position to know. He was a veteran of more than one hundred professional fights, and since coming to the academy in 1919, had created a boxing program that was among the nation's best. In one incredible eleven-year span, his teams never lost a match. He was one of the most popular coaches at the academy, a man so committed to his profession that he volunteered in his spare time in Baltimore to work with underprivileged boys. Among those he trained was Walker Smith who changed his name to "Sugar" Ray Robinson and eventually became world middleweight champion.

On the gridiron, Cutter lived up to his moniker, "Whataman." He was easily the biggest man on the team and became a skilled left tackle, accurate place kicker, and backup for the first-team center, who was prone to concussions. Cutter's status was jeopardized one Saturday morning at the training table prior to the varsity clash with powerful Columbia University in the fall of 1933. "A guy by the name of Holman Lee was sitting next to me. He was a 140-pound quarterback, but a third stringer, and he was all guts and smart. But his nickname was 'Holy,' and he was the most unholy person in the whole class. In those days when we would get up to leave breakfast, they would say, 'Rise, parade rest,' and at parade rest, we would say the Lord's Prayer in unison. Well, at the training table Holman Lee was saying the Lord's Prayer. I had never heard him pray—ever—and I looked at him, thinking, what the hell's going on? I didn't say anything to him; that's all there was to it. So we were dismissed, and I went to the first class. I came back, and there was a note saying, 'Report to the director of athletics.'" Without a clue, Cutter appeared before head coach Edgar "Rip" Miller, Lt. Cdr. John L. Hall Jr., and Capt. John W. Wilcox Jr., director of athletics. They informed Cutter that he had committed a Class A offense as reported by Lt. Robert H. Smith, of the first battalion of midshipmen. Smith, because of an earlier falling out with his counterpart in Cutter's battalion, had been keeping a close eye on the rival battalion for a chance at revenge. "This was it, really—just childish as hell—the two of them," said Cutter. "So R. H. Smith, whom we called 'The Beagle,' had caught Cutter in this situation where he put me down for a class A: 'This midshipman was grimacing and apparently directing the grimaces at another midshipman.' Directing a grimace—now how the hell are you going to do that?"

The result was that Cutter would not be able to play in the game against Columbia that afternoon, ten demerits were to be affixed to his academic record, and he would be confined as punishment to the academy's brig, the old Spanish cruiser *Reina Mercedes* stationed at the school. The football team was outraged; there was no one that could back up the center if he was knocked out of the game.

Just before game time, a deal was worked out: The "grimace" was reduced from a class A to a class B offense. Cutter could play that afternoon and would not have to go to the brig. But he would have fifteen demerits added to his academic record and would be forced to walk extra duty from the end of the football season until the beginning of the boxing season—two hours on Wednesday, two hours on Saturdays, one hour the other days except Sunday. Cutter also got a lecture from his battalion officer, Commander Mahlon S. Tisdale. "He called me to his office and said, 'Cutter, I am terribly disappointed in you. When you get out in the Fleet and stand the deck watch under the stars in the Southern Hemisphere, you'll be close to God. And you'll feel regret that you did this sort of thing.' He made me feel like I was completely without religion."

In the game against Columbia, Navy's center predictably suffered a concussion and Cutter replaced him on a team budding with talent. All-American Fred "Buzz" Borries was the running back, All-American Bill Clark was the fullback and punting specialist, and Robert "Dusty" Dornin, known as one of the academy's best all-around athletes, was the tight end. The team seemed poised to carry Navy far. Though capable of beating any team on a given Saturday—and having just beaten Notre Dame by a 7–0 score the previous week to bring their record to 5–1 and a national ranking—the middies were not so lucky this time. Columbia won, 14–7. The following week, Princeton shut Navy down, 13–0. And to the academy's continuing chagrin, the team lost its season finale to Army for the third time since Cutter arrived, a winless streak that stretched back thirteen years.

Throughout his years at the academy, Cutter dated only one

woman, Franny Leffler, whom he met at Severn. Her best friend, Ruth McCracken of Philadelphia, was the regular date of Slade's friend and teammate, "Dusty" Dornin. Ruth often drove down from her Main Line home on weekends, picking Franny up at her house in Baltimore, then continuing on to Annapolis to double-date the two midshipmen, who intended to marry them.

The year ended ceremoniously for Cutter, as it did for all second classmen, with the annual Ring Dance. It was one of the academy's most romantic traditions. The ceremony came into being in 1925 to replace an earlier tradition of second classmen putting on their class rings right after their final navigation exam. Typically, graduating first classmen dragged them to the banks of the Severn and tossed them in to mark the occasion. However, in 1924 one of them drowned after striking his head on a seawall. The Ring Dance was introduced by the administration the next year. The dance, attended by second classmen and their dates, occurred after final exams. The highlight of the evening for Cutter, as it was for all the middies, was approaching a gigantic replica of the class ring. With Slade's ring in hand, Franny Leffler dipped it in three basins containing water from the Caribbean, Atlantic, and Pacific Oceans. She then slipped it on Slade's finger as the couple passed through the replica ring, then sealed the occasion with a kiss.

Slade returned home for a brief visit by carpooling with other midshipmen who lived in the Midwest. But he could hardly wait to return for what promised to be an interesting training cruise to Europe, including stops in England, France, and Italy. He was also looking forward to the upcoming football season, one in which the team vowed revenge against Army. For Slade, it would be his last chance to beat the cadets. The game would immortalize Cutter for a singular event on a muddy field in Philadelphia before eighty thousand spectators.

Whataman

THOSE WHO looked back on the summer of 1934 thought that the middies' training cruise to Europe perhaps had something to do with Navy's remarkable football season in Cutter's senior year. Happy omens seemed to follow the midshipmen everywhere, especially the football team aboard the battleship *Wyoming*. The voyage in July and August with the battleship *Arkansas* was memorable for a number of reasons, as noted in the *Lucky Bag*, the academy's yearbook.

The midshipmen made their first stop in England where they toured the sights, gawked at "long-haired haranguers" on soap boxes in Hyde Park, and attended a luncheon with Hollywood movie star Douglas Fairbanks Jr. and "a bevy of English beauties." The middies also shared tea with Lady Astor before the battleships set sail for the Mediterranean with a first stop in Villefranche, where the middies enjoyed the glitz and glamour of Monte Carlo and Cannes. Next stop was Naples, where they were intrigued by Mount Vesuvius, ominously belching smoke. Then on to Rome where Italian midshipmen manned the rail to salute them, a rare occurrence. Afterwards, the men from Annapolis gave a startled Benito Mussolini a spirited "4N" cheer—*NnnnAaaaVvvvYyyy!*—vocalized in a quick stutter that echoed loudly through the Venetian Palace. They also visited Vatican City where they had an audience with Pope Pius XI, who smiled benignly as the sailors greeted him with another 4N. Cutter, the varsity place kicker and tackle, and fellow first classman William Clark, the fullback and punter, seized the moment by sticking out their kicking toes as the Pope blessed the assembled midshipmen. On the return voyage, the battleships stopped in Gibraltar, allowing the middies to visit nearby Tangiers, "a Ripley's Believe It or Not" experience, for its camels and crosscurrent of Arab, Spanish, and British influences. Recrossing the Atlantic, a school of porpoises —a lucky omen—greeted the *Wyoming* and the football team off the Virginia capes and followed them to Norfolk ("a whirl of dances, dinners, girls, touched with real Southern hospitality"). The ships continued north to the mouth of the Potomac River where they anchored for three days, long enough for President Franklin D. Roosevelt to come aboard ("we greet him with a 4N").

Returning to the Severn, Slade and his teammates prepared for a football season in which a national championship seemed possible. The team had a new head coach, Lt. (jg) Thomas J. Hamilton, who abandoned the favored Notre Dame double-wing backfield and its time-consuming reverse and end sweep formations. Instead, he adopted the single-wing, which was built around the speed of star running back "Buzz" Borries, and his ability to break runs straight ahead through opponents' lines. In addition, fleet receiver "Dusty" Dornin provided an effective target for quarterback Richard R. Pratt. The team retained former head coach "Rip" Miller as its line coach. Hamilton never interfered with Miller, who developed an awesome defensive and offensive front wall, anchored by Slade Cutter. Miller was a master, having been an All-American tackle at Notre Dame in the 1920s where he was one of the "Seven Mules," the offensive line that played in front of the famous backfield known as the "Four Horsemen" under coach Knute Rockne. Navy also had the talents of its incredible punter, Clark, and field goal specialist Cutter. Thus in September 1934, Navy was poised to use all its strengths—speed on the offense coached by Hamilton, tough-as-nails line play conceived by Miller, and a solid kicking game destined to make Cutter famous.

The middies made a statement in their first game against the College of William and Mary. On the first play from scrimmage, Borries scored on a long touchdown run. Five minutes later, the team scored again.

"They looked fast and smart, and played heads-up football," noted one reporter. Nevertheless, penalties snuffed out many other chances, leaving the final score: Navy 20, William and Mary 7. Next came the University of Virginia. On a wet field, the middies unleashed a powerful first quarter attack, with Borries scoring on a fifty-yard scramble. Bill Clark, who could boot punts sixty yards with pinpoint accuracy, kept Virginia pinned deep in its own territory as Navy scored two more touchdowns. Cutter anchored the defense and kicked three straight point-after placements to beat Virginia, 21–6.

The University of Maryland fell as well in a 16–13 defensive struggle keyed by Cutter's dominating line play. By mid-October, Navy faced talent-rich Columbia University, one of the elite teams in the East. Before a record thirty-two thousand fans at Baker Field in New York, the middies rallied to a 18–7 win, as they did the following week, downing the University of Pennsylvania by a 17–0 score that featured Cutter kicking a field goal, leading the run blocking, and helping stifle the Penn running game.

Navy's next test was against Washington and Lee University. Sports pundits predicted a Navy defeat. Again, the midshipmen were relentless, posting a stunning 26–0 triumph. The victory made the middies the favorite for their impending confrontation with vaunted Notre Dame. However, man-for-man, Notre Dame outweighed the middies. Moreover, the game was to be played at South Bend where the Fighting Irish were nearly unbeatable. For Navy, the game was huge. A possible national championship was within its grasp. Only six major colleges still were undefeated and untied: Minnesota, Alabama, Princeton, Syracuse, Illinois, and Navy.

From the opening kickoff, Notre Dame flexed its muscle and drove deep into Navy territory. However, the offense sputtered short of field goal range. The Fighting Irish repeatedly threatened to score in the first half but were denied. Meanwhile, Cutter's toe (blessed by the pope) gave the middies an early 3–0 lead. A blocked punt led to another Cutter field goal and a 6–0 halftime lead. Incredibly, the midshipmen clung to that lead as the fourth quarter opened with Notre Dame on the march for what could be the winning touchdown. However, an interception led to a Navy touchdown and a 13–0 lead. With time running out, Notre Dame scored a late touchdown. By then it was much too late. Navy 13, Notre Dame 7.

With a perfect 7–0 record and only two games left in the season, passion at Annapolis ran high. Only once had Navy gone undefeated in a football season. But the 1926 campaign was ruined by a season-ending 26–26 tie with Army. Now, the middies faced the University of Pittsburgh, whose only loss was its season opener to Minnesota, the Number 1 team in the country. Since then, the Panthers had posted six straight wins and outscored opponents by a 154–27 margin. The key to Pittsburgh's success was three huge linemen whom sports writers described as "savage" and "unstoppable." Navy was counting on its overall team speed and a variety of trick plays, such as using forward laterals, in a "basketball" style of razzle-dazzle offense. The middies kept it close in the first half, but Pittsburgh unleashed a crushing onslaught in the last half, scoring three touchdowns to win the game by a 31–7 margin.

Some blamed the loss on Navy's spending itself emotionally in the stiff battle with Notre Dame the previous weekend. The midshipmen also were looking ahead to the final game of the season. The annual battle with Army on the neutral ground of Franklin Field in Philadelphia on 1 December was the most anticipated Army-Navy clash in a generation. "The Army game meant a lot to a lot of people. It means a great deal which it doesn't in a lot of schools, but it does at the academy," Cutter said of the annual contest for service academy supremacy. "To go through four years as we were on the verge of without seeing your team win is pretty tough."

Army was 7–2 on the year. But the record was deceptive. The cadets had lost by a single point, 7–6, to Illinois and dropped a heartbreaker to Notre Dame by a 12–6 score. The cadets outweighed the middies by twelve pounds per man and had every intention of continuing a dominance over Navy that had lasted thirteen years. For Slade, the game was especially poignant because his father, who was gravely ill with cancer, traveled to Philadelphia to see him play for the first time. Accompanying him was Dudley Edwards, who loaned Slade the six hundred dollars that put him on the path to Severn and the academy.

The night before the big game, a fierce storm pummeled Philadelphia, turning Franklin Field at the University of Pennsylvania into a sea of mud. The Associated Press termed it "a mass of slime, a shiny, slippery table, and as green as pea soup and just as gooey." At game time, the rain came down in sheets. Fierce gales shredded pennants atop the bleachers, unroofed umbrellas, and ravaged chrysanthemums. Nevertheless, eighty thousand screaming midshipmen, cadets, former gridiron legends, congressmen and senators, VIPs, and fans from afar thronged the stadium at noon for the kickoff. They filled every nook and cranny in the horseshoe-shaped, Greco-Roman coliseum. Among the many notables were Admiral William H. Standley, chief of Naval Operations, and General Douglas MacArthur, chief of staff of the Army.

On the second play of the game, Navy halfback "Buzz" Borries, who had been named that day to the Associated Press's All-American team, galloped around right end for a twenty-two-yard gain. It would prove to be the longest run of the game. What ensued was a titanic battle for field position in mud so thick it obliterated uniform numbers. The soggy, heavy pigskin football was nearly impossible to pass, and running was difficult because cleats got hung up in the mud. Players had the appearance of clay figures. Slowly, Navy kicker Clark out-gunned celebrated Army punter "Texas" Jack Buckler. Near the end of the first quarter of a scoreless tie, Clark booted a punt down near the Army end zone where Dornin knocked it out of bounds at the one-yard line. The cadets were unable to move the ball in three running plays, forcing a kick that Cutter tipped at the line of scrimmage. Navy took over at Army's thirty-five-yard line. Borries blasted between the tackles play after play, slowly gaining yardage until the middies reached the Army six. On third down, he tried for the end zone on a sweep but was tackled for a loss to the Army fifteen. On fourth down, Pratt, the quarterback, called the next play—"Cutter back to place kick."

"I thought he was out of his mind in the damn mud," recalled Cutter who called for a time out. According to the Associated Press, "The midshipmen gathered around their mastodonic tackle, Cutter. He tossed off his head guard and his curly brown hair glinted in the sun that had broken through the drip and the fog for a few moments. He wiped his hands and he wiped his right foot. The ball lay to the left of the uprights as Cutter, the biggest man on the team, squinted down the sights as though he were about to fire a 6-inch gun."

On the sidelines, Navy coaches Hamilton and "Rip" Miller waited in nervous anticipation. They had developed a trick play for the game, a fake kick in which Cutter would line up for a field goal but Clark, in handling the hike from center, would run the ball in for a touchdown. Collegiate rules in force in the 1930s forbade coaches from sending in plays. So, according to the prearranged script, the team wiped off the muddy football while building a little mound of mud for use as a place to spot the ball. It was thirty yards from the goal posts at the back of the end zone. Coaches Hamilton and Miller eagerly awaited the chicanery to unfold. "They were sure it was a fake place kick—the play they had been working on for the past two weeks," explained Cutter. "Then, when they saw I was going to kick it, they said, 'The goddamned fool! He's going to kick it!'"

They had reason to be concerned. Cutter had been practicing place kicks before the game and had not made a single one because of mud sticking to the long cleats on his lineman shoes. "You groove a kick like a golf swing," he later explained. "My cleats were catching the dirt as I kicked." What the coaches did not know is that between the warm-up period and kickoff, Slade obtained a shoe with much shorter cleats for his right foot—just in case.

Out on the field, the team set in position with Clark back to receive the pass from center and spot it on the mound for Cutter to swing through. Time stood still for the mudmen and the spectators as Clark barked out the signal to hike. "The ball arched back from center, a perfect pass from Louis Robertshaw of Haverford, Pennsylvania, a tower in the middle of the line," reported the Associated Press:

> The kneeling Clark held it. Slade Cutter drew back his foot and struck. The ball sailed low, whistling past a couple of frantic Army hands stretched up to get it. It was still rising, almost whistling like a shell, as it cleared the crossbar, with feet to spare, squarely between the uprights, and sailed on and up into the stands back of the playing field for three points. The wet, chilled, bedraggled crowd clothed in

anything but the finery that usually makes this a glittering picture, huddled under umbrellas and papers, shrieked with glee. Cutter pulled on his helmet again, went back into the line, and for the rest of the afternoon all this magnificent lineman did was thunder Army backs into the muck, uproot plays and players.

Cutter seemed possessed. He slashed through the big Army line to drag down runners. Bill Clark emerged as a heroic figure by continually keeping Army backed up near its goal line with tremendous punts, one of which traveled sixty-eight yards. Through the stormy afternoon, Navy made only three first downs and gained 109 yards from the line of scrimmage. However, Army made only two first downs and seventy total yards.

In the end the 3–0 score held up and brought victory to Navy for the first time in more than a decade. News of the triumph made Slade Cutter a household name. Front-page photos showed the flight of the ball as it rocketed off his foot toward the goal posts. The lead on the Associated Press's story said it all: "The boom of Slade Cutter's mud-encrusted boot, like the crash of a battle cruiser broadside in some far rolling sea, roared out the end of Army's thirteen-year football domination over Navy today as eighty thousand hysterical, rain-drenched partisans howled at as fine a battle as these great service rivals ever have staged."

In the delirium of the dressing room, a beaming coach Hamilton rushed up to his giant tackle. "You not only won the game with a field goal, Slade," he said, "but you also played a whale of a game at tackle." Many proclaimed him the greatest lineman ever at the academy. However, Cutter deflected praise in his typically humble fashion, choosing to give most of the credit for the victory to Clark. "Shucks," he said in the crush of reporters around him, "anybody can kick a field goal with a fellow like Bill Clark holding the ball. Clark deserves as much credit for that goal today as I do—more in fact." He added, "I wasn't nervous when I was waiting for that pass. I was just afraid that the ball might be too heavy to boot high." In the pandemonium, Slade's father, bursting with pride, congratulated his son. For Watts Cutter, the final score was a gift seemingly heaven sent. He had been rooting for Navy not to score another point after his son's field goal—so that Slade would win the game all by himself, which he did.

The regiment returned to Annapolis early the next morning. Most of the town was up to give the midshipmen a tumultuous reception at the train station. At the academy, the old Army-Navy victory bell had been hauled onto the steps in front of Bancroft Hall. The Emperor of Japan had presented the bell to Commodore Matthew C. Perry when he forcibly opened Japan to world commerce in 1854. Since the great service rivalry began, midshipmen had tolled it only on the occasion of an Army defeat. From the moment the 3–0 final score was announced, a plebe was posted to ring it thirteen times every fifteen minutes—to mark the fact that Navy's thirteenth victory in the service series came after a wait of thirteen years in the thirteenth minute of the first quarter of the game in Philadelphia. The day after the victory, Cutter and his teammates climbed aboard a fire engine and proceeded to the athletic field. The entire school followed behind on foot, the victory bell in tow. Each player lined up and struck the bell three times as the regiment cheered wildly. Capt. Dick Burns, choked up, expressed the team's feeling in four words: "Damn it, we won!" Cutter shrugged, "On a dry day we could have beaten 'em 23 to 0!" Said "Dusty" Dornin, "Army asked for it and we gave it to them!"

The academy yearbook later noted the middies defeated Army in five sports in the 1934–1935 school year. The football triumph was the sweetest of all, "Navy—Three, Army—Swabo!" In the final Associated Press poll, Navy finished third—behind only Minnesota and Pittsburgh.

For Cutter, the national spotlight would continue to follow him, this time into the boxing ring. The winter sport was one of the premiere collegiate activities in the 1930s, though it was rugged and bloody. Fighters were equipped with boxing gloves but no headgear except during practice. They fought three-round bouts, the format followed in Olympic games. Competition was keen, drawing capacity crowds to indoor arenas. Normally, there were eight individual contests in every meet, ranging from the 115-pound flyweight category to the 185-pound heavyweight class. As a heavyweight, Cutter had never lost a bout in two years of intercollegiate competition. Coach "Spike" Webb was so impressed with his protégé that he viewed the midshipman as the best heavyweight prospect in America. Webb believed he was faster and more powerful than heavyweight champions Jack Dempsey, Max Schmeling, Primo Carnera, and Max Baer. Several professional offers came Cutter's way, including one from a fight manager in Philadelphia known as Bill "Slim" Brennan. Reportedly, he and some backers were offering as much as fifty thousand dollars. At least that is what was relayed to Cutter through Webb. That amount of money was an absolute fortune for a young man in the mid-1930s. Slade considered the idea and discussed it with his father. "But my father said, 'No, you owe it to the Navy to stay in the Navy.'"

It did not take much convincing. "It was a good thing I didn't turn pro, because I would never have beaten Joe Louis the best day of my life," said Cutter. "He was too quick, and speed is everything in boxing. I saw Louis, and I was pretty objective about it; he was just too good. Why not be honest? I was good in my league, but he was out of my league."

As a first classman, Slade's reputation was so formidable that he won his first two intercollegiate bouts against Western Maryland College and Richmond College by forfeit. Next up was the powerful University of Virginia, working on a string of twenty-one consecutive bouts without a loss. A capacity crowd filled Macdonough Hall at the academy to witness the spectacle. Virginia easily won the first two bouts, but Navy took the third. Entering the match, Cutter was undefeated after eighteen intercollegiate bouts since arriving at Annapolis. This time, however, his record was in jeopardy because of a perforated eardrum suffered in practice. His sparring partner landed a blow to one of the ear holes in Slade's training helmet, causing the air to compress and break the eardrum. Though in excruciating pain, Cutter refused to see a doctor, realizing the physician would not let him box powerful Virginia heavyweight Freddie Cramer. Coach Webb knew about the injury and wanted to cancel the bout. However, Cutter pleaded with him to let him fight, fearful that it would look like he was afraid of Cramer if he forfeited. "So, Spike says, 'Okay, but you'll have to get him in the first round. If you don't, I'm pulling you out.'"

"Normally boxers throw a lot of jabs, testing each other slowly at the beginning of the first round," said Cutter. "But I came out into the ring fast and caught Cramer with a left hook and he went down. He got up at the count of eight while I was yelling to the ref that he was out. So the ref motioned us to come in and I hit Cramer again with a left hook and he was out."

It took all of thirty-eight seconds.

In the last four meets of the season, Navy defeated Penn State, New Hampshire, Syracuse, and Pittsburgh to finish the season 7–1. Cutter won all of his bouts by knockout or forfeiture, leaving him undefeated and with multiple collegiate boxing crowns.

Cutter ended his academy career as one of its most famous athletes —a somewhat dubious distinction in his mind. "It put me in the category of a 'jock'—you know, 'this dumb fool.'" But that was hardly the case. He graduated 309th in a class of 610 that entered the academy four years earlier. The administration was acutely aware of Cutter's leadership ability and named him one of only nine graduates to get a letter of commendation for his "officer-like qualities and positive characteristics." He also was one of seventeen honored for rifle marksmanship. For all his accomplishments, he earned three shoulder stripes out of a possible five. Every midshipman got at least one. To earn two, he had to command a squad of middies. However, to achieve three, it was necessary to command one of the academy's eight companies. It was quite an honor, only excelled by three midshipmen—two midshipmen with four stripes for commanding the two academy battalions, and a single midshipman with five stripes for command of the entire midshipman regiment.

By mid-spring of 1935, Cutter was preparing for his final examinations when his mother called from Oswego urging him to come home: his father's health was failing rapidly due to cancer. Watts Cutter, though having lost considerable weight, was still lucid. He could get around on his own and kept a stiff upper lip throughout the visit, as did Slade. Afterwards, the elder Cutter drove Slade back to the train and saw him off, both men holding their emotions in check.

Slade's absence from the academy had cost him because he missed several tests and classroom exercises and faced a make-or-break final examination with no chance of make-up tests to offset the score in the final. He had no choice but to concentrate: which he did, scoring a near perfect score on the exams. "I finally realized just what I could have done if only I had applied myself to my studies rather than played so much bridge and cribbage," he said.

On graduation day—6 June 1935—Slade Deville Cutter had climbed the mountain that looked so impossible before Mrs. Loomis entered his life. Now, as the national anthem sounded, he stood proudly in his dress whites not far from where Sam Loomis Jr. also stood at attention. Slade thought of his father, wishing he could have been there. Graduation concluded with the playing of the class song, "No More Rivers." The middies' white caps went flying as the "anchor man"—the midshipman standing last in the class—was borne off the field on the shoulders of his classmates to awaiting girlfriends and mothers who pinned shoulder stripes on the graduates' uniforms. They were now commissioned ensigns.

Watts Cutter died three weeks later. After the funeral, Slade would resume his military career. Soon he would do the unthinkable. Resign.

Turning Point

SLADE CUTTER'S first choice upon graduation was to become a Marine. It was a yearning dating back to the summer of 1917 when a distant relative visited the family farm. "His name was Arthur Lake, who was about a second or third cousin of mine. He was in the Marine Corps. He came in his uniform and sat on the front porch and he was going overseas. He was killed in the Argonne, not too long before [World War I] was over. He was an only child, and it was very sad for the family. Still, I just wanted to be a Marine from that experience of seeing him. I was five years old at the time."

Cutter's dream was within sight. Each of the 445 graduating first classmen listed the service of his choice. Cutter chose the Marine Corps but did not obtain one of the twenty-six available billets. So, Slade took aim at his second choice—naval aviation—which had as an enticement hazardous duty pay, very appealing to a young man without means in the Great Depression. However, this time the hurdle was weight. At 230 pounds, Cutter had to shed twenty pounds if he was to make it in under the wire. "In those days, 193 pounds was your top level in naval aviation. I couldn't get to 193 and hold it. I could starve down to there, but I couldn't stay there. So I was ordered to the USS *Lexington*. At the time, the carrier was the largest in the world, later to be sunk in the Battle of the Coral Sea in the Pacific War."

Unbeknownst to Cutter, the captain of the *Idaho,* Arthur G. Stott, had an influential friend in the Navy who pulled some strings to get the ensign transferred to the battleship so Slade could form the nucleus of the ship's football team. The warship was stationed in Long Beach, California, meaning a forced separation from Franny. She was the only girl he had dated through all four years at Annapolis, yet they could not marry. Both knew the consequences of doing so. "In those days," said Cutter, "ensigns were on probation for two years and were forbidden to get married. If they did get married, they would have to resign. The rule had only been in place a few years, the whim of some senior officers who wanted to save midshipmen from going off and getting married too soon."

Therefore, at his graduation, Slade and Franny faced two more years of courtship during a period of high stress for her. As an only child, she grew up in a privileged, nurturing environment in the exclusive Roland Park subdivision of Baltimore. She had a sweet, reserved disposition, and was an impeccable dresser. During his academy years, Slade often spent leave at the Lefflers' expansive two-story home. It was on one such visit in Cutter's third year at Annapolis that Franny's family life began to unravel. In the middle of the night as Slade was asleep in the guest-room, her father frantically woke his daughter in her bedroom, telling her to come quick. Slade, awakened by the commotion, also ran to the master bedroom where he was shocked to see Mrs. Leffler lying prone and unresponsive on her bed. "Franny's mother had died in her sleep and her body was still warm. Franny threw herself on her mother, sobbing uncontrollably," said Cutter. After a few moments, Franny's father asked Slade to take her from the room. Gently, he lifted her off her mother and, cradling her, carried her from the bedroom, consoling her.

Cutter assuaged her grief in the months to come as the couple drew closer emotionally. Compounding Franny's sense of isolation was the fragile health of her aging father, who was in and out of the hospital with various illnesses. Slade's orders to join the *Idaho* arrived in the summer of 1935, just as Franny's father suffered a stroke. Slade had no choice but to go. But when Franny's father was well enough, Franny went to California to visit Slade and stayed with his mother, who had moved to Hollywood with her daughter, leaving the boys behind to run the farm.

"Franny was so distraught. It was a hell of a situation," said Slade, who thought it best to resign from the Navy for her sake and return to Baltimore where they could be married. There was a promise of a job at Baltimore Electric as soon as Cutter's resignation became effective. "So, I decided to get married and submitted my resignation from the Navy," explained Cutter. "I just made it one sentence: 'I hereby resign, because I'm going to be married in the near future.'"

Cutter believed the Navy would accept his decision. But the resignation came back "disapproved" from the Bureau of Navigation, presenting the ensign with a strange irony: The Navy would not accept the resignation, but if it found out that Cutter was married, he would be dismissed. "So, I thought, 'To hell with them. If they won't let me resign, then I'll get married.'"

To keep news of the wedding out of the newspapers—so it would not cause a big row aboard the *Idaho*—the two drove to Tijuana and were married there on 4 April 1936. "I was honest," said Cutter. "I told the Navy I was going to get married; therefore, I resigned. They said, 'You can't resign,' so I got married. I didn't put in for a marital allowance or anything like that and didn't flaunt it in any way. I never rubbed it in their faces. Franny's father was very upset because we were not married by an Episcopal priest and not in the United States."

Inexplicably, the Navy acted as if the marriage never took place. The *Idaho*'s commanding officer, Captain Stott, knew about it but took no action, perhaps because of Cutter's popularity as a sports icon. However, the mother of another ensign who wanted to get married sent a letter to Maryland senator Millard E. Tydings, who forwarded it to the Bureau of Navigation and the desk of Admiral Chester Nimitz. The woman insisted that it was common knowledge aboard the *Idaho* that Slade Cutter had violated the Navy's probationary period by getting married and if he could, why couldn't her son? Nimitz wrote back to the senator, "If you can provide the proof of [Cutter's marriage], he will be dismissed." The admiral knew such proof would be difficult to come by without knowing where the couple got married. Predictably, that was the last the bureau heard of the matter. The Navy finally dropped its marital ban in 1942.

"Well, the war was coming along, and they realized they would need every man they could get," theorized Cutter. "Though several resignations were accepted up to the time I asked for one, the decision was made not to accept any more. I was twenty-five years old, and I had gone with this girl for six years. It was ridiculous."

So Cutter went about his business learning to be an officer aboard the *Idaho,* an experience he found as enriching as his four years at the academy. The 33,400-ton battleship was home to eight hundred men and a Marine detachment of forty. It was one of three sister ships—the *Idaho, New Mexico,* and *Mississippi*—authorized by Congress in 1913. They were constructed during World War I to augment the U.S. Navy in the Pacific, where Japan's growing navy was a threat to U.S. and European economic interests in Asia. With the power of the British Navy severely drained by the war, unrest was spreading. Thus, the three American battleships were launched with an eye to keeping Japan from making a move. They were based, along with the rest of the Pacific fleet, in Long Beach.

The tradition was for all graduating ensigns to rotate duty stations every few months so that in two years they had a taste of all the various departments and responsibilities aboard. Had Cutter not been a gridiron and boxing star, he might have followed the usual track. However, because of Captain Stott's desire to keep Cutter involved in football, Slade became assistant navigation officer and served in that role for nearly half the time he was aboard the *Idaho.* It was the one position that allowed him time off to play with the ship's team whenever the battleship was in port—and that was almost every weekend except during fleet exercises in the early spring of each year. "Football took up an awful lot of the time," said Cutter. "We would start our season in May, working out physically, and that would stretch through Thanksgiving. And then in the winter I had the boxing team."

Every capital ship had football, boxing, and baseball teams that competed with one another. An officer was assigned to each, normally as a coach/player. The teams were drawn from each ship's complement of enlisted Marines and sailors. Cutter was the *Idaho*'s player-coach of the football team and quickly assembled a top-caliber group. The starters were six Marines and four sailors, many of whom had been involved in fleet football for a decade or more. Each ship had its own song and colors, with the *Idaho* adopting orange and black. *Idaho* crewmen dyed their hats orange for the games. "It was good, it was real good for the esprit de corps," recalled Cutter.

The *Idaho* nearly went undefeated in 1936. The team met the Army's all-star team in Tacoma, Washington, before thirty thousand fans in a much-anticipated clash on 11 November—Armistice Day. Whitey Grove, an All-American quarterback at West Point, took the snaps for Army. Supporting him was an all-star team brought together from bases all over the country. "We weren't able to do that," said Cutter. "We just played with what we had. But we were so cocky we thought we could beat any damn Army team."

Cutter was awarded the privilege of kicking off with a ceremonial football signed by President Franklin Roosevelt just before game time. The ball was retired after the first play. During the game, Grove was intercepted by the battleship team four times and the *Idaho* prevailed 14–0, adding to Slade's laurels throughout the Navy.

In the eight-game regular season, the *Idaho*'s only loss was to the *Arizona* in October. Slade's good friend and academy All-American "Buzz" Borries was *Arizona*'s halfback. "Still," recalled Cutter, "we thought we would beat them by three touchdowns. We were overconfident and thus had a letdown. It was a close game but we lost. Boy, that made me mad and disgusted with myself."

During two off-seasons that he was aboard, Slade's training gave him experience in engineering, communications, and deck management. As a deck officer, he was in the *Idaho*'s gunnery division, including service in one of the big gun turrets outfitted with a catapult used to launch the *Idaho*'s complement of amphibious airplanes. "They'd land at sea and the ship would pick them up. Lt. William H. Hamilton took me up one time with him and we were catapulted off the number three turret. We had a bombing exercise, and the bombing run consisted of the passenger, that was me, throwing a bag holding dye into the water. They'd mark where the dye hit. He would tell me over the intercom in the plane when to throw the thing out."

Aviators were considered nuisances by many *Idaho* crewmen because the flyboys got the decks dirty and did not have to clean them. "Having to pick the planes up and launch them and all that, plus the fact they were prima donnas and were getting pay and a half—that rubbed the men the wrong way," Cutter explained. "Not only did they get the pay for this, they also got a chance to go up and fly around, which was fun. I was jealous."

Maneuvers off Long Beach and spring voyages to Panama and Hawaii kept the fleet battle ready. "We didn't know what was going on most of the time; we never did," Cutter said of his fellow ensigns. "In maneuvers, all we worried about was standing watches and keeping five hundred yards from the ship ahead at night. And watching fuel oil consumption."

The Navy was so worried about the expense of operating its ships that it put them in competition with one another for coveted "E" awards for efficiency. Sparing use of fuel oil was key. The new assistant engineering officer aboard the rival *New Mexico* was determined to do something about his battleship's previous eighth-place ranking. The lieutenant, future admiral Hyman Rickover, carefully analyzed all data aboard the ship and then took action. He restricted the flow of water to wash basins and showers because they were oil-heated. The ship's heating system was throttled back as well. Rickover replaced light bulbs with fifteen-watt filaments to conserve energy. Despite complaints from the ship's crew and an admiral's staff officer, Rickover stood firm with the support of his superior, the ship's engineering officer. The tactics soon made the lieutenant notorious. "He had special plugs made and inserted in the shower heads and it cut the water down to a trickle," recalled one of the *New Mexico*'s junior officers. "Then he fixed the valve that held the water on so that you had to use an awful lot of your strength just to get the trickle of water. Then he started timing junior officers' showers. If he thought you were taking too long, he would actually pull you out of the shower."

To those aboard the *Idaho*, Rickover seemed unscrupulous. "For the fuel situation, he bribed the oiler who came alongside [the *New Mexico*]," recalled Cutter. "He'd give him a bottle of booze or something so he would give them one hundred extra gallons of fuel and take them away from the next ship. He turned off many lights and turned down the ventilators so people would be miserable, but it would save oil—anything to win that efficiency pennant for engineering."

It worked. In the three years that Rickover was aboard, the *New Mexico* won all three annual awards.

In his various duty stations, Cutter began to notice a difference among the officers aboard the *Idaho*. Some at the top were exceptional, like Captain Stott and his executive officer, Commander James Rutter. However, others left Cutter disappointed. "The promotion process was brutal," he explained. "Until an officer reached lieutenant commander, promotion was not by selection, a weeding-out process. The result was that every officer in the rank below lieutenant commander was advanced to fill a vacancy created by someone retiring. Very few people got command of a major combatant as a captain, and the ones who did were very outstanding people. But the rest of the officers, down the line, we had some real dumb-dumbs. I think maybe they were discouraged over their inability to get promotions."

Cutter was impressed, however, with former submarine officers attached to his battleship. Their love of the undersea service began to rub off on Slade. Two of them—turret officers on the battleship—were former S-boat skippers. Cutter's division officer also had been a submariner. "We would get down there standing watch in the engine room together. And he would tell me about submarine duty. He loved it. All of the officers who had been in submarines were top-flight people on the ship, every one of them. There were about five of them. I finally decided to put in for submarine service. It was due to these people."

When his two years of probation ended on 6 June 1937, Slade and Franny marked the date by getting married—this time officially. "My father-in-law didn't think his daughter was [officially] married, and he couldn't wait until we could get married. So we got married. We didn't send out any invitations to anybody back East. Franny's father wasn't well so he didn't come. It was an Episcopal church wedding, like he hoped. My mother was there and my aunt, my sister, and a couple of close friends aboard the ship."

Captain Stott and his wife, dressed in hat and gloves, called on the couple the next day as part of Navy protocol to formally accept an officer and his bride as a married couple. The calling system was formal and common throughout the armed forces. It was a rite of passage, signaling acceptance of newlyweds within the military hierarchy. Commanding officers typically made a formal visit lasting from fifteen minutes to no more than half an hour whenever a junior officer got married in a church. He reciprocated by paying a return call with his bride within twenty-four hours. In each case, an engraved calling card with the names of the couple was left behind. The system was rigidly observed because diplomatic and military relations between countries throughout the world hinged on such formalities, Capt. A. P. Niblack observed in 1915. "The exchange of visits and of visiting cards," he noted, "implies a *recognition,* which forms the entire basis of social or official relations, and any one who belittles it is a nonentity."

Slade had decided on submarine service, applied for a billet in the summer of 1937, and waited for orders to New London, Connecticut, to the Navy's submarine training school. However, his plans took an unexpected detour back to the academy—as a football coach.

Harum Scarum

SLADE CUTTER'S detour to Annapolis turned out to be a hiccup on the road to New London. It was made clear to him before he left the *Idaho* that he would stay at the academy as coach of the plebes only through the end of the football season, then start submarine training. For the Navy, it was more practical that he lend his talents to shaping up the academy recruits before heading off to submarine school. Slade did not mind, as it was a chance to renew old friendships at the school. Unfortunately, the varsity campaign was a disaster under new head football coach Hank Hardwick. The team lost to Army 6–0 and finished 3–4–1.

With the season behind him, Slade packed his gear, and with Franny headed up the coast 350 miles to the submarine school. The couple arrived in New London on a cold January afternoon in 1938. The picturesque town on the south bank of the Thames River was a colonial shipbuilding center and carried on a thriving trade via tall-masted clipper ships that once lined its waterfront. The Cutters rented a cottage in the city located five miles inland from Long Island Sound in an area known for its rolling pastures, sleepy country villages, and foggy weather. The submarine school sat on the opposite side of the river on a hillside overlooking the Thames. Originally a ship-coaling station, it was converted into a training base in 1917, the year the Navy launched its first government-built submarine, the L-8. By the time of Cutter's arrival, the base appeared much like any other college campus in New England—tidy lawns and stately red brick classroom buildings and dormitories. But it differed from college campuses in a couple of aspects, not the least of which was a 150-foot-high submarine escape tower, looking much like a grain silo with a stairway winding around its exterior to a windowed, octagonal cupola at its peak. The cylindrical tank was filled with 240,000 gallons of purified water, steam-heated to 92 degrees. Submariners practiced solitary emergency ascents inside from the deck of a mock submarine at the bottom of the tank. Also unmistakable was the school's small fleet of stubby World War I—era submersibles used in training and docked at slips along the river.

Cutter's class of 30 officers joined about 170 enlisted men in a training program that turned over every six months. Just as Cutter had been impressed by the *Idaho*'s former submarine officers, he was equally pleased by the caliber of his class. Among them were some who would become renowned wartime skippers: Richard H. O'Kane, Charles E. Loughlin, and old friend "Dusty" Dornin. "Most of them were just good leaders, topflight people," said Cutter. "Practically all of them were stripers, showing leadership as midshipmen." There were also a few who had not fared as well at the academy but distinguished themselves as ensigns, including Sam Loomis Jr., who had finished near the bottom of his class at Annapolis. However, he achieved outstanding fitness evaluations in the fleet.

Much of the training at submarine school was classroom instruction in diesel mechanics, electrical systems, submarine tactics, torpedo weaponry, and communications (with an emphasis on Morse code). Each man had to pass rigorous oral and written examinations to graduate. Exhausting hours were spent taking apart and putting together practically every item on a submarine, one of the most complicated weapons ever devised. Diesel engines were dismantled and rebuilt. Motors and generators were rewound, and students observed acid-lead electrical storage cells emitting deadly chlorine gas when drenched with seawater, a constant concern on the boats. The men diagramed all the electrical, pneumatic, and hydraulic systems and practiced using them. Instructors taught them how to use Momsen Lungs, self-contained breathing devices that would allow them to escape from a stranded submarine. Each lung consisted of a spring-loaded nose clip, a mouthpiece, and an oxygen bag from which to breathe. To qualify for submarine duty, each officer and enlisted man had to make an ascent from a waterproof chamber at the bottom of the escape-training tank. After partially flooding the compartment, each man made an ascent of one hundred feet straight up through the middle of the column of water to the surface. The students had to do so on a knotted line stretched between the mock submarine's deck and a buoy deployed to the surface. The men methodically ascended from one knot to the next, pausing at each to allow decompression of gases in their lungs to avoid rupturing them. Divers, working in pairs in air-filled vestibules that ran the length of the tank, waited to rescue anyone who ran into problems. Cutter and his class conquered the tank with no problem. "It gave you a little sense of security," said Cutter. "But when you are out there in the Pacific with the bottom at two thousand fathoms, you don't worry much about Momsen Lungs."

Twice a week, the students boarded the school's antique "O" and "R" class submarines in small groups for lessons in diving, surfacing, and maneuvering the vessels in the river and Long Island Sound. Under the careful scrutiny of the regular crew, the students experienced for the first time the complexity of submerging, beginning with the explosive *ah-oo-gah* of the Klaxon diving alarm. In unison, crewmen cranked open huge Kingston valves to flood ballast tanks to start a boat down on a typical ten-minute dive. Simultaneously, the deafening clatter of diesel engines stopped as electrical motors took over for undersea propulsion, drawing power from the electrical storage cells lining the keel (and making up nearly a third of the submarine's weight). With split-second timing, crewmen sealed all hatches and valves throughout the vessel to prevent interior compartments from flooding. Helmsmen manned two large, hydraulic-powered hand wheels at midships that controlled the stern and bow diving planes, mechanical wings deployed from the craft to maneuver it up and down in the sea. Everything was timed; everyone aboard had to carry out his duty unerringly to perfect the dive. The lessons emphasized teamwork and the critical nature of it: one mistake could cost the lives of every man aboard.

Football players like Cutter and Dornin could identify with submarine service. "Football is getting into the details," explained Cutter. "The best football teams are those who pay attention to the details—blocking and tackling and timing and running the plays with precision and running the pass patterns properly. It is a team effort; if one guy falls down the whole team suffers. That is exactly what happens in a submarine. The engineman has to shut off the engines at the diving alarm. The man on the hydraulic manifold in the control room closes the outboard induction valve by hydraulic power. When the engine room personnel hear the outboard valve close, they close the inboard inductions. The guys in the maneuvering room have to shift to the batteries for propulsion. The fellow in the control room opens the vents, and then he closes the vents after the submarine is submerged. All these things have to happen independently. Nobody is supervising them; nobody can be there. The officers have their own responsibilities. All these things have to be done and you have to count on the people doing them in the proper sequence. It's teamwork."

The submarine class of 1938 was important to the Navy because it helped form the command nucleus for the service's new fleet boats, the long-sought answer to how to deal with the growing might of the Japanese military. For three decades, the United States had viewed with concern the threat posed by the Japanese Navy, which in a single day in 1905 sank the entire Russian Baltic Fleet in the Straits of Tsushima between Japan and Korea. Tokyo posed a strategic threat to U.S. trade interests in China, as well as U.S. territories in the Pacific. In 1907, Japanese immigration to California provoked racial conflict and government-ordered segregation in San Francisco. To deal with the possibility that Japan might retaliate by seizing Hawaii or the Philippines, the U.S. Navy developed its so-called "Orange War Plan." Initially, it projected the U.S. fleet steaming from harbors on the East Coast through the Panama Canal and into the Pacific to stymie Japan. After World War I, the plan was modified to create a new command in the Pacific as well as plan for the deployment of U.S. battleships, heavy cruisers, and supporting ships from San Diego and Long Beach (instead of the East Coast) to enable them to respond to a crisis more quickly. To do so effectively required a submarine fleet that could carry enough firepower, travel across the Pacific, patrol the coast of Japan, and return without resupply.

Admiral Hart, the superintendent of the Naval Academy during Cutter's years there, proved in 1921 that existing American submarines were incapable of doing that. He took a flotilla of ten S-class boats, accompanied by a tender, on a voyage from New London to Hawaii, then southwest to Manila in the Philippines. The entire journey was beset by breakdowns, forcing overhauls in Hawaii and overtaxing the submarines' mother ship. The flotilla's ineffectiveness convinced the Navy of the need for a long-range submarine that would not be tied to a tender and would be capable of patrols lasting as long as three months at a time.

The Great Depression of the 1930s led to the collapse of the post–World War I power balance and initiated an arms race. By 1936, Japan served notice it would no longer adhere to any restrictions on a military buildup. In retaliation, President Roosevelt authorized construction of twelve submarines, six destroyers, and two new thirty-five-thousand-ton battleships, the *North Carolina* and the *Washington*—the first to be built in the United States in twenty years. This exacerbated hostilities in Japan, putting the two countries on a collision course. The situation further escalated when Japan invaded China in 1937, pillaged the old Chinese capital city of Nanking, and attacked U.S. vessels on the Yangtze River. Tokyo declared that a "New Order" existed in Asia. To support its troops in China, Japan was desperate for the oil and raw materials abundant in British, French, and Dutch colonial territories in Malaysia, now weakened by the growing conflict between Germany and its neighbors in Europe. Only one thing stood in the way: U.S. control of the Philippines.

Meanwhile, the Orange War Plan was revised again. Instead of the fleet steaming directly to Manila from its base in Hawaii at the outbreak of war, it would move in stages, first to bases in the Marshall Islands, then to the more westerly Caroline Islands before moving into Philippine seas. The new tactic required U.S. and Philippine troops to stand their ground longer and retreat, if necessary, to the rocky fortress of Corregidor at the mouth of Manila Bay until the fleet arrived. In tandem with this strategy was a compelling need for new long-range submarines to interdict troops and supplies from Japan.

Plans for the first of these amazing submarines, called "fleet boats," had been finalized and the first generation was scheduled to arrive from shipyards in New England and California in the mid-1930s. The contrast to the old S-boats was astonishing. The older vessels were 211 feet long; the fleets, 310. The S-boats contained four torpedo tubes; the fleets, ten. The S-boats could dive to a test depth of two hundred feet; the fleets, three hundred. The S-boats had a maximum surface speed of fourteen knots; the fleets, twenty-one. The S-boats carried a crew of forty-two; the fleets, seventy-five. The S-boats had a range without refueling of five thousand miles; the fleets, twelve thousand. Moreover, enough food and water could be stored aboard a fleet submarine to enable a crew to patrol for nearly three months without resupply or refueling.

With the accelerated push for an undersea fleet, most Navy officers envisioned war with Japan in the not-too-distant future, heightening the risk to submariners. Few professions were as unforgiving. When a submarine disappeared, inevitably it meant the loss of the entire crew. In just eight years, between 1927 and 1935, ten submarines from five countries—Italy, France, Britain, Russia, and the United States—were lost in peacetime accidents, claiming the lives of 408 crewmen. Nevertheless, given the number of submarines in operation and the growing fleets around the world, disasters statistically were actually rare. In wartime, survivability was another matter. The discovery and development of sonar as a means of locating and destroying submarines posed a significant threat. During the latter stages of World War I, an Allied group known as the Anti-Submarine Detection Investigation Committee discovered an electronic method of locating German submarines. The resulting echo-ranging system known as ASDIC (from the committee's initials), or sonar, came into being. With it, a sound pulse ("ping") was transmitted from a surface vessel. When the pulse hit a submerged metallic object, it bounced back as an echo.

Cutter was vaguely aware of sonar from his studies at the academy. At the submarine school, he learned from Lt. Donald McGregor, the thirty-five-year-old officer in charge of the Communications Department, that sonar meant certain destruction of submarines. McGregor believed that a properly equipped destroyer, operating in tandem with other vessels, could determine the precise location of a submarine with sonar and deliver a coup de grâce. "He believed all this stuff," said Cutter. "He was a proponent of it in the school, and I think he really believed that it was impossible for anybody to successfully attack a convoy protected with a supersonic screen."

Still, Cutter and his classmates shrugged off the potential hazards. "That's the beauty of being young," he said. "You stick your head in a buzz saw and hope for the best. You don't worry about things like that. It isn't going to happen to you what happened to the other guy."

In Cutter's class, competition for class rank was intense because of the consequence of finishing last: assignment to the S-boat squadron patrolling the Chinese coast. "Nobody wanted to go to China, because you couldn't take your family with you," explained Cutter. "Everybody fought like the devil to stay out of the bottom of the class, because two people had to go to China, and then some had to go down to Panama, where they didn't particularly care to go either. So there was keen competition, but it was all aboveboard. Everybody liked everybody else, and we were just in there cutting wood, to do the best we could and learn as much as we could. We knew war was coming. Most of us were newly married, and we were all serious-minded young officers."

For Franny Cutter, the thought of her husband entering such a dangerous profession may have bothered her but she never let on. "Franny was for anything that I was for. She was a tremendous support always. Anything I wanted to do, she wanted to do," said Cutter. She was six months pregnant when the couple arrived in New London. Daughter Anne was born on 6 March in the middle of Slade's training. The thought of leaving his family behind for duty in China or Panama now was even more unimaginable, inspiring Cutter to hit the books with determination. "I studied harder at the submarine school than I ever did at the Naval Academy. I had to," he said. He finished fifteenth in his class of thirty. Loomis, despite his best effort, finished second to last academically, drawing the unenviable China station.

Upon graduation, Cutter was ordered to the new fleet submarine *Pompano* (SS-181) based at the Mare Island Navy Yard in San Francisco Bay. However, he was again detoured temporarily back to the academy for summer duty aboard the S-30, a training vessel for midshipmen, after which he would coach football in the fall.

The purpose of the S-30 (SS-135) was to give every midshipman a taste of what it was like to dive a submarine. Cutter, as one of the junior officers, served under mild-mannered Lt. Cdr. Robert H. Rice, his first skipper. The captain was unflappable in the face of calamities—and there were many. "That was some harum-scarum outfit," Cutter recalled. "It was really the worst. I don't know why they put Rice in there; he was too good to be in that boat. But we did need it for the midshipmen."

The boat was unique because of a mistake made during a previous overhaul in the Philippines in which diving controls were installed backward. "Everything was bass-ackwards. They couldn't transfer anybody off the S-30 because nobody else knew how to operate it. It wasn't like any other boat," explained Cutter who was unaware of the problem until a near disaster while on an initiation dive with a group of midshipmen. A crewman, a veteran of submarine service assigned to the mechanical controls for the dive, had been on leave in Baltimore for two weeks. It was his first day back and he had forgotten about the reverse installation of levers that drove the propellers during submergence. Instead of going ahead when the levers were pushed forward, the S-30 went backward. "Well, this guy wasn't thinking. So when they said, 'Dive,' he pushed the levers ahead." To the consternation of most aboard, the watertight boat started diving astern as the order came to throttle up, causing the submarine to accelerate in reverse.

"So we made this dive and all of a sudden we got a big down angle, a real big down angle by the stern, not the bow—by the stern and finally we got almost to the bottom and the diving officer says, 'Blow everything!' So we blew all main ballast, but that didn't stop us from hitting. In the meantime, the midshipmen were sliding all over the place, and the trashcans that hadn't been emptied were all over, and it was one horrible mess. Bob Rice was standing in the control room. I was in the control room, too. I didn't know what was going on. I had no idea what was going on. I was kind of scared."

The only one aboard observing the spectacle calmly was the captain who knew there was no real danger. "Bob Rice didn't say a word," said

Cutter. "When we got down, hit the bottom of the bay [at a depth of one hundred feet], he said to the controller man, 'Jim, do you know what happened?' 'No, I don't know,' was the reply. 'You were going astern,' said the captain."

Throughout the summer, Rice retained his cool, even when Slade accidentally misjudged a shipping channel while at the helm. "The first thing I know, we had a hell of a starboard list, and the captain didn't say a word, except, 'Left full rudder,' just quietly. And I put the rudder amidship and got back on the course, and Rice said, 'You know what happened?' 'No, Sir,' I replied. He said, 'You were aground.' The channel had silted up over the years, and our bilge keel on the starboard side dug into the bank of the channel and caused this heel. The captain knew what it was, and he didn't get the least bit excited or upset. I know a lot of skippers who would have just had a fit over something like that."

After the summer of training dives, Cutter rejoined the football team as the assistant varsity line coach. It was another deplorable season. The team finished 3–3–2 and, again, lost to Army (14–7). It would be Hardwick's last season as head coach. "When the football coaches didn't do a good job, of course, the alumni would rise up in wrath and demand that the coach be fired," explained Cutter. "The problem with the naval football team is not coaching; it's academic standards. You are taking a bunch of boys with brains, who are pursuing a degree in a tough academic environment, and you're pitting them against people who are functionally illiterate at other colleges. They're only interested in football."

For Slade, the new year was a chance for a new beginning as the junior officer aboard the submarine *Pompano*. That experience would test him in ways he thought not possible under a commander who was an opinionated zealot, a man who despised reserve officers and minorities, and had a reputation for rule-flouting that made him a legend in the undersea Navy.

Parks

SLADE CUTTER'S first view of the submarine he would call home for the next four and a half years was less than auspicious. Slade and Franny and their baby daughter arrived in San Francisco in the winter of 1939, then crossed the bay on a ferry boat to the Mare Island Navy Yard —fifteen miles north of Oakland on the upper reaches of San Francisco Bay. The long, flat tidal island hummed with activity in 1940 with scores of ships under construction while others were in for routine maintenance and overhaul, including the *Pompano.*

While Franny settled into the couple's second floor apartment in the nearby military enclave of Vallejo, Cutter headed for the docks to visit the *Pompano.* From the blunt, hollowed-out bullnose of its bow, the black vessel tapered aft along its narrow slatted, teakwood deck the length of a football field, hiding most of its bulbous bulk beneath the waterline. The tall white numerals "181" painted on both sides of the conning tower amidships identified it as the tenth and last in the *Porpoise* class of fleet submarines, one of only twenty modern fleet boats in existence though dozens were under construction in government and private shipbuilding yards around the nation. The submarine's half-inch-thick pressure hull enclosed eight compartments, separated by bulkheads and watertight doors. The forward torpedo room contained four 21-inch torpedo tubes and the after torpedo room had two tubes for stern shots. This was four fewer than future fleet boats. Between the torpedo rooms moving aft were

> the forward battery room containing the officers' quarters sitting above half the ship's electrical storage cells lining the keel;
> the control room, the nerve center of the submarine beneath the conning tower, and containing a machine shop in the keel;
> the crews' galley with food storage area in the keel;
> the after battery, containing the mess hall and crew's quarters;
> the engine room, containing the four diesel engines; and
> the maneuvering room, below which in the keel were the boat's electrical motors for submerged propulsion.

The submarine's sleek design was enhanced by extensive use of stainless steel throughout the compartments. The fleet boats were unique for being the first submarines to be air conditioned, not so much for the comfort of the men but to cut down on electrical short circuits caused by the high humidity of the tropics. The vessels were also the first to be outfitted with a fire-control system. The Mark I Torpedo Data Computer was capable of automatically calibrating the trajectory of a torpedo based on information drawn by the computer from a submarine's periscope and sonar system.

Despite its modern construction, the *Pompano* was beset by problems with its propulsion. Built at Mare Island and commanded by Lt. Cdr. Ralph E. Hanson, who put it into commission in June 1937, the submarine had returned to the yard from Hawaii where yard workers gutted the submarine's four diesels. Though most of the new fleets got reliable diesels from the Winton Engine Company (later absorbed by General Motors) and Fairbanks-Morse, the Navy designated the *Pompano* and a few other submarines to receive the first of a slightly more powerful German configuration manufactured by the Hooven-Owens-Rentschler Company of Hamilton, Ohio. The new engines proved disappointing: Extraordinarily high pressure and temperature caused piston rods to score and freeze. Generators periodically threw off sparks, creating dangerous conditions, and the engines produced so much smoke it tended to reveal the *Pompano*'s position at sea. Stressed-out crewmen were continually dismantling one or more of the engines to repair them. The submarine's black gang (engine mechanics) derisively referred to the engines as "whores," after the manufacturer's initials—a moniker that stuck. Still, the Navy was not about to give up. The prototype engines were shipped back to Ohio for overhaul. Charged with overseeing the overhaul was brilliant young naval engineer Lewis Parks, the service's resident inspector at the H. O. R. factory. It was his job to determine what caused the persistent breakdowns and how to overcome the deficiencies—if he could. He then accompanied the rebuilt diesels back to Mare Island where he assumed command of the *Pompano* to prove the H. O. R.s' worth by, in effect, living with them.

Parks approached the challenge with fire and determination. The contrast between him and Captain Hanson whom he relieved was dramatic. Hanson projected a kindly demeanor and was known as "Pops" because he was in his late thirties, whereas the wiry Parks oozed intensity. The New York native and son of an Episcopal clergyman was a veteran of difficult S-boat duty off the Chinese coast. Standing just short of six feet with dark hair and thick eyebrows, he was relentless in his demands on his officers and was a stickler for regulations and details. Any mistake made by a crewman drew an instant, scathing rebuke of the officer in charge. At captain's mast, said Cutter, "Parks was pretty rough on his officers with a tongue lashing for any perceived shortcomings on the boat. But the crew really worshiped the guy; they didn't know how tough he was on us." The enthusiasm that Parks brought to the boat resulted in an aggressive, skilled crew that stayed together for years as the skipper doggedly resisted transfers.

Cutter was the junior officer, or the "George"—meaning he was assistant engineering officer, communicator, commissary officer, and "all the odds and ends that 'George' gets in a submarine," said Cutter. The submarine also had an engineering officer, a torpedo and fire control officer, and an executive officer invested with day-to-day supervision of the entire seventy-man crew.

During the time it took to modify and reinstall the diesels in *Pompano*, the Navy once again modified its Pacific war plan. President Roosevelt decided to relocate the Pacific Fleet to Hawaii because the Nazi invasion of Poland in 1939 had deepened the crisis in Europe. The European powers were preoccupied in Europe, but the president believed moving the warships closer to Japan would dissuade Tokyo from offensive moves in the South Pacific. Congress also authorized the Navy to strengthen U.S. bases on Johnston, Midway, and Wake Islands—but not Guam, which it thought might provoke Japan.

It was in the spring of 1940 that the *Pompano* returned to Hawaii to join Subron 6, composed of new fleet-type submarines of the *Porpoise* and subsequent *Pickerel* and *Salmon* classes. Each new advance in the fleet submarine design was given a class designation and all boats in that class were named for fighting fish. With the submarines continually operating out of Pearl Harbor, the Cutters relocated from California to a rented apartment in nearby Honolulu where Slade enjoyed leave every ten days.

Aboard *Pompano,* Parks was eager to prove his mettle as a submarine captain. He was certain that conflict was coming and wanted his boat to be ready and his crew trained to the zenith. "He was a taskmaster," said Cutter. "He was a hard man to please, very tough, and not very popular with other submarine commanders because he was extremely competitive. And all these little tricks that he had, they were all his. He wasn't about to share them with his counterparts on other boats. He wanted the credit all to himself when the shooting began. Parks was going to make admiral come hell or high water. Everything he did was geared to making flag rank."

One of his accomplishments was developing a means of taking photographs through a periscope. "When Parks zeroed in on something, boy, he pursued it to the bitter end," said Cutter. "He learned an awful lot about photography and learned a lot about periscope photography. He was the first one to have one installed that you could look through the camera and through the periscope at the same time. Others had tried it. Parks was a pioneer. He was the first. He was first in a lot of things. And this was before the war. But he kept those secrets to himself."

Cutter was the antithesis of his skipper. Reticent to accept personal praise, Slade routinely credited the skills of others with his own success—

just as he shrugged off accolades for kicking the winning field goal against Army in 1934. Nevertheless, he scrupulously studied Parks, who became a role model for him in many other ways. "He protected his crew; he protected his officers and men. He was like a mother hen. Nobody ever better criticize anybody in the *Pompano;* that was a criticism of him. He wouldn't tolerate that." If any of his crewmen got in trouble with shore patrols, Parks stepped in to bail them out, telling military police, "I'll take care of that; that's my problem, not yours." The result, said Cutter, was unity aboard the boat. "We all knew Parks was behind us, and we had a very high esprit de corps, in spite of the fact that he was tough. A lot of tough skippers didn't have any esprit de corps. They didn't have the qualities of leadership that Parks had. He wasn't mean at all. And he was always very loyal, and he expected loyalty too."

The major problem for the *Pompano* continued to be its engines. The overhaul had done little to make them more reliable. It was not unusual for one or more to be disabled and for the boat's engineers and mechanics to be slaving to fix them. Despite the impediment, the submarine participated in war exercises, often with one diesel out of commission.

Rear Admiral Thomas Withers Jr., a veteran of World War I submarines, established a rigorous program of practice dives and torpedo drills for the nearly four dozen submarines under his command at Pearl Harbor. Realizing a whole generation of undersea sailors had come of age with no experience in combat, he made practice as realistic as possible. He insisted the boats dive to their maximum test depth—250 feet for the *Pompano.* He took his skippers up in aircraft to demonstrate just how clearly an enemy pilot could see a submarine at the normal operating depth of one hundred feet. Crewmen were subjected to depth-charge explosions from a safe distance to give them a sense of an enemy counterattack.

The U.S. Navy believed Japanese antisubmarine warfare was formidable, employing heavy depth charges and sophisticated hydrophone equipment. Navy strategy required submarines to make submerged attacks on all targets and not to show their periscopes in the presence of enemy destroyers. Instead, each submarine commander was told to depend on undersea listening gear to detect the cavitation of the propellers of enemy craft, and to send out an electronic "ping" to more precisely locate the hull of a target the moment before firing a torpedo. Skippers were schooled not to risk their vessels unnecessarily, to remain submerged during daylight, and only run on the surface at night. The effect was to produce overly cautious commanding officers on the eve of war. "They drilled this into you at the Naval Academy. You pay a price for everything you do wrong. We read all the court-martial proceedings in the Courts and Boards course we had at the academy," said Cutter. "So you tended to hesitate to do anything. You didn't want to make any mistakes."

Parks on the *Pompano* viewed such protocol with a jaundiced eye. He did not put much credence in Japanese capability and believed the submarine force could wreak havoc if employed aggressively. Many of the undersea boats were outfitted with a secret weapon the Navy believed would be decisive: magnetic exploders on the tips of newly designed Mark XIV torpedoes. The new torpedoes were longer, faster, heavier, and had twice the explosive power of previous models. The magnetic feature worked on the principle that all vessels create a magnetic field around them that would trigger the exploder if a torpedo penetrated that field. When Parks heard the weapon had never been test fired at a target vessel, he formally requested a live demonstration in Pearl Harbor. If he had to take the weapon into battle, he wanted absolute assurance it would work. The Navy turned him down, explaining that the ordnance factory at Newport, Rhode Island, was only producing ten Mark XIVs per month. The Navy did not have the luxury to "waste" them in target practice. Instead, a laboratory test was authorized. "The way they demonstrated its effectiveness was to set one up in the torpedo shop at Pearl Harbor and pass a charged wand over it," explained Cutter. "It would go *click,* and they would say, 'See, it works.' This was supposed to simulate a torpedo going through the magnetic field of a ship." The Navy clung to the laboratory tests as proof the weapon would work. It was a decision with disastrous consequences for submariners in days to come.

In the spring of 1941, the fleet practiced wartime maneuvers around Hawaii for ten days at a time, separated by three days of liberty at Pearl. The submarines participated in mock attacks on battleships screened by destroyers. At one point, Parks managed to get inside the escorts during a night surface approach on the battleship *California*. What the skipper did not know was that the ship was among the first to be outfitted with radar. "What a shock it was when all of a sudden they opened up with a thirty-six-inch searchlight on us," said Cutter. "They didn't get us until we got within about two thousand yards, but when they did they were right on. That was very unnerving."

Whenever the *Pompano* sailed into Pearl, Parks sent Cutter to the docks at Aloha Tower in Honolulu to observe Japanese merchant ships. Hawaii had a thriving trade with Japan, and magnificent white Japanese merchant ships were frequent visitors. "Parks wanted me to see if there were any features or anything on those ships that was unique that would help estimate the angle on the bow," explained Cutter, who by early 1941 had been promoted to torpedo and fire control officer on the *Pompano*. Knowing the angle on the bow from a submariner's viewpoint would help sink a ship if and when the war began.

While Cutter was spying on Japanese ships, the Japanese consulate in Hawaii had its own spies making note of the regularity of U.S. maneuvers—ten days out to sea, three days in Pearl. Relations between Tokyo and Washington continued to sour as the Navy prepared for the inevitability of war in the Pacific. Meanwhile, the *Pompano* had become an enigma to the rest of the undersea fleet. Inexplicably, Parks had not qualified any of his junior officers for submarine duty. To Cutter, it was a bit of an embarrassment after two years under Parks. "When I graduated from submarine school," recalled Cutter, "we were supposed to be qualified in submarines within one year, or else the skipper had to explain to the Bureau of Navigation why you weren't qualified. One year went by; two years went by; two and a half years went by, and I wasn't qualified. Neither was Lt. Earle C. Schneider, who was ahead of me in sub school, nor Lt. David R. Connole, who was after me; the three of us were not qualified."

Parks knew from the increasing pace of submarine construction that the Navy would transfer off the *Pompano* any qualified officers to form the command nucleus of all the new boats. Empty billets on Parks's submarine would likely be filled by reserve officers. Nothing earned Parks's disdain more than a reserve officer. He had a rabid hatred of them because there were too many of them in the peacetime Navy and, in his opinion, they clogged the service with deadwood and hindered promotions of younger men like him. "So Parks told us, 'If we don't qualify you guys, you won't get pulled off. We're going to war, and I want to be ready.' So he just poured this stuff into us," said Cutter. "He worked our tails off, and he wouldn't qualify us. And he said, 'The bureau will never check up on us.' This was a Rickover trick. Rickover would say, 'You don't submit the report, and they will never check up on you. You know the bureaucracy.' Well, this is true. Parks said they wouldn't check up, and they didn't. But my peers were going around with submarine pins, and here I am with a clean chest. Kind of hurt my ego."

Though the bureau never got wise to Parks, in mid-1941 Merrill Comstock, commander of Submarine Division 13 put it to him bluntly: "You've got to qualify these people or else." Parks did so in a remarkable exhibition of prowess, using the old destroyer *Litchfield* as a practice target. The ship was making twenty-five knots on a zigzag course as the *Pompano* tracked the vessel in a submerged approach, with Cutter and his fellow "unqualified" officers taking turns trying to "sink" the destroyer with dummy torpedoes. "Parks taught us how to solve problems in our heads. Not too many people could do this. We never used what is called the 'is-was,'" explained Cutter, referring to an instrument similar to a slide-rule that was used on most submarines to determine the proper torpedo trajectory. Nor would Parks allow his officers to use the torpedo data computer and the "banjo," devices that solved trajectories automatically. The officers could use nothing but the plot of the target's course taken from the periscope's stadimeter, eight horizontal lines etched into the lens. Parks taught the officers a formula he had devised that could be used to accurately attack a surface ship, if the course of the vessel was known, by looking at the plotting table in the conning tower. Always conscious of raising his stock with his superiors, the skipper was determined to put on a show for Commander Comstock, who was aboard as an observer. Parks told his officers in private, "I don't want you to do anything except say, 'Make the tubes ready,' and then, 'Fire.' You can say, 'Come right or left' so many degrees by compass, but don't give a course."

One by one, junior officers Cutter, Connole, and Schneider took their turns firing at the *Litchfield.* Schneider was first but missed when the destroyer zigged as he gave the order to fire. Connole was next and got a hit. Cutter followed him and also got a hit. A beaming Parks then bellowed, "Make ready another tube for Mr. Schneider" who subsequently got a hit on the *Litchfield.* "The division commander was sitting there, and he didn't know what the hell went on. All he knew was that they signaled back a hit from the destroyer but he didn't know how it happened," said Cutter. "So Parks turned to the division commander while we're all right there, and he said, 'Commodore, I think these officers are ready to be qualified for command, too, don't you?' And we were, so the division commander had to agree after our show. We were qualified for command the same day we qualified for submarines. That was Parks's moment of glory too. And he deserved it, because he had worked our butts off and he taught us all these things. We had learned everything from him, not from submarine school. We got that from Parks. It helped out later on. It helped me sink ships."

While the crew of the *Pompano* continued to practice for war, Admiral Husband Kimmel had assumed command of the Pacific Fleet. It was his responsibility to phase in a new operational plan. The old Orange War Plan was scrapped for the Rainbow Five War Plan which was a defensive holding pattern to secure Hawaii and American interests east of Midway Island. The plan envisioned the Philippines falling to Japan and a retreat from the western Pacific by the U.S. Asiatic Fleet commanded by Admiral Thomas Hart, who had been superintendent of the Naval Academy when Cutter was a midshipman. The plan was a practical document because battleships, cruisers, destroyers, and carrier *Yorktown* were being siphoned away from the Pacific to strengthen the U.S. Atlantic Fleet now guarding merchant convoys supplying raw material to Britain in its war with Germany. The strategy was a "fight to win in Europe first" if war broke out; the United States would let Japan have its way in the early going, then reassert itself offensively at a later date.

In July 1941, relations between Tokyo and Washington further deteriorated when Japan peacefully occupied French Indochina after the fall of France to Nazi Germany. The Japanese Army established bases in Saigon and Da Nang while the imperial navy began patrols in the Tonkin Gulf. Suspecting a move on the oil-rich Dutch East Indies, both the

Netherlands and Britain banned the sale of oil to Japan, aggravating the situation. The U.S. Navy had consistently urged President Roosevelt not to join the embargo because it would confront Tokyo with one of two choices: either give up its ongoing war to conquer China or wage a wider war for oil. Roosevelt believed he had no choice and joined the embargo, quickly denying Japan 80 percent of its supply. Subsequently, Tokyo planned a vast military campaign to seize and hold Burma, the Philippines, Malaysia, and the main prize, the Dutch East Indies. The Japanese Army and Navy believed that by securing these territories, Japan could complete its conquest of China and establish an impregnable defensive line around its newly acquired empire.

By August 1941, war seemed imminent. In Manila, Admiral Hart ordered all civilians and families of naval personnel to evacuate the Philippines. He also deployed his old S-boats and some fleet submarines on scouting missions around the island nation. Several squadrons of new, long-range B-17 Flying Fortresses arrived to help buttress the islands against attack. In Hawaii, the *Pompano* and the Pacific Fleet prepared for the worst. Submarines drilled constantly and were deployed on scouting missions around the coast of Hawaii. A dawn air patrol extended five hundred miles seaward from Oahu and covered all sectors to the west of the islands. Adm. Husband E. Kimmel ultimately scaled back aerial surveillance to two hundred miles and reduced the number of sectors covered because he and other naval strategists believed that if Japan attacked, it would be from the west or southwest. The admiral had the added security of the Army Air Forces to protect the fleet if Japan some-how launched an aerial attack; such an attack seemed unlikely because the Army had positioned aircraft at bases all around Pearl Harbor. "We depended on the Army Air Force to protect us," explained Cutter. "The only reason we had the Army in Honolulu was to provide a haven for the Navy so we could come in and do the things we had to do in order to keep ships running, such as opening up the bilges in order to paint them to reduce rust; or to do other maintenance repairs which required watertight integrity to be broken. For instance, the submarine had electrical cables that ran the whole length of the submarine during upkeep, so you couldn't close your watertight door between compartments. And if you even got a hole in any one of your compartments, you'd sink. I'm not condemning the Army; the Navy felt secure in the defenses it had. Admiral Kimmel and the people in charge of the Navy had us all prepared."

Roosevelt expected the Japanese to strike the first blow. The question was where and how such an attack might be handled with the least damage. The president cautioned that "the Japanese are notorious for making an attack without warning." Based on intercepts of Japanese intelligence, the administration believed it would come as a raid on the Panama Canal or the U.S. base at Wake Island. Admiral Kimmel discounted a Navy scenario prepared in early 1941 that concluded it was possible for Pearl Harbor to be attacked by carrier-based aircraft from the northeast in the early morning. There was no evidence that Japan was contemplating such a move; U.S. code breakers were reading high-level Japanese intelligence and there was no mention of Pearl Harbor in any of the intercepts. The concern in Hawaii was that the Fleet might be the target of Japanese submarines or land-based saboteurs. As a result, the entrance to Pearl Harbor was draped with antisubmarine nets and patrolled constantly by sonar-equipped destroyers. Furthermore, the Army grouped its airplanes close to one another in the center of its airfields around Pearl Harbor to better protect them from sabotage.

In October, the *Pompano* and two other submarines returned to Mare Island for modifications to their conning towers, including installation of degaussing equipment, which would neutralize the submarine's magnetic signature so that it could operate in minefields off the coast of Japan. "People say the Navy was asleep; we didn't know war was coming," said Cutter. "But that's a lot of nonsense. These alterations were purely for war."

Back in Hawaii, anxiety swept the islands. Slade's wife, who had suffered a number of miscarriages and whose health was poor, was worried. He wrote back she need not be overly concerned. "There is no danger of evacuating personnel yet, and I don't think that there is any danger of it in the future. You are bound to hear all sorts of stories at a time like this. . . . It is a hell of a life, honey, but you have something called character, and a lot of it. Take real good care of yourself for me, sweetie, and give my little girl a big hug and kiss from her daddy."

Modifications to the *Pompano* were completed in November. Cutter had been promoted to executive officer, second in command on the boat.

The submarine was about to return to Hawaii when another letter arrived from Franny. She wrote how surprised she was when Rear Adm. Isaac Kidd, commander of Battleship Division One (whose flagship was the *Arizona*), had visited her. Kidd, a former heavyweight boxer at the Naval Academy, was fond of the Cutters, having gotten to know them when Slade was a midshipman. During his visit, Kidd told Franny that if she ever needed anything not to hesitate contacting him. "I wonder what he means?" Franny wrote.

On 1 December 1941, the *Pompano* cast off for the return voyage to Pearl Harbor, in company with the *Pollack* (SS-180) and *Plunger* (SS-179). The submarines were due to arrive at the entrance buoys at Pearl Harbor at 0630 on the morning of 7 December. En route, the *Pompano* again developed engine problems. Two diesels had to be taken off line for repairs. That forced the two other submarines to slow down as well. "So we sent a dispatch to the submarine base that we couldn't get to the Pearl Harbor entrance buoys at 6:30 in the morning as planned and we couldn't rendezvous with the destroyer that was supposed to take us in," recalled Cutter. Then everything changed.

"We were steaming along on the surface 135 miles northeast of Oahu on the morning of December 7 about five minutes to 8 A.M. when the radioman came up to the bridge, up the hatch, and handed a message to the Officer of the Deck, and it said, 'Air raid on Pearl. This is no drill.' We had aboard two officers we were transporting to Pearl to take command of submarines. And they had served in China like Parks, and they got talking about the Japs: 'That's just like those yellow bastards. They'd do something like that.' And they believed it right away."

With the prospect of being attacked at any time, the *Pompano* was suddenly in peril with limited ability to dive. Because of the H. O. R. engines, the crew had been forced to pump as much water from the *Pompano*'s variable water tanks as possible to make the submarine lighter so it could go fast enough to keep up with the other two submarines. Variable water [water that could be pumped into and out of ballast tanks quickly] was a necessity in making a quick dive. Now the water had to be pumped back into the tanks—and fast. "Rig ship for dive and compensate!" yelled Parks. "Get the water back in so we can dive."

As the men at the inboard pumps worked feverishly, one of the lookouts sighted aircraft approaching from the south. They were Japanese Zero fighters returning to their carriers after leading the first wave of dive-bombers that devastated Pearl Harbor. The aircraft, camouflaged with green and gray splotches and emblazoned with a red Hinomaru rising sun on both sides of the fuselage, were the most advanced aircraft in the world at that time—fast, maneuverable, well-armed, and high-flying. The airplanes had been cruising at two hundred miles per hour at twenty thousand feet over the crystalline Pacific when pilots noticed the three submarines. The *Pollack* and *Plunger* immediately dove and were completely submerged within fifty-five seconds. The more buoyant *Pompano* was not so lucky. Lookouts jumped through the conning tower hatch where the officer of the deck dogged the watertight seal. In what seemed like an eternity, the *Pompano* began sliding beneath the waves. However, the boat was still too shallow as one of the Zeros screamed down out of the clouds. The pilot took aim with his 20-mm cannon, determined to hole the *Pompano* and send it to the bottom.

"We dove and we couldn't get all the way under," said Cutter. "We heard the machine gun bullets hitting the water above us." A few "thuds" shook the submarine as bullets ripped into the *Pompano*'s teakwood deck. The vessel plowed downward, finding safety at 250 feet. The boat leveled off and remained submerged as the crew looked for damage. Fortunately, it had survived unscathed. After an hour, Parks took the boat up to periscope depth to search the horizon for any more airplanes. He radioed Norman Ives, commanding Submarine Division 43, in the *Plunger*. "Commodore," said Parks, " I think we had better tell Pearl Harbor that we were attacked."

A cryptic reply came back: "Negative. They have enough problems."

10

War Patrol

MILITARY LEADERS in Pearl Harbor dispensed with the tedious job of encoding military broadcasts in the aftermath of the Japanese raid. Time was of the essence: "Air raid on Pearl. This is no drill." Soon reports of an enemy invasion of Hawaii hit the airwaves. Aboard the *Pompano,* the crew faced a quandary. "Everything was frantic," said Cutter. "The only urgency was to get the message out of what had happened. So the fifth column [Japanese operatives in Hawaii] took advantage by sending out phony radio warnings of Japanese fleet movements against the islands. The one I remember is 'Enemy main body off Kauai. Carriers speed 25 course 090. All ships Hawaiian Area attack.' That meant they were coming towards Pearl Harbor. So we started for Kauai. A little later, we got another one from these fifth column sources . . . 'Enemy transports unloading off Barber's Point. All ships Hawaiian Area attack.' We knew then that these messages were spurious and we ignored them."

The *Pompano* and its two traveling companions soon received encrypted orders to go to an area west of Maui near Lahaina Roads where the submarines were to remain submerged. The next morning, 8 December, the destroyer *McFarland* met and escorted them to Pearl Harbor. Those topside on *Pompano* were in disbelief. "We started up the channel and dead ahead of us was the battleship *Nevada* with her bow in the mud bank with the keel of the ship jutting into the channel," said Cutter. "And there was an American aircraft that had been ditched. Apparently, the pilot had made a landing on the reef in the shallow water there. And then we passed Hickam Field on the starboard side and everything was gutted, leveled and burning. We turned the corner at Ford Island on our port side and Ford Island was devastated and it was burning too. Then came the battleships. The *Utah* was upside down and the rest of them were cantered one way or the other. The *Arizona* was still burning and there were several inches of fuel oil on the surface of the water. The destroyer *Downes* was in dry dock blown up, and the *Oglala* was on her side next to Ten-Ten dock over in the shipyard."

The damage was unimaginable. In just two hours, two waves of torpedo airplanes, dive bombers, high-altitude strategic bombers, and escort fighters—353 airplanes launched from six carriers 230 miles north of Oahu—sank the battleships *Utah, Arizona, West Virginia, Nevada, California,* and *Oklahoma,* and seriously damaged the destroyer *Downes.* The battleships *Tennessee, Pennsylvania,* and *Maryland,* and cruisers *Helena* and *Raleigh,* the destroyer *Shaw,* and the service ships *Vestal* and *Curtiss* all suffered damage. The Navy and Army Air Forces lost 188 combat aircraft with another 159 damaged. Bunched together at airfields to prevent attack by saboteurs before the raid, the airplanes were easy targets for enemy bombers. Most sobering of all was the human toll—2,335 military and civilian personnel killed and 1,143 wounded. Rear Admiral Kidd, commander of Battleship Division 1, who had offered encouragement to Franny days earlier, went down with the *Arizona.*

The Japanese had hoped to sink the aircraft carriers *Saratoga, Lexington,* and *Enterprise* but they were not in port. *Saratoga* was on the West Coast while the *Lex* and the *Enterprise* had been sent out a few days earlier to deliver aircraft to U.S. bases on Midway and Wake Islands. Amazingly, the Japanese did not send a third wave of bombers to destroy oil depots at Pearl containing 4.5 million barrels of precious fuel oil, as well as ammunition dumps and machine shops nearby that, if destroyed, would have stymied the U.S. war effort for months. The submarine base, including three fleet submarines tied up at finger piers, was also ignored.

As the *Pompano* made its way through the harbor, the submarine base came into view. "There were people from the battleships sleeping on the dock, and the lawn was covered with people and their bedding," said Cutter. "When we tried to tie up, we couldn't get anybody to take our mooring lines. They were standing there in a stupor." One sailor finally took the line. He was a first class torpedoman off the *Pompano* who had gotten drunk and into trouble and was left behind in the brig when the submarine returned to Mare Island. After the attack, he was released and went looking for the *Pompano.* The captain welcomed him with open arms.

Also greeting the *Pompano* was Thomas Patrick McGrath, who had played football at the Naval Academy when Cutter was a coach. After graduation in 1940, he joined the battleship *California* and was on the signal bridge during the attack, firing a pistol at dive-bombers. He was one of the lucky survivors who slept on the submarine base's grassy field the night after the attack. "All he had on was a .45[-caliber pistol] strapped to his waist, a pair of khaki shorts and open sandals. That was all he had," recalled Cutter. "His clothes were lost on the battleship. I invited him down in the wardroom to have lunch with us."

McGrath was angry. "I want to go out on the first ship that's going out after those bastards," he told Cutter. Parks, who was in his cabin next door, overheard him and asked, "Young man, do you mean that?"

"Yes, sir!" replied McGrath.

Parks immediately left the boat, went to see Admiral Kimmel, even though McGrath had no submarine training whatsoever. Fifteen minutes later the captain returned. "Son," he said coolly, "you are a member of the *Pompano* crew."

The submariners in Pearl were the only real hope for quick retaliation against Japan. In addition to the *Pompano, Plunger,* and *Pollack,* the submarines *Gudgeon* (SS-211) and *Thresher* (SS-200) brought the submarine force to seven serviceable vessels, all of which refueled and took on ammunition, drinking water, and food stores for extended voyages.

In Washington, the War Department ordered the Navy and Army to "execute unrestricted air and submarine warfare against Japan." To Parks, the meaning was clear: show no mercy. He whipped up unbridled hatred of the Japanese. Cutter, as executive officer, joined the chorus as a dominating presence aboard the boat, burning with intensity and being physically larger by thirty pounds than any other crewman. "The saying goes that the exec has always got to be a son of a bitch," explained Cutter. "He doesn't have to be that, but he's got to lay down the rules and see that they are observed and arrange for the administrative operation of the boat."

Besides getting the submarine ready for combat, Cutter had his wife and daughter to worry about. Orders had been issued to evacuate all Navy dependents from the islands as a precaution in case Japan invaded. Franny, bravely facing the uncertain future, began making arrangements to leave for San Francisco with her daughter. "A lot of wives of officers were terrified of their husbands going out on war patrol. Not Franny," said Cutter. "She had confidence in the *Pompano* and especially Parks who she had gotten to know well. She never said 'Be careful.' She always said goodbye by telling me to 'Be smart, Slade.'"

On 17 December, nine days after the submarine's arrival at Pearl, the *Pompano*'s engines roared to life in a blast of blue smoke just after noon. The submarine pulled away from its mooring pier, passed the wrecked battleships, and rendezvoused with the *Litchfield,* which escorted it fifty miles west to protect it from accidental friendly fire. Because the Navy was following a "win in Europe first" strategy, the fifty-one submarines in the Pacific would have to carry the brunt of the Pacific offensive for some months to come. The Navy, however, was confident the magnetic exploders on its new torpedoes would inflict a high toll on Japan.

The *Pompano*'s orders were to travel alone to the East Caroline Islands in the vicinity of Truk Atoll, fifty volcanic peaks bristling like ragged teeth in the deep waters of the Central Pacific nearly three thousand miles west of Hawaii. Tokyo had taken control of the atoll after World War I and converted it into a Japanese Gibraltar, the suspected staging area for its invasion of the Philippines, which was already being pounded by enemy bombers. Because there was concern an armada might embark from Truk to attack Hawaii, the *Pompano* was to radio back whatever intelligence it could gather.

Parks could not wait to demonstrate the *Pompano*'s lethal skill. "It was a new ball game and Parks was very happy," said Cutter. "He could now demonstrate all these tricks he knew and then pass them along." One such twist was the installation of a special device on the periscope eyepiece that would allow Parks, an amateur photographer, to attach still and 8-mm motion picture cameras. Navy rules at the time prohibited cameras aboard submarines but Parks paid no attention.

The crew was just as excited as Parks to get underway. "You'd have thought we were going on a picnic," said Cutter. "The men were singing and whistling at their work as I made a routine inspection. It felt like the night before the Big Game. Our submarine was no plaything however. She was twenty-five feet wide and three hundred feet long—as long as a football field—and every cubic inch of her insides were fairly crackling with electric excitement."

The captain hoped for a quick transpacific crossing. But problems hounded the *Pompano* from the outset. First, a serious leak developed in the after battery deck hatch, threatening to sink the boat. It took two hours for the problem to be fixed as the *Litchfield* circled to protect the submarine as it bobbed on the surface. No sooner had that problem been solved than the H. O. R. engines began to act up as the destroyer returned to Pearl. One diesel had to be taken out of commission. The other three created so much vibration at high speed that they threatened to blow apart. Exhaust valves occasionally sprouted leaks as well, requiring frequent pumping of the submarine's bilges to keep seawater from flooding the engine room. More delays were caused by sightings of aircraft. On the second day of the patrol, the *Pompano* had to make five quick dives to avoid unidentified airplanes. On the third day, another airplane forced an early morning dive. The airplane dropped a bomb that exploded close to the submarine but caused no damage. Parks immediately brought the vessel back to the surface to continue it on its way. Seven hours later, three warplanes in attack formation from the U.S. carrier *Enterprise* returning to Pearl screamed down out of an overcast sky at nightfall. Lookouts did not notice until it was almost too late. Three bombs fell toward the submarine as it dived. The first flew over the *Pompano*, exploding on the far side.

In the control room, the quartermaster looked at Cutter with a peculiar expression.

"Hear that, sir?" he asked.

"No, what?"

"The second bomb, sir. I heard it hit the water. Close, too. It—"

A shattering explosion interrupted, followed quickly by another, so close that the quartermaster and Cutter were not conscious of the sound, only the concussions. "For the first time," said Cutter, "we heard a noise that was to become familiar to all of us—the whooshing and gurgling of disturbed water being forced along our hull and through the apertures of the superstructure over our heads. This whooshing was the worst part of the bombing, although after a time it became possible to estimate the distance of the explosion by the force of the surge of water."

Cutter looked at Captain Parks who was grinning, nodding an unspoken order for Slade to make a tour of inspection. The compartments were illuminated by ruby bulbs, used by photographers in darkrooms, to minimize surface glow at night. Faces of the men seemed ashen in the unearthly light, but every man was at his station as Cutter passed through.

"Any damage here?" Cutter asked.

"No, sir." . . . "All fast here, sir."

At first, Parks and Cutter believed the *Pompano* had escaped unscathed. But within a few days, lookouts noticed an oily film trailing the submarine. It was obvious one of the bombs had split the seam in one of the submarine's ballast tanks, used to store fuel. However, it was a slow leak, so rather than return to Pearl, Parks pressed forward, too eager for combat to follow a more prudent course.

En route to Truk, the *Pompano* was diverted to Wake Island, about two thousand miles due west of Honolulu. All contact had been lost with the base there. The Navy feared it had been overrun.

Before dawn on 1 January, the *Pompano* arrived off the coast of Wake. "Parks, of course, got in real close to look it over and he saw the Japanese flag flying over the Pan Am building," said Cutter. "He was going at dead slow speed; it was a flat calm sea and with just a little bit of periscope up. We started to go down below periscope depth, thereby making the captain blind. Parks said, 'Bring her up, bring her up, goddamnit, bring her up!' He didn't want to speed up to do so, so he said, 'Put a bubble in negative tank.'" The auxiliary man assigned the task made a crucial error however. Instead of blowing water out of the negative tank, he had his hand on the crank for the bow buoyancy tank. "What he didn't realize was he was blowing bow buoyancy by mistake," said Cutter. "The next thing we knew we were on the surface, right off the damn island; we weren't four hundred yards off the beach in daylight."

Miraculously, no one noticed. The *Pompano* quickly dived and moved off submerged. Later, making another periscope search, Parks examined the wreckage of two beached U.S. destroyers. The boat surfaced at nightfall and radioed confirmation that Wake had fallen. Meanwhile, another H. O. R engine broke down, creating more setbacks for the crew. Cutter, exasperated, noted in the *Pompano*'s war patrol diary that the engines "are entirely unreliable and unsuited to wartime operations. Although only two weeks of the patrol have elapsed, the engineers are almost exhausted from standing watch and making continuous repairs of both a major and minor nature." Still, the *Pompano* pressed on.

Parks concluded that they did not have enough fuel to reach distant Truk. "Everything was theoretical," explained Cutter. "Before the war, they never tested these things. They never sent ships out to really see—can you make it to Truk and back? So as soon as we started on patrol, Parks kept a graph on our fuel consumption and how much we had left, and also on our food—how long we can endure out there. Well, we couldn't possibly get to Truk and get back to Pearl Harbor, no way." The submarine base in Pearl, advised of the boat's dilemma, radioed Parks to proceed to Wotje Island in the Marshalls, which was much closer.

The submarine arrived submerged on 11 January and found the 16,500-ton luxury liner *Kamakora Maru* at anchorage in a narrow channel between Wotje and another island. The liner had been converted to a troop transport, thus making it a valuable target. As the *Pompano* waited offshore, a patrol boat made hydrophonic sweeps of the sea near the entrance to the strait but could not detect the lurking submarine six hundred yards away. Parks preferred to wait in the hopes of sinking the transport when it left port. More problems cropped up. The periscope began to fog up due to lack of nitrogen, the gas used to keep it clear of moisture. And something on deck started banging around, threatening to disclose the submarine's location. That night, the *Pompano* surfaced and Cutter sent a crewman topside to find the cause of the noise, which turned out to be a loose rail. During the operation to secure it, a wave crashed over the boat, smashing the seaman against the deck. He was pulled back inside where he was treated for deep cuts and serious bruises.

The *Pompano* submerged just before dawn and moved in toward the anchorage, so close to the island's coral reef that the boat's sound operator became alarmed. Nevertheless, Parks held his position just as the *Kamakora Maru* left its anchorage at five knots. Nearly a month after leaving Pearl Harbor, the captain finally was in position to wreak havoc. His success now hinged on Lieutenant (junior grade) Ralph F. Pleatman who had joined the crew before the war—to Parks's chagrin. Pleatman was a Jew from Cincinnati who had not attended the Naval Academy. He had graduated at the top of his class in college in the Reserve Officer Training Corps program before enlisting in the Navy. Parks was an old-line WASP and a virulent anti-Semite. "I don't want you aboard," he told Pleatman in private, "and I'll have you off in a month for two reasons—one, you're a reserve officer, and two, you're a Jew." But Pleatman's technical skill soon ingratiated him to the captain. Explained Cutter, "I was the TDC (torpedo data control) operator. That was the guts of the fire control system, and Pleatman was my assistant. He was sharp as a tack. He caught on to it very quickly and he was very aggressive." Those were qualities that Parks could appreciate, so he accepted his junior officer. So now, at 1123 off Wotje, the skipper gave the order to fire four torpedoes at the unescorted *Kamakora Maru* via a setup on the TDC made possible by Pleatman.

Through the periscope, Parks saw the effervescent wakes of the torpedoes closing on the target as it turned to evade. But it was too late. "We heard the hits and Parks saw the splash of water through the periscope, so he assumed that it was going to be sunk and went to deep submergence," said Cutter. The torpedoes, however, proved to be duds. The liner accelerated, leaving the scene. Parks mistook the noise of the ship's propellers for the sound of it sinking. When the *Pompano* came back up, the big ship was nowhere in view. Parks reported the "sinking" to Pearl Harbor.

The *Pompano* remained off Wotje Island for the next four days. Deteriorating weather made it impossible to attack any ship. Nevertheless, Parks insisted on getting in close to the anchorage under cover of nightfall. "Well, he almost made a nervous wreck out of me, taking sights at night," explained Cutter. "I would have the sonar, the listening gear, lowered [beneath the submarine] and would stop every so often as we closed in so we could listen. We could hear the reef, and when we got close I wouldn't go anymore. We would always be pretty close to where Parks wanted to be in the morning, because he didn't want to have to run in submerged. He wanted to be close to the harbor entrance when we submerged."

Two destroyers routinely patrolled nearby, looking for the *Pompano.* The captain decided to go after them while submerged. "Parks maneuvered all day long, trying to get in position to hit them, but they never settled down to get a good firing position," said Cutter. "I was operating the TDC, and he was up in the conning tower. So finally, in desperation, he decided to shoot. He took a 60-degree gyro angle, which was much too much for those torpedoes at that time. And we fired two torpedoes with magnetic exploders, and both of them exploded before they could hit the target. The sub readied for a third shot. Jeez, I'm on TDC and I got from Parks, 'Range twelve hundred yards, speed 25, angle on the bow 2 degrees port, stand by.' And I put on the solution light, 'Fire!' About this time Parks came down, 'Slade, did you ever have so much fun before with your clothes on?' And over the loudspeaker system. Well, I wasn't worrying about having fun with clothes on or off about that stage of the game."

The third shot also detonated prematurely. The destroyer bore down on the *Pompano* so fast that there was little time to escape. A dozen depth charges exploded near the boat, battering it and terrifying the crew. Few had experienced the terrific concussion of such powerful undersea detonations. One blast raised the bow several degrees and personnel in the forward torpedo room froze as seawater rushed past the *Pompano.* The *swoosh* through the boat's superstructure frayed nerves. "I knew then what it was like to face death," said Cutter. "We thought we had been holed. So I thought, that's the end and you don't feel anything."

A chief petty officer was catatonic. "He just sat there and stared. He didn't scream or anything like that; he was just immobile. Parks was gentle with him, just took him off his duty station," said Cutter. Lieutenant McGrath, the *California* survivor, took over, and efficiently and quickly opened and closed ten valves that make up the manifold. "His knees were knocking together," said Cutter. "But he was functioning 100 percent, scared as hell. We all were. But he did the right thing. Then it was a matter of maneuvering to get away from this destroyer.

"We abandoned the conning tower, and to this day I can see Lew Parks. He got on the annunciator controls in the control room and the wheel. He maneuvered the submarine around, all ahead full, starboard back full and port ahead full, to cut down the turning circle to evade these guys up above dropping their depth charges. He shifted to hand steering to reduce our ship's noise and had two men turning the wheel. Parks thoroughly enjoyed it. He was having a hell of a time. God, it was funny."

Though the destroyer continued to drop depth charges, they were off target. The submarine made its escape in the noise of the concussions. McGrath later sat at the crew's mess with a cup of coffee. "I love to be bombed," he deadpanned to Cutter. "It feels so good when they stop."

The *Pompano*, suffering only minor damage, resumed the patrol, heading for neighboring Maloelap, Reuter, Taron, and Aur, a group of islands thought to be the epicenter of enemy activity in the Marshalls. For several days, Parks kept Maloelap under surveillance. A number of merchant ships were anchored not far from several island warehouses, hangars, and barracks. Parks radioed details to Pearl, noting that the buildings were out in the open and would make excellent targets for an air raid. With no targets to shoot at and fuel running low, the *Pompano* headed for Pearl Harbor.

On 31 January, the *Pompano* became the first submarine to return from an extended war patrol. The boat moored at the submarine base in the early afternoon. To have completed the forty-five-day voyage seemed miraculous, given all the calamities—the fuel leak, persistent engine breakdowns, attacks by U.S. aircraft, and depth charges. The high command considered the sinking of the Japanese troop transport off Wotje Island a significant achievement. But even more valuable was the radio intelligence used by Vice Admiral William F. Halsey Jr., commander of Task Force 8, to launch bombing raids on 1 February against the Marshall and Gilbert Islands. Enemy facilities identified by Parks on Maloelap were obliterated in the first major counterattack of the war. The raid was a significant morale boost for Americans back home and staggered the Japanese. Parks was roundly applauded for the aggressiveness and persistence of his patrol. The skipper was mildly rebuked, however, for risking his submarine by continuing to remain on patrol despite the fuel leak. "The loss of a submarine in war time is a very serious matter," noted his squadron commander, who nevertheless strongly recommended giving the Navy's highest award, the Navy Cross, to Parks for his accomplishments under trying circumstances.

Cutter's note about the "utter unreliability" of the magnetic torpedoes in the ship's log was dismissed. The Navy blamed the crew for improper maintenance. Still, premature explosions were being reported by submariners everywhere. Sub captains, including Parks, begged Admiral Withers, commander of the undersea fleet, to allow them to deactivate the magnetic feature. But Withers absolutely forbade it. He cited the shortage of torpedoes and the Navy's belief that one magnetic warhead could sink a ship, whereas it would take two or three contact torpedoes to do the same job. The skippers were appalled at the decision, given so much evidence the warheads were defective. Some, including Parks, decided on their own to deactivate the magnetic function without Admiral Withers's approval or knowledge.

The much-ballyhooed secret weapon was in fact completely unreliable for a number of reasons. The triggering mechanism had never been tested in southern latitudes where the earth's polarization flattened out the magnetic fields around metal-hulled ships, causing the warheads to go off too far from their intended targets. Also, because of peacetime cost-cutting measures, the Navy had only practiced with dummy torpedoes and had not accounted for the additional weight of live warheads. As a result, the torpedoes ran ten feet deeper than predicted, causing many to pass under their targets. Finally, the torpedo firing pins in the nose of the Mark XIVs had not been thoroughly tested. In the months to come, field commanders were to discover that when the nose cone came in contact with a ship's hull, the crushing impact trapped the firing pin, thereby disabling it. Only those torpedoes making contact with a target at oblique angles were likely to go off. Ironically, direct contact at 90 degrees—the perfect setup—ensured failure.

At Pearl, the squadron commander recommended that new engines be installed in the *Pompano* before its second war patrol. But he was turned down. Every available submarine was needed to keep pressure on the enemy. Yard workers in Pearl did their best to repair the diesels. They also installed a prototype radar unit capable of detecting incoming aircraft.

The work took two months, during which time Cutter spent time with his family, still in Honolulu while awaiting transport back to the States. The risk of a Japanese invasion remained, and Slade was afraid the enemy would use poison gas. Thus, he was anxious for his family to leave. However, because of wartime censorship, he was unable to learn the exact departure date for the ocean liner and thus missed seeing his wife and daughter off in March. In a letter written to Franny from the *Pompano,* Slade recalled the poignancy of their last goodbye. "It was a very depressing moment when I turned to go to the car after hearing Anne tell me, 'Have a good time, Daddy.' On the way in Sunday morning the captain and I stopped off and passed by the ship you left on. It was evident that you would not be there very long from the preparations that were being made, and I found out later that you left—damned censorship. I have thought of my two dear ones constantly, and hope that everything is well. . . . This was no place for you and Anne to be, and I am very happy that you are now safe on the Mainland. All we worry about now is how soon we can get out after the bastards again."

On 20 April, the *Pompano* headed for the South China Sea. This time, because of a shortage of magnetic exploders, the boat was outfitted entirely with older Mark X torpedoes with contact exploders—perfectly fine to Parks and Cutter, given their skepticism of the Mark XIVs.

The radar unit aboard proved to be useless: it needed a special vacuum tube that could not be procured before the patrol because of a strike by the manufacturer, the Bendix Corporation back in the States. "The crew was angry," said Cutter. "And I'll never forget getting down there in the control room and talking to them and saying, 'Look, we are out here to protect our country.' I was trying to get them over this anger at Bendix Corporation and at the United States government that it would tolerate such a situation when we were out there risking our lives for people who didn't care. My point was, 'Well, your family cares. Your mothers and brothers and sisters and grandparents all care, so you are fighting for them. To hell with the rest of them!' They bought that, making it like a family affair."

The submarine proceeded west four days to Midway Island where it anchored briefly to top off its fuel supply, then resumed its mission. On 2 May, as the *Pompano* neared Japanese-held Wake Island, a biplane spotted the submarine on the surface and dropped a bomb, which just missed. As the boat made an emergency dive to three hundred feet, the immense sea pressure caused a gasket in the after battery toilet to break in half. Seawater gushed into the submarine. "It was serious," recounted Cutter. "We had to do something about it. We were not far off Wake but had to surface to stop the leak. Fortunately it was night because we had to remain on the surface until the problem was fixed."

A work crew discovered the gasket had been installed backward by workers at Pearl, causing it to rupture. Now, it was necessary to get inside a narrow pipe to fix it. Someone with exceptional strength was needed to saw through the metal discharge line to get to it. The man chosen for the job was Motor Machinist's Mate First Class Herbert A. Calcaterra. "They called him 'Chainfall' because you didn't need a chainfall with him aboard," explained Cutter. "He was strong as an ox, and I was pretty husky in those days, too. So he and I were the ones who sawed through that discharge line which is tough metal. We used a hacksaw blade held in our hands with a rag because we couldn't get a hacksaw in there. We were motivated. We couldn't dive and were on the surface for six hours in enemy-controlled waters. We finally cut through it, and they put the correct flange on, and we went on our way." Though the leak had been fixed, the toilet—one of only two aboard—could not be used for the rest of the patrol.

Resuming the mission, the submarine entered its patrol sector on 9 May in the shipping lanes between Japan and Malaya, now under Japanese occupation. Two weeks went by as the *Pompano* made its way down the east coast of Formosa (Taiwan). Four lookouts, the officer of the deck, and Cutter or Parks stood watch on the bridge. Soon Slade became concerned the lookouts were getting bored and decided to give them a pep talk down in the control room.

"One thing you have to remember," he began, "is that we have only fifty-some submarines, and the people in our country are counting on us to do a job. And if we get knocked off, why, it's a great loss, and you've got your shipmates who are counting on you. You've got that one sector, the 90-degree sector that you're responsible for, and if somebody comes in on that sector and you don't see it and we get sunk, why, that's a pretty bad thing to think about."

To which one of the lookouts replied, "Yes, sir, Mr. Cutter, and I'm aboard, too."

On 24 May, the re-energized lookouts sighted a fifty-ton fishing vessel, which was too small to attack. But the vessel's crew saw the submarine in the darkness and moved toward it, thinking it was Japanese. The *Pompano* attempted to evade but the trawler kept moving forward, as if to make friendly contact. Parks worried that the ship might radio others about the *Pompano*'s presence. When the ship continued to approach, the skipper gave the order to fire fifty rounds of tracer bullets to warn him off. A frantic crewman, still thinking the *Pompano* was Japanese, held a lantern up to show the rising sun on the ship's flag. That inflamed Parks. "So Parks said, 'Let them have it!' I gave the order to the gun crew to open up again, and that time we just kept firing. Finally the thing caught fire. That's one of the terrible things of war. He was harmless, and he thought we were friends. He was coming over to exchange information or whatever. I was quite upset about that afterwards. But that didn't bother Parks in his interpretation of our orders to wage unrestricted warfare. They were enemy to him. He said, 'Don't worry about that. They're feeding the enemy, and they are fair game.'" There were no survivors.

The following morning, the *Pompano* identified a five-thousand-ton oil tanker. The submarine surfaced, then charged after the vessel. During a seven-hour chase, a fire broke out in the engine room, disabling a generator. Then an airplane forced the submarine to dive. Parks tenaciously resurfaced and overtook the tanker, taking position ahead of it. When it came into view, he launched a fusillade of torpedoes. At 1601, one of them exploded against the tanker, turning it into an inferno. The *Pompano* surfaced among survivors but quickly dived when another aircraft was sighted.

For the next two days, the submarine patrolled the west side of Okinawa, looking for more action. On 30 May at 1510, smoke was sighted on the horizon. The *Pompano* surfaced and raced after the target. An hour later, the submarine submerged to periscope depth ahead of a large transport escorted by a destroyer. Parks fired two torpedoes at the transport from his stern tubes at a range of only 540 yards. Both hit with devastating consequences. Parks, to fool the destroyer commander, increased the boat's forward speed and made a sharp turn back in the direction of the sinking ship to pass close by it while submerged, one of his favorite techniques. The destroyer counterattacked, dropping the first of twenty-two depth charges. But they were well off target and the *Pompano* escaped. Two and a half hours later, the creaks and groans of the transport's superstructure collapsing were picked up by the submarine's sound equipment, foretelling the death of the ship as it headed to the bottom.

For the next four days, the *Pompano* angled eastward to conserve fuel for the return trip to Pearl. En route, it gave chase to a four-hundred-ton inter-island ship. Surfacing, Parks ordered gun action, and filmed the action with the motion picture camera. The firepower of the submarine quickly destroyed the vessel, leaving two dozen survivors afloat. Two days later, the *Pompano* sighted a one-hundred-ton trawler. Again, the boat surfaced and crewman opened up with the deck cannon, sinking it as it tried to escape. Parks filmed the entire episode. There were no survivors.

On 7 June, news arrived of the Battle of Midway in which a Japanese carrier task force attempting to seize the island was defeated by a U.S. carrier force in a duel fought by aircraft. During the height of the battle, the enemy submarine I-168 sank the crippled carrier *Yorktown* and the destroyer *Hammann* alongside it. Similarly, the U.S. submarine *Nautilus* (SS-168) sent the damaged Japanese carrier *Soryu* to the bottom. The good news for the United States was that the battle ended further attempts by Japan to seize Midway or pose a threat to Hawaii.

The crew of the *Pompano* was jubilant as it changed course and headed for Midway Island to refuel. The submarine arrived on 13 June, two days after the battle. Parks and Cutter, in accordance with Navy custom, went to call on Captain Cyril T. Simard, commander of the base. "Simard was taking a shower," said Cutter. "He said, 'Come on in.' And he came out there bare-ass naked after his shower and we sat there while he got dressed. And he was very upset about the Army Air Force because of the claims they had made about the Battle of Midway, which were false." The Army airplanes were based on the island and did take off during the battle but were inconsequential in the succeeding air battles. Some got lost over the ocean and had to be directed by carrier-based Navy fighters back to Midway where the Army pilots boasted about their heroics, angering Simard.

While at Midway, a Japanese prisoner picked up by another submarine was transferred to the *Pompano* for transit to Pearl Harbor for interrogation. After a voyage of five days, the submarine met the *Litchfield*. "I was up on the bridge and the skipper was down below taking a shower," recounted Cutter. "And the skipper on the destroyer got on the voice radio, called over and wanted to know how the patrol went. We were just batting the breeze back and forth, and I mentioned we had a prisoner aboard." As a favor, the destroyer skipper said he would signal Pearl so Marines would be on the dock when the *Pompano* arrived to take the prisoner into custody without delay. Cutter thanked the captain, then called down the hatch to inform Parks.

"Jeez, the next thing I know, up comes Parks, face covered with lather and a towel wrapped around his waist, no other clothes on except sandals. And boy was he fit to be tied," said Cutter.

"What the hell do you mean by doing that?" Parks demanded.

"Captain," replied Cutter, "what would you have done?"

"That has nothing to do with it. Do I interfere with your operating the internal mechanism of this ship? I don't expect you to interfere with the external affairs of the ship. That's my responsibility."

With that made clear, the submarine arrived in Pearl Harbor where a booze-laced celebration by Parks and his officers was to make headlines in Hawaii—and make Slade Cutter's name infamous.

11

The Hooligan Boat

WITH TWO combat patrols behind them, the crew of the *Pompano* basked in glory for sinking 32,985 tons of enemy shipping while providing crucial intelligence for the air raid on the Marshall Islands. Captain Parks and his men had accomplished this despite persistent engine problems, leaking fuel tanks, bombings by U.S. aircraft, depth charges by Japanese destroyers, and faulty torpedoes. "It is particularly gratifying," concluded the commander of Submarine Squadron 4, "to note the aggressiveness and efficiency displayed by the commanding officer in conducting both his torpedo and his gun attacks." Cutter earned Silver and Bronze Stars for skill and gallantry. And the crew was singled out for praise for their truculence at a time when other submarines returning from patrol posted disappointing results—the first hint of a brewing "skipper problem," a sense that commanding officers were reluctant to press the fight. Parks not only pursued the enemy with dogged determination, he brought back motion pictures and still photos that earned him further acclaim—and a promotion to the staff of Commander Submarines Atlantic in New London.

Cutter was happy the skipper was moving up, but regretted he could not make another run. "It's just a crime that he didn't have a good submarine with good torpedoes because he would have made a killing out there," he said. "He had this old submarine with these torpedoes that weren't worth much." The performance of the Mark XIVs was scandalous. Many were going off prematurely, traveling too deep, or striking a target but not detonating. Frustrated captains complained bitterly, but the Navy's Bureau of Ordnance stood by its weapon, thus putting the submarines in great jeopardy. By July 1942, three had disappeared after firing duds—the *Grunion* (SS-216), the *Shark* (SS-194), and the *Perch* (SS-176).

Because of wartime secrecy, veterans of the "Silent Service" could only discuss among themselves the particulars of their heroics. Within hours of the *Pompano's* arrival, alcohol flowed as freely as the yarns in the officers' club at the submarine base where Parks, Cutter, and Connole were happy to see Commander Willis M. Thomas, the former *Pompano* executive officer who had been detached in 1940 to take command of mothballed destroyers being loaned to Britain for its war with Germany. Now he was back in Hawaii, angling for command of his own submarine.

"As usual we got drunk as we always did just coming in from patrol," said Cutter. The binge continued into early hours of the morning and resumed the next afternoon at the club, crowded with military personnel. Parks, in an expansive mood, purchased a couple cases of cold beer, placed them on a large aluminum mess tray, and passed them around. As the afternoon wore on, he and Cutter tried to get two Army lieutenants, former enlisted men, to give them a ride in their staff car to the Royal Hawaiian Hotel, the luxury hotel in Honolulu leased by the War Department as lodging for submarine sailors. But the Army officers turned them down. "That's the trouble with the Navy," said one. "You have no morale. Here we are, we are just second lieutenants, and we have a command car."

Angered by the rebuff, Parks left the bar at dusk, Cutter, Connole, and Thomas in tow. Outside, they noticed the Army car. "The lieutenants made a mistake," said Cutter. "They stayed in the bar. And they left the keys in the car. So Parks got in. Of course he was the skipper, so he got behind the wheel." Cutter jumped into the passenger seat while the other two got in back. Parks started the car and tried to put the five-speed gearshift into reverse but could not find it. "We kept inching ahead and went through a hedge in front of the officers' club. Finally, he got her into reverse, backed out into the street, and we went out on the highway into town," said Cutter.

No one was feeling any pain as the stolen car roared along beneath sodium vapor lights that illuminated the highway. Thomas noticed a rifle in the back with a bandolier of tracer and armor-piercing bullets. He passed them to Cutter. "See if these are the same as the Navy's, Slade," Thomas said to the Academy rifle marksman. "So I loaded the rifle, and what the hell was I going to shoot at? Well, I tried to hit those sodium vapor lights as we went through. But none of us could see the tracers because we were moving. Then we got into town and right as you make the turn onto Beretania Street, Dole Pineapple had a water tower made like a big pineapple. That was a good target, I thought, so *whammo, whammo* as we were going by. The next thing we knew, a green Marine car with MPs in it pulled up alongside and motioned us over."

Because the Navy yard was changing shifts, traffic was too heavy for Parks to comply. So he kept driving with the Marine car racing alongside until the road split. "The only place the Marines could go was up King Street and we went down Beretania," said Cutter. "They couldn't get us." Parks sped on toward Honolulu's Aloha Tower monument where territorial guards manned a traffic checkpoint. Cutter, worried the Marines would catch up, urged the skipper to abandon the car. But the captain would not hear of it. It was beneath his dignity, he said, to walk from Aloha Tower along the Ala Wai yacht basin about four or five miles to the Royal Hawaiian. "So we stopped at the checkpoint and Parks took out his wallet," said Cutter. "We didn't have ID cards in those days. I don't know what he showed them, member of the Elks or whatever. That was enough for these guys, and they waved us through."

The car rumbled on, and Cutter resumed target practice. "I hadn't been able to spot my shots yet but now we've got a yacht basin with these white balls for anchors and now I could spot them in the water. Boy, here I was. We were going along and *whammo, whammo.* The next thing I knew we were up over the curb and into a palm tree. We didn't hit it but stopped next to it." Simultaneously three military Jeeps screeched to a halt. Marines with guns drawn surrounded the seemingly crazed submariners who stumbled out of the hijacked Army vehicle.

"Don't shoot!" shouted Parks. "We're not mad!"

The Marines ordered the men into a paddy wagon for a trip to the local police station, which was jammed with cops, craning for a look at the dangerous characters who had raised such an alarm. News of the incident quickly got back to the submarine base where Lt. "Dusty" Dornin called the police station. He volunteered to drive over to vouch for the *Pompano* officers. "You come down here and we'll lock you up too!" shot back the desk sergeant.

During interrogation on the second floor of the lockup, Parks received permission to telephone General Delos Emmons, the military governor of Hawaii, who was Parks's neighbor on Diamond Head. He also telephoned his brother, John Parks, who happened to be the federal prosecuting attorney in Hawaii.

"So these birds were in a quandary," explained Cutter. "I was just sure they were not going to lock us up. They knew we were going back out on war patrol. I didn't worry about it. I got a kick out of their discomfort. They didn't know what to do. They wanted to let us go but they didn't know how to do it. So finally they wanted to know where the evidence was; they needed some evidence. Where are the shells? Well, I had some in my pocket, empties—two, as I recall. Before anything had happened I had gone to the toilet and tried to flush them down the toilet. But .30-caliber cartridges won't flush down the toilet, so I fished them out."

One of the detectives now wanted to know where they were.

"I don't know," said Slade.

To which Connole whispered, "Christ, you had these things. Why don't you give them to them? What did you do with them?"

"I threw them out the window," Cutter replied beneath his breath.

A detective reading lips from forty feet away shouted, "You threw those away. Whereabouts?"

Cutter, believing there was nothing to be gained by continuing to stall, replied, "Out in the parking lot." An MP marched him outside where Cutter got down on his belly. Crawling under a car, he found one but could not locate the other. The single shell was evidence enough for the authorities, who let the suspects go, subject to being recalled.

Parks abruptly left for the States. No punishment was ever handed down nor any formal report filed, thanks to the intercession of Parks's brother and the governor, which enraged the shore patrol commander who wanted to make an example of the *Pompano* crew. He gave Thomas, the senior officer in the group, a tongue-lashing. "Parks is no longer around, and you won't have the protection of his brother and the governor the next time," he warned.

Parks hoped no one would find out about the escapade. But it had already become the stuff of legend. "Hell," said Cutter, "everybody knew about it. You can't keep something like that quiet. But, you know, we didn't give a damn. In those days, I didn't care at all what happened. I didn't expect to survive the war. I don't think anybody did, really. That's why I never kept a diary, never took any pictures, never kept any pictures of anything. But we weren't as bad as we were made out to be. You know, terrors of the beach. Normally these things would happen just when we came in from patrol. We would get unwound, and then we would settle down and be reasonable."

Fanfare over the incident and Parks's aura as maniacal and reckless on war patrol enhanced the submarine's reputation as a boat filled with hooligans. Crewmen who got inebriated in the first few days after arrival did not help matters. One of them—Herb "Chainfall" Calcaterra—had gotten drunk at the Royal Hawaiian and for some reason had begun throwing furniture and clothing from his sixth floor window. The manager of the hotel called Cutter, demanding he do something. "They were afraid to go in there," said Cutter. "So I went into the room and Calcaterra started crying, 'Oh, Mr. Cutter.' He was just as docile as a lamb. He didn't have any clothes to put on; everything was out of the room. We took him out to base and put him in the relief crew for the rest of the refit period."

The big news for the *Pompano* was the appointment of a new commander. But the reception for Dudley "Mush" Morton, who was to become one of the top wartime skippers, was less than enthusiastic. Crewmen knew he had been passed over for executive officer in peacetime. "He hadn't made it so we didn't want him," said Cutter of the general attitude aboard the submarine. "Somehow, someone recognized his potential, and they ordered him to the *Pompano* because he was pretty experienced. I was getting ready to command, and Connole was one year behind me. And the other officers aboard were McGrath and Pleatman. We had some talent there. I think they figured that if they put Mush there with that talent, he would have a better chance."

After only two days, the Navy thought better of the idea and transferred Morton off the boat to take command of a new submarine. Thus Thomas, the former *Pompano* exec, took over. "We were all good friends. Thomas knew us, we knew Thomas, we all respected each other and it was perfect for him to be assigned as skipper," said Cutter. The new captain made it clear that because he had not made a war patrol, he would have to rely on Cutter and Connole, perfectly acceptable to them.

The *Pompano* cast off on 19 July 1942 for its third patrol, a two-month mission to the heavily traveled shipping channel in the middle of the Sagami-Wan Bay, below the entrance to Tokyo Bay. Daily gunnery drills and training drives occupied the *Pompano*'s crew en route, along with the usual problems with the boat's H. O. R. engines. As navigator, Cutter often stood watch on the bridge with the lookouts. There he pondered the future as the submarine neared the coast of Japan. "Before sunup, before morning twilight, I remember taking a look at the stars and wondering if I would see them again."

On 1 August, the *Pompano* made contact with a small trawler and a fishing boat posted as sentries five hundred miles east of Tokyo—a precaution after a force of B-25 bombers, led by Army Air Forces Lt. Col. James Doolittle, bombed the city on 18 April 1942. U.S. submarines had been ordered to attack the screen. But Thomas wanted to enter Sagami-Wan Bay undetected, and chose not to attack. Five days later, the submarine slipped into the bay and made contact with a torpedo boat. Thomas wanted to sink it but Cutter and others talked him out of it; the target had a shallow draft and the torpedoes could not be set shallow enough to ensure detonation. The following night, 7 August, the *Pompano* spotted another torpedo boat that turned and made for the submarine's position at high speed. The submarine evaded attack and later that night encountered a large, unescorted freighter. Thomas maneuvered the submarine into position and fired four torpedoes. All missed.

At 0300 prior to submerging for the day, the *Pompano* received encrypted radio intelligence from code breakers in Hawaii that a large enemy warship, perhaps a battleship or carrier, would pass through the shipping channel the following night, probably bound for the naval base at Yokohama. Sixteen hours passed as the crew waited for darkness so the submarine could surface and begin the hunt. By then, the boat's electric storage batteries were nearly spent; the struggle to maintain position against the great current that flows north through the bay toward Tokyo had drained them. They needed a recharge, but that could only be accomplished on the surface where the air-breathing diesels could be powered up to turn the generators.

At 1900 hours, Thomas surveyed the bay through the periscope. Standing by his side was Cutter, ready to relay orders to the crew while fixing his gaze on the depth gauge and the bubble in the boat's inclinometer to ensure the submarine did not accidentally broach. The periscope sweep revealed darkness had descended over the bay. Thomas had Cutter also take a look through the dim illumination of the periscope. He too reported a dark, glassy sea with no apparent surface traffic. At 1915, Thomas gave the order to surface.

Cutter and six lookouts hurriedly climbed the ladder leading to the bridge as the submarine bore upward with the release of high-pressure air into the boat's ballast tanks. The *Pompano* broke surface and the boat's diesel engines came to life. In a flash, the lookouts and Cutter who had been wearing night vision goggles to acclimate their eyes to seeing in the dark scrambled through the hatch to the bridge. "My God, we thought we were naked. It was daylight," said Cutter. "Nobody was around so we decided to wait it out because it was going to be dark in a little while. All of a sudden on the starboard quarter searchlights illuminated us and six shells came out from 8-inch gun turrets."

It was a Japanese cruiser, half a mile away. Cutter sounded the alarm. "Clear the bridge! Dive! Dive! Two hundred feet! Cruiser firing at us! Rig for depth charge!" The bridge party plunged through the open hatch as the deafening *ah-oo-gah* of the diving alarm reverberated and the first shells screamed past overhead. "We heard them hit the water. We were going down the hatch by that time, all seven of us in a stream, and we dived so fast there was no time to fasten the conning-tower hatch," explained Cutter. "As the water closed over us, four men were hanging from the inside of the hatch to hold it shut. They took a shower as the water streamed in, but after a moment the outside pressure seated the hatch." It took less than a minute for the *Pompano* to clear the surface.

"Sound reported destroyers closing in—five of them," said Cutter. "For the first time on the cruise, watertight doors were sealed throughout the ship, isolating all compartments. The whole ship became a taut, listening unit."

The destroyers searched the sea with sonar pulses, and quickly established the *Pompano's* location. The situation was as bleak as Cutter could imagine. "The air was bad. The battery was down, because we had been bucking that current, so all we could do was hope to God they weren't lucky. We couldn't take much evasive action. We didn't have enough battery for it." In stony silence, crewmen stood at their posts. In each compartment, talkers listened on the boat's battle telephones for reports from the tracking team in the conning tower.

"He's turned toward us. . . . He's coming in. . . ."

The sound of propellers was faint at first, a slight throbbing outside the hull. But it grew in intensity. The destroyer's screws cleaved the ocean in a hypnotic rhythm that rose to a scream. The splash of depth-charge canisters hitting the water could be heard as the warship passed over. The *Pompano* dropped below two hundred feet. The first bomb exploded with an audible "click"; then the anvil-like concussion of seawater smashed the boat. More than a dozen charges ripped the ocean at thirty-second intervals. Shock waves battered the submarine. Intermittently, heavy objects hit the hull and deck and bounced off. Broken glass showered the compartments. Chunks of insulating cork fell from the overhead. In the engine room, a diesel exhaust valve ruptured, spewing a fountain of seawater. Crewmen fought to control the flood but little could be done against the sea pressure. Bilges in the engine compartment began to fill.

The boat slid deeper.

At 403 feet, the compression of seawater on the hull caused more cork insulation to buckle loose and fall, littering the deck. The superstructure crackled ominously, threatening to rip apart. Thomas ordered more speed from the electric motors to keep the boat from passing below crush depth. He also powered up the bilge pumps to expel seawater that threatened to flood the engine room. The noisy equipment and the high-pitched squeal of the boat's rotating propeller shafts soon betrayed the *Pompano*'s location, and the destroyer charged anew with a fresh rack of depth charges. All it would take was one to detonate beneath the submarine or next to it to break its back and it would be no more.

Thomas secured the pumps for silent running as his sonar operator counted down the approach. "He's at 180 . . . 170 . . . 160 . . . 150 . . . he's coming in."

Depth charges fell fast. Detonations shook the submarine wildly. Ventilation pipes vibrated, threatening to break loose. The leak in the engine room became more pronounced. The boat took a sharp up angle.

The *Pompano* was alive . . . barely. Officers moved through the compartments, whispering encouragement and gathering status reports. The silence was nerve-racking as the sound of a heavy ship with a four-ship escort could be heard overhead. The convoy moved past on the port side—the *Pompano*'s intended target that night. Unable to attack, a gunnery officer muttered, "Damn him!" Even Cutter was mad. But there was a silver lining. "The ship gave us a chance to elude the destroyers which were still listening for us," he explained. "We got directly under it and started off in the same direction, headed straight for the Japanese port. The destroyers couldn't hear us, and so we slipped away. In twenty minutes we had lost them. In another ten minutes the big ship had run away and left us. We were alone, under the surface of an island-studded, tide-ripped channel on the coast of Japan. Beyond that, we had only a general idea of where we were."

Minutes later, the submarine ran aground 294 feet down, crushing its sonar pod and leaving the boat electronically blind. Seawater in the engine room had reached the deck plates, swamping the two aft diesel engines and short-circuiting the boat's electrical generators. The motors, the only means by which the *Pompano* could attack, subsequently short-circuited and shut down.

Thomas summoned Cutter and Connole to his quarters. He told them he had decided to scuttle the *Pompano*. Cutter pleaded with him to give the boat a fighting chance, to stay submerged for as long as humanly possible. But Thomas was resolute, turned and went into his stateroom where he stayed. "I guess he had given up," said Cutter. Before long the captain emerged however, agreeing to one more try. But the boat had no power. It would be at the whim of the sea, adrift and with no listening gear to evade hunter-killers above.

Connole, the diving officer, managed to get the vessel off the bottom, using blasts of compressed air. It was now up to Cutter, the navigator, to plot a way out. But he had no idea where the submarine was, just the knowledge that the five-knot current in the Sagami-Wan Bay was strong enough to keep the boat moving north toward Tokyo, or, if he was lucky, west toward the coast of Honshu. If the boat could remain submerged long enough, if the flooding in the engine room could be slowed, he reasoned, the *Pompano* might surface out of range of the warships, then make a getaway before daybreak using the boat's two serviceable engines. It was a slim chance. But at least it was a chance.

As the boat drifted in the bay, the helmsman steered a westerly course by hand-turning the large wheel controlling the boat's rudder. Before long, the *Pompano* came to a grinding halt on the bottom, spinning the wheel and flipping the helmsman. With the submarine again stranded at a depth of 145 feet, Cutter reasoned the *Pompano* was near the coast and probably out of range of enemy ships. Thomas gave the order to blow the remaining ballast, but cautioned a quick scuttle might be necessary. "Be prepared to carry out your orders," he told his officers.

"I felt for my weighted sacks of confidential papers. They were where I had tucked them inside my shirt," said Cutter. "Then we blew the last drop of ballast water."

The submarine made a steep ascent, the crewmen holding their breaths. The boat burst into the open at 2345. Cutter and the lookouts threw open the conning tower hatch and scrambled onto the bridge. "I was the first one out the hatch as the navigator," said Cutter. "I looked up and a brilliant beam of light hit me full in the eyes. Jeez, I thought it was a searchlight right on us. I said, 'Oh, shit!' I thought it was a cruiser with that searchlight up there, high above us."

It turned out to be the coastal Mikomoto lighthouse guarding the entrance to Tokyo Bay. The submarine was less than a thousand yards from the base of the stone sentinel whose beacon lit up the boat. Luckily, the submarine had not been detected. Cutter looked out to sea and saw nothing but blackness—and a way out. Quickly, the crew fired up the two diesels and the boat began moving away from the coast. The engine room raised an alarm however. "For God's sake, don't dive because we are done!" shouted the intercom talker. The electric fuel pumps had grounded out. The only thing keeping them running were the diesel engines. If they shut down to dive, there would be no way to restart them. "We had this big up angle, and the after engines and both generators were flooded. So we had to stay on the surface and get the hell out of there," said Cutter. But the two operating H. O. R.s could only go at half speed because power had to be diverted to recharge the batteries and run the bilge pumps to expel seawater taken into the engine room. "So we limped southward toward the open sea," said Cutter. "All we could do was keep going and trust in the luck that had carried us through so far."

Just before dawn, the recharge was sufficient for the boat to dive and remain submerged the following day, giving crewmen time to make repairs and recuperate from the ordeal. Engineers removed an undamaged motor from the boat's crushed sonar pod and attached it to the fuel pump so the diesels could be restarted after surfacing. They also repaired the engine exhaust valve leak. Meanwhile, the crew was shaky. Of the seventy-five aboard, twenty-three suffered from nausea and vomiting. Most were veterans who had made all three war patrols on the boat. By nightfall, the *Pompano* had surfaced, virtually back from the dead and ready to resume its patrol. With few enemy sightings, Thomas rested the crew for another day, then resumed the hunt in earnest. From periscope depth, he sighted a freighter escorted by a destroyer on 12 August. The destroyer reversed course to come between the lurking submarine and the freighter after the *Pompano* fired two torpedoes. Thomas saw a huge column of spray blot out the destroyer's bow as heavy explosions rocked the ocean and the submarine dove. The noise of a ship breaking up could be heard. At 1207, the *Pompano* came to periscope depth. The destroyer had disappeared and the freighter was seen listing to port and sinking—proof that the torpedoes had succeeded in sinking two ships.

For the next nine days, the submarine made numerous contacts with small patrol craft, freighters, and destroyers but could not get into position to attack them. Then, on the night of 22 August, while the *Pompano* patrolled the surface, Thomas sighted a large, armed troop transport and fired three torpedoes, all of which missed. Sailors manning the ship's afterdeck gun returned fire at the *Pompano*. Sixteen shells splashed down around the boat as it submerged. A minute later two depth charges exploded nearby but caused no damage. Over the next six hours, thirty-three depth charges exploded in the sea over the boat but not close enough to do substantial damage.

After dusk, the *Pompano* surfaced and sighted a destroyer. In the moonlight, the enemy noticed the submarine and sped toward it, driving it under. The warship dropped eighteen depth charges, severely shaking the boat, but again it escaped. Thomas decided to stay down the following day. It was a good thing, said Cutter. "The crew was tired and jittery. For twenty-five hours, they had heard sixteen projectiles, two bombs, and fifty-two depth charges go off near them."

Captain Thomas decided to continue the patrol down the coast for a few days, but heavy seas made it difficult. Attempting to maintain periscope depth was useless in the heavy surf of a typhoon. One of the boat's two periscopes malfunctioned and had to be taken out of commission for the remainder of the patrol. On 2 September, the skipper decided to head for home.

At dawn, five hundred miles east of Japan, the *Pompano* came upon a naval auxiliary patrol boat. In accordance with previous orders to sink any enemy ship serving as a sentinel off the coast, Thomas submerged for an attack. Undetected, the submarine circled the target, which was armed with a 20-mm cannon, machine guns, and depth charges. The draft of the boat was too shallow for a torpedo attack, so Thomas battle surfaced at 0938 only two hundred yards from the ship, hoping to take it by surprise. The submarine's 3-inch deck cannon and seamen on the conning tower using machine guns raked the enemy craft, which returned fire. In the ensuing gunfight, one Pompano crewman was creased by a bullet and another—the indestructible "Chainfall" Calcaterra—was wounded while he fed ammunition to the 3-inch cannon. The *Pompano*'s blistering assault overwhelmed the patrol boat, leaving it in flames and sinking as survivors abandoned ship. Thomas directed a boarding party, armed with revolvers, to row over in a rubber boat in an attempt to take a prisoner for interrogation. It was not easy. "Our men in the boat would approach them, and the Japanese would just open their mouths, and down they would go," explained Cutter. "These were all naval ratings; they were not civilians. Finally one of our men hit this guy over the head with a .45. I don't think he was knocked out, but he acted like he was. He was stretched out over the gunwale of the rubber boat as it came alongside. We took him down below, and the crew started knocking him around. They were shoving him around, up against the gyro table and against the hydraulic manifold until one of the officers got down there and stopped it. It was all because of Chainfall."

Calcaterra had taken a bullet in the shoulder. Though the wound did not seem life-threatening at first, he began coughing up blood. The bullet had penetrated his lung and there was nothing anybody could do about it. "We put him on a cot in the forward torpedo room," said Cutter. "I went in to see him at the close of the battle. I asked how he felt. 'Pretty good, sir,' he said. When I went back to see him an hour later, he was flushed and half delirious." His condition continued to worsen through the afternoon. "He was an only child. His father was a doctor who died during World War I in the flu epidemic. And his mother was a lovely lady, and I could understand why he was such a fine young man," said Cutter. "It was very sad."

Drowning in his own blood, Calcaterra died just before midnight. With his dying breath he motioned toward the prisoner and gasped, "Mr. Connole, kill that son of a bitch."

NOBODY SLEPT that night. Crewmen sewed Calcaterra into a length of clean canvas and draped a U.S. flag across his body. A machinist found a heavy wrench and fastened it securely to Calcaterra's feet. Toward morning, Captain Thomas called Cutter to his stateroom.

"Slade, do you know any prayers?" the skipper implored.

Cutter said he learned one in childhood, "Now I lay me down to sleep . . ."

"No, that won't do," the captain replied.

"There's the Lord's Prayer," Cutter recalled. "Ah," replied Thomas who took down the Bible from a shelf and started thumbing through it. The two located the prayer after a brief search, nudging Thomas's memory. "There was a Psalm that I used to like. Was it the twenty-third?" "Maybe," Cutter replied. The two quickly found it to the captain's satisfaction.

At daybreak, the *Pompano* came to a complete halt far out at sea. "All of us who were not on duty gathered on deck," said Cutter. "The captain had put on a fresh uniform and he had the places in the Bible marked with white pipe cleaners. There was no noise aboard and very little wind on the sea, and his voice sounded unnaturally loud. 'The Lord is my Shepherd. I shall not want . . .' The words came back to mind as he read them. He started on the Lord's Prayer, and all at once we were all chiming in. And finally he said, 'And now, we commit our beloved brother to the deep.'"

Two men lifted Calcaterra by the shoulders. His feet, weighted down by the concealed wrench, slid gently over the side. They lowered him down and let him slide away. He disappeared gently into the deep blue sea. "I think he'd like that," said McGrath, clearing his voice. Moments later, the submarine continued on its way.

"Chainfall" never got his final wish. The crew developed an affinity for the prisoner. "We found out that he was a merchantman and he'd been to San Francisco and he knew a few English words and was a very affable, nice guy," said Cutter. "The crew got to love him. They called him Tojo, of course."

The *Pompano* made the transit to Midway and then on to Hawaii in seven days. It was a somber journey, marking the end of the boat's longest war patrol, spanning 10,700 miles. The battered submarine arrived to heavy fanfare, having once again miraculously survived. Thomas turned the prisoner over to the Marines but with a most unusual gesture: "First the crew got the last cigarettes they had and some sugar, which this poor Jap loved. He hadn't had sugar in a long time," said Cutter. "They gave him sugar and whatever we had that they thought he might want. They put them in a pillowslip, slung it over his shoulder and pinned a note on it: 'To the Marine: Tojo is a good guy. Treat him right.'"

Capt. Slade Deville Cutter.
Courtesy of Paul Stillwell

DEC. 1, 1934 CUTTER KICKS FIELD GOAL
NAVY-3 ARMY-0

All-American tackle Slade Cutter kicks the winning field goal in the mud to beat Army before eighty thousand spectators at Franklin Field in Philadelphia, 1934. The final score marked Navy's first victory over Army in thirteen years. *Courtesy of U.S. Naval Academy*

Though he was compared to the great Joe Louis, collegiate boxing champion Slade Cutter turned down a lucrative offer to turn pro so that he could remain in the Navy. *Courtesy of Paul Stillwell*

Undefeated heavyweight boxer Slade Cutter chats with Sir Guy Standing from Paramount Studios, which was filming "Annapolis Farewell" in 1935. Boxing coach "Spike" Webb (*bottom right*) and the Navy boxing team encircle Cutter and Standing. *Courtesy of U.S. Naval Academy*

Midshipman Slade Cutter with senior officers of the various midshipmen companies on the steps to the Naval Academy chapel in Annapolis, spring 1935. *Courtesy of U.S. Naval Academy*

Ens. Slade Cutter and his bride Franny Leffler Cutter in Bremerton, Washington, 1936. Because the Navy banned marriage at the time, Cutter had resigned to get married but the Navy did not accept his resignation. *Courtesy of Anne Cutter McCarthy*

Ens. Slade Cutter (*front and center*) with the quartermaster gang he headed on the battleship USS *Idaho,* 1935. *Official U.S. Navy photo*

The Submarine School Officers' Class January–June 1938 poses at the Groton, Connecticut, facility. *Third row, fourth from right,* Slade Cutter. To his left is his pal "Dusty" Dornin. *Second row, extreme right,* Sam C. Loomis, whose mother encouraged Slade to attend the Naval Academy when she visited him at his boyhood farm in Illinois. *Official U.S. Navy photo*

From the left, Lt. Frank Fisher, Capt. Lewis Parks, and Lt. Bill Budding in Hawaii. Their ship was the USS *Pompano. Courtesy of Bill Budding*

Franny and Slade Cutter with his best friend, Lt. David R. Connole, at
the officers' club at Pearl Harbor. Connole, the commanding officer of
USS *Trigger*, lost his life when *Trigger* disappeared in the East China Sea in 1945.
Courtesy of Anne Cutter McCarthy

USS *Seahorse* slides
down the ways at
Mare Island Naval
Shipyard, California,
9 January 1943.
Lieutenant Budding's
father supervised the
construction of the
submarine that would
become his son's
home during the war.
Courtesy of Bill Budding

The *Seahorse* at her commissioning in San Francisco Bay, June 1943.
Official U.S. Navy photo

From the left, Lt. Cdr. Slade Cutter, USS *Seahorse;* Lt. Cdr. Ray Davenport, USS *Haddock;* and Joseph L. McGrievy, former *Seahorse* chief signalman, at an awards ceremony on Midway, 12 October 1943, prior to *Seahorse*'s second war patrol. *Courtesy of Ruth Cutter*

Adm. Chester Nimitz pins a Navy Cross on Slade Cutter's uniform for his exploits during *Seahorse*'s second war patrol. During the fifty-three-day mission, Cutter sank two oil tankers, one transport, three freighters, and three trawlers—a record at that point in the war. In subsequent patrols, Cutter would earn consecutive Gold Stars in lieu of three more Navy Crosses plus a Presidential Unit Citation, placing him among the Pacific war's most formidable submarine captains. *Courtesy of Anne Cutter McCarthy*

Lt. Cdr. Slade Cutter *(left)* talks with his officers at the Pearl Harbor submarine base following *Seahorse*'s third war patrol. *Courtesy of Anne Cutter McCarthy*

A determined Slade Cutter on *Seahorse*'s bridge during the boat's fourth war patrol off Saipan. The submarine patrolled the surface to draw antisubmarine warfare vessels so that USS *Greenling* could scout Saipan's southern beaches for a planned invasion in June 1944. Cutter not only made his boat's presence known but sank four enemy freighters and a Japanese submarine. *Courtesy of Anne Cutter McCarthy*

Seahorse comes alongside the heavy cruiser USS *Louisville* to take on supplies during the naval bombardment of Satawan Island, 1 May 1944. *Courtesy of Joseph McGrievy*

The *Seahorse* crew on deck at Pearl Harbor, 19 July 1944, after the boat's fifth and Slade Cutter's last war patrol as the boat's captain. Lieutenant Commander Cutter is the largest man in the front row. *Official U.S. Navy photo*

Franny and Slade Cutter Jr., Norfolk, Virginia,
spring 1960. Slade Sr. was commanding officer of the
flagship cruiser *Northampton*. During the Bay of Pigs
operation, the cruiser was posted off Cuba, and it
was later converted into a national command post for
President John F. Kennedy. *Courtesy of Anne Cutter McCarthy*

Slade Cutter at home in Annapolis, Maryland, with a collage of his famous
kick that beat Army in 1934. *Courtesy of Ruth Cutter*

Ruth Cutter and her husband at home, 2002. Ruth was Franny Cutter's best friend when the two dated "Dusty" Dornin and Slade Cutter, respectively, through the men's midshipman years. After Franny's death in 1981, Ruth, a widow at the time, married Slade. It was Franny's dying wish that he do so.
Photo by Mary Anne LaVO

12

Schism on the *Seahorse*

REAR ADMIRAL Robert English viewed the report of the *Pompano's* third war patrol with satisfaction. Promoting Thomas to command seemed an obvious success in the admiral's "youth experiment." English, commander of the Pacific submarine fleet, had relieved twelve skippers in their late thirties or forties because of mediocre or unproductive results. Most of the replacements, such as Thomas, were six years younger, and were uninhibited by the cautious peacetime habits of their predecessors. Nevertheless, many in the Silent Service believed English had not acted as purposefully as he could have in terms of his promotions. Aggressive leaders like Slade Cutter and "Dusty" Dornin had proven themselves, yet the admiral was reticent about pushing his luck. Moreover, with Thomas in command, the *Pompano* not only sank a freighter and a destroyer, but also surfaced to destroy an armed patrol boat during an arduous voyage that cost the life of a seaman. "The Commanding Officer is to be commended for his aggressiveness," noted English, adding: "The loss of a member of the gun crew is regretted but casualties in war must be expected and accepted. Damage cannot be inflicted on the enemy without taking a calculated risk."

The *Pompano* began its long-delayed major overhaul at Pearl, a process that would take months during which yard workers finally would replace the boat's worn-out H.O.R.s. Meanwhile, the Navy detached Slade in November 1942, giving him extended leave to return home to his family. There was no explanation of why. "I was very unhappy," recalled Cutter. "But shortly after I got back to Mare Island, I was very happy. I was back with my family which meant a lot more to me." It had been ten months since he had seen his wife and daughter. The couple had stayed in touch through letters that Cutter carefully numbered and mailed at the completion of each patrol. "I would mail twenty letters or more to Franny every time we got in from war patrol, and I would get that many back from her," said Cutter.

By early 1943, the Pompano's overhaul was nearing completion, and Captain Thomas was preparing for the boat's fourth war patrol. Slade, however, was still without a submarine. In January, the death of Admiral English in an airplane crash on the northern California coast led to a shake-up in the submarine command. Rear Admiral Charles Lockwood, "Uncle Charlie" to many submarine veterans, took over. The admiral had most recently commanded U.S. submarines in the southwest Pacific and defended his submarine captains who insisted their torpedoes were defective. In 1942, he solved one of the problems by proving that the Mark XIV torpedo ran too deep by shooting them into a net in the harbor in the Australian port of Albany. Subsequently adjustments were made. Nevertheless, duds and premature explosions still bedeviled the submarine service. Lockwood, who taught seamanship to Cutter when he was a midshipman, had an electric personality—energetic, brisk, tenacious, and known to fly in the face of Navy rulebooks. He was among the first to jump aboard a returning submarine so he could be the first to talk to the crew. He also was known to relieve submarine captains he thought were not doing the job.

As Lockwood flew to Pearl from Australia to assume command of the undersea fleet, Cutter received orders to become executive officer of the Seahorse (SS-304). The vessel, about to be commissioned in Mare Island, was the latest of the new Balao-class submarines being built (at the rate of three a month) in government and private shipyards. They were much more formidable than Pompano—bigger, faster, with more weaponry (including four additional torpedo tubes). They also were "thick skinned"—shielded by welded, high-tensile steel hulls that allowed them to dive well below the capability of Cutter's old boat. The *Seahorse* was also special in one other way: It was built by the father of the boat's new ensign. Twenty-one-year-old William A. Budding Jr. was the submarine's brilliant junior officer who graduated near the top of his class and was one of the youngest officers in the submarine service. Budding's father was Mare Island's shipbuilding superintendent. "I'll tell you nothing was too good for the submarine," said Cutter. Every inch of the hull was X-rayed to spot any imperfection in the welds so they could be fixed. All equipment installed was of the best quality and was carefully checked. The *Seahorse* was also the first submarine to have an experimental, rubberized packing material installed around its twin propeller shafts designed to keep them from squealing when at deep submergence. Though the new substance had yet to be authorized by the Bureau of Ships, Budding's father had it installed anyway. "We never had a squealing propeller in the *Seahorse*," said Cutter. "The father was looking after his son."

The biggest surprise for Cutter was the man chosen to be the submarine's first captain. It was Slade's former submarine school instructor, Donald McGregor, the man who insisted to his students that any surface ship protected by sonar and listening devices could thwart submarine attack. "He firmly believed it was suicidal to attack a convoy protected by a screen of destroyers with supersonic sonar gear," said Cutter, who had defied such measures aboard the *Pompano*. "I said, 'Well, Captain, in the *Pompano* we went right smack underneath, and they didn't pick us up'. And we did. A ship had passed right overhead off Okinawa. The sonar operators picked up so many schools of fish and whales and all sorts of things that they became slap-happy, ping-happy listening to that ping going out. They didn't pick us up as a result."

McGregor was far from being a novice at war patrols. He had been captain of the *Gar* (SS-206) when war broke out and was attached to a submarine squadron based in Fremantle on the west coast of Australia. Though he made four patrols in *Gar*, he sank only one fifteen-hundred-ton ship, unescorted at the time. He blamed the lack of results on the poor quality of his officers. But the thirty-nine-year-old captain seemed to typify the "skipper problem." Lockwood, who was commander of southwest Pacific submariners in mid-1942, concluded the soft-spoken, well-mannered McGregor did not have what it took to be a wartime skipper and relieved him. The Bureau of Naval Personnel, however, prodded by Rear Admiral Ralph Christie, who succeeded Lockwood in Fremantle and was McGregor's friend and former golf partner, gave him another chance by transferring him to Mare Island to take over the *Seahorse.*

This time the crew would not be blamed if the submarine was unsuccessful. The bureau appointed Cutter as McGregor's executive officer. Also assigned to the boat were Lt. John P. Currie as diving officer and Lt. Elbert C. Lindon as torpedo and TDC operator. Currie had just come off the *Growler* (SS-215), which had been attacked by a Japanese gunboat in February 1943. The boat's skipper, Howard W. Gilmore, was on the bridge and gravely wounded. He ordered Currie, his executive officer, to "take her down," thus sacrificing his life to save the *Growler.* It earned Gilmore the nation's highest military award, the Medal of Honor. Lindon was a veteran of the *Saury* (SS-189), which had seen strenuous action in the South Pacific. With Budding, that made four officers who were Annapolis graduates. "No other submarine had the luxury of that. They would have a couple of Naval Academy officers, and the rest were reserves. So we were really loaded, and they did that purposely for their pal, McGregor," said Cutter. "Except for Budding, the rest of us were war tested."

Capt. John H. Brown, the submarine force training commander who assigned or relieved officers on all the submarines, was confident that Cutter would push McGregor. "Brown knew me; he knew Parks, he knew I had been with Parks; he knew what we had done in the *Pompano,*" said Cutter. "And he knew damn well that I was not going to be quiet if McGregor played it safe and that there was going to be friction. He just intuitively knew it."

The *Seahorse,* commissioned in March, left for Pearl Harbor in July. During training exercises, Cutter was favorably impressed by McGregor's ability in day-to-day operations of the submarine. He was typical of the older submarine commanders, men who were selected because of their knowledge in engineering and administration, rather than their ability as combat leaders. During the *Seahorse*'s shakedown period, McGregor excelled and got high marks from his superiors and the crew. "He organized *Seahorse* like the very experienced naval officer he was," said Cutter. "I was very pleased and expected that we would do well in combat."

The captain had one glaring deficiency. "For McGregor, the TDC was a mystery—the solution of the fire control problem," Cutter explained. "McGregor recognized that I was good. I wouldn't have been if it hadn't been for Parks. But I was better on approaches than McGregor was, so he put me on the periscope."

The captain and his exec, though they did not meld well personally, accorded each other professional respect. McGregor was somewhat intimidated by his huge executive. McGregor had read all the patrol reports. He thought the *Pompano* acted with reckless abandon. And his private view was that his new exec had come from what he would later refer to among *Seahorse* crewmen as "the Hooligan Navy."

With the boat thoroughly sea tested, the *Seahorse* departed Pearl on 3 August 1943 for its maiden war patrol with a crew of seven officers and seventy-two enlisted men. McGregor's orders were to patrol the shipping lanes of the Palaus, a group of two hundred islands in the Carolines north of New Guinea and east of Mindanao in the Philippines. Japan seized the islands in 1914 from Germany and had converted them into a major naval base. It was here that Japanese convoys assembled before proceeding to New Guinea, Guadalcanal, and other enemy strongholds. It was also a transit point for tankers bringing fuel to Tokyo from the oil fields in the Dutch East Indies. The Palaus were rich in targets. "We were elated and felt honored to be assigned such a good area for our first patrol," said Cutter, anxious for action after his long absence from the war zone.

At the time, the undersea offensive seemed to have turned a corner. Though a handful of submarines had not returned from patrol, there were more than thirty new vessels on patrol, swelling the fleet from fifty-two at the beginning of the war to more than eighty. Despite continuing problems with torpedoes, the aggressive tactics of certain skippers had electrified the undersea Navy. Chief among them were the exploits of Lt. Cdr. Dudley "Mush" Morton, who had command of the *Pompano* for two days before being assigned to the *Wahoo* (SS-238). On his third patrol from Brisbane between 16 January and 7 February 1943, Morton not only entered a shallow harbor to sink a Japanese destroyer, but in a subsequent fourteen-hour sea battle wiped out an enemy convoy of three freighters and a troop transport attempting to resupply troops in New Guinea. Morton earned a Navy Cross for the patrol and the *Wahoo* received a Presidential Unit Citation from President Roosevelt. Morton and the *Wahoo* on their fourth war patrol in March 1943 did even better, entering the Yellow Sea to sink nine enemy ships.

It was that kind of action that made Cutter salivate at prospects for the *Seahorse*. For two weeks in early August, the submarine's southwestward voyage was uneventful, occupied by regular drills and an otherwise normal routine. On 17 August, the submarine entered its patrol sector off the eastern entrance to Malakal Harbor in the Palaus. The next day two small patrol boats located the boat by echo ranging and turned toward it. An hour later a third antisubmarine vessel emitting a powerful sonar beam joined the hunt. Fearing depth charges, McGregor took the *Seahorse* below 275 feet, where a layer of cold seawater deflected the sonar, enabling the boat to escape. The incident rattled the captain, who noted in the ship's log that the enemy's sonar seemed to be much better than he encountered on the *Gar* a year earlier. "The echo-rangers put out a sharp, powerful signal while their receivers, presumably mounted in a separate unit from the pinger were considered rather effective. Their sound operators apparently have improved with experience. Tactics varied between a pinging and a listening search depending on conditions."

For the next several days, numerous sightings of enemy aircraft and warships made McGregor edgy. On the night of 24 August, the *Seahorse* sighted a patrol boat on the edge of a rainsquall. McGregor was the officer of the deck, having spelled Cutter who had gone below for a nap. From a range of fifteen hundred yards, the submarine chaser opened fire on the submarine using flashless powder. The first two shots whistled over the bridge, exploding abeam as the submarine made an emergency dive. Six subsequent depth charges, two fairly close, caused the gasket around the main air induction valve to leak as the boat descended

to four hundred feet. The *Seahorse* eluded the submarine chaser and surfaced at dawn to repair the leak. Over the next several days, patrol craft
and observation airplanes continued to hound the submarine. Finally,
at midday on 28 August, a periscope search revealed that a three-ship
convoy was leaving Malakal harbor.

At 1800, the *Seahorse* surfaced and began an "end around," a term
derived from football where the submarine raced at flank speed to a
point ahead of the convoy, then submerged to await its approach. It
took nearly twelve hours for the submarine to overtake the convoy and
submerge at dawn "in excellent position," reported the captain. Again,
one of the escorts located the submarine through sonar pinging and
turned in its direction, unnerving McGregor. He took the boat deep as
fifteen depth charges exploded over the boat, causing the induction
piping to spring another leak. Later the submarine surfaced so crewmen
could repair the leak. By then, the convoy was gone.

McGregor charted a new course to the vicinity of Toagel Mlungui
passage in the Palaus. On the late afternoon of 31 August, a large ship
came into view. The *Seahorse* was in perfect position to attack just as
the ship's lights went on, revealing it to be a Japanese hospital ship.
McGregor called off the attack in accordance with international rules.

For the next four days, no contacts were made. The crew became
increasingly restless. The submarine had been at sea for a month and
had yet to attack anything. "There was general disappointment and much
discussion among the crew regarding Captain McGregor's lack of aggressiveness," recalled Chief Torpedoman's Mate Ralph Fiscus. Cutter,
though upset, kept his opinions to himself. "I'm sure Slade Cutter still
has indentations in his lips from the times he bit them so hard to keep
from saying what he really wanted to say to the captain," said Roy Hoffman, the boat's veteran sonar operator.

On 6 September, while submerged near the passage, the submarine
sighted two transports escorted by a patrol craft and a gunboat. McGregor
chose to fire four torpedoes from a distant two thousand yards at one of
the ships, a seventy-five-hundred-pound vessel that he later noted "was
loaded to the gunnels with NIP troops." They were the first shots of the
war for *Seahorse*. Rather than wait to confirm a hit, the captain took the

submarine deep where the sound of distant explosions convinced him that the torpedoes had hit and sunk the target. Others including Cutter doubted it. The wakes of the four torpedoes revealed the *Seahorse*'s location and within minutes the escorts began an attack that disabled one of the boat's torpedo firing tubes and damaged the packing material around the bow plane's operating shaft. There were also numerous leaks the crew fought to control.

The enemy broke off the attack seven hours after it began, after which the submarine surfaced to effect repairs, then resumed the patrol. The narrow escape seemed to unnerve McGregor, who refused to take the *Seahorse* close in to Toagel Mlungui the next day because of his fear of persistent sonar pinging from patrol boats. "They seem to be angry about something," he concluded. Cutter's mood grew darker at the captain's worsening timidity. The executive encouraged him to move in closer. "If we try to do all the things you want to do," snapped the captain, "we will all get killed." In frustration, Cutter appealed to Lieutenant Lindon to talk to McGregor. "I tried but he politely rebuffed me," the gunnery officer said later. "McGregor was one of the nicest guys to come down the pike but he was overly cautious. That wasn't really his fault though because caution was ingrained in the older skippers."

For the next few days, McGregor withdrew from the coast of Toagel Mlungui so additional repairs could be made. Then on the afternoon of 10 September, he took the boat back to Toagel Mlungui Passage where contact was made with an armed merchant vessel, an oil tanker, and a freighter. None of the ships were escorted. Nevertheless, McGregor feared enemy airplanes might attack the submarine so he remained submerged, not even risking exposing the periscope. For thirteen minutes the submarine closed on the suspected track of the tanker without taking another look through the periscope. "This mistake," McGregor later admitted, "was costly as the next exposure [of the periscope] showed the target to have zigged about fifty-five degrees away and range had opened to forty-two hundred yards." The result was the tanker and the rest of the convoy safely reached the island harbor where the *Seahorse* could not attack them.

The submarine still had no confirmed sinkings in almost six weeks at sea while encountering numerous targets. Only four torpedoes had been fired out of twenty-four aboard. Anxious to vindicate himself, the captain reasoned the convoy soon would leave port and head north. Therefore, he positioned the *Seahorse* to intercept the ships. The next day, 11 September, contact was made with a five-ship convoy including a ten-thousand-ton, three-stack troop transport led by two submarine chasers. McGregor declined to initiate an attack, however, preferring to wait for sundown when the boat could surface and race after the ships. Two hours later, the submarine encountered another oiler with a freighter steaming for Toagel Mlungui but the submarine could not reach attack position.

As darkness fell, the *Seahorse* surfaced and set out after the five-ship convoy which had been making about ten knots toward the Philippines. During the nocturnal end-around, the submarine quickly overtook the slow-moving targets. "The captain went down into the wardroom, and there he stayed, and he let me maneuver and keep ahead of them," recalled Cutter, noting the convoy had stopped its defensive zigzagging, making the setup easy for the *Seahorse*. "So I would keep going down to the wardroom from the conning tower to say, 'Captain, we are in position to dive and fire our torpedoes'. From early evening I recommended to Mac that we should dive and attack the troop transport. He either did not acknowledge my remarks or said that we should wait awhile. This went on all night while he sat in the wardroom drinking coffee. He also was not wearing red goggles to preserve his night vision. I mentioned this to him, too. Spud Lindon, who was the TDC operator, and I wore our red glasses all the time below decks, as did all personnel who needed to be able to see in the dark."

With the moon about to set, making it more difficult to see the transport, Cutter again urged the captain to attack. McGregor finally agreed. "Go ahead and dive," he told Cutter. But as the boat flooded down to launch the torpedoes, the sonar pinging of a destroyer could be heard. The captain came up to the conning tower and said, "Up periscope." After a quick scan of the surface, he blurted, "I can't see a thing. Down periscope, three hundred foot depth."

"I couldn't believe my ears, nor could Spud Lindon," said Cutter.

"The convoy went right over us, and we didn't do a thing about it. We let them get away; I was sick."

After the convoy passed, the *Seahorse* surfaced in daylight and started another end around. After a chase of six hours and ever so slowly gaining on the convoy, an exhausted Cutter, who had been awake for thirty-six hours, asked Lindon to relieve him as watch officer on the bridge so he could grab a nap. "I had been in my bunk for about three hours when a messenger awakened me and said Mr. Lindon wanted to see me on the bridge. I got up there and Spud told me that Mac had relieved him as watch officer on the bridge shortly after I had gone to my bunk." During that time, the submarine lost contact with the convoy.

"Mac had deliberately lost contact," said Cutter who made a final try at finding the ships but failed. "There was nothing to do but return to Toagel Mlungui. This was the most frustrating of all the bungled affairs."

The submarine made its way back to the island with the demoralized crew, although they continued to get new chances. On 13 September, lookouts sighted a three-thousand-ton freighter. Again McGregor called off the attack after spotting a patrol boat near the freighter. The next day presented the crew with its best opportunity in the approach of a ten-thousand-ton oil tanker. There were neither escorts nor airplanes around and the sky was overcast. The officer of the deck was the first to see the ship and sent for Cutter rather than the captain. "So I came up to the conning tower and took a look and said, 'Right full rudder, all ahead two-thirds'. I took another look, and we were about twenty-five hundred yards off the track, range ten thousand yards. We were in a beautiful spot. All we had to do was keep coming around, get ourselves on a ninety track, go dead slow speed and wait for him to come on, and we were going to fire at about eight hundred yards range—like shooting fish in a barrel because he wasn't zigging. I did not send for Mac until I had all the dope on the target and a solution had been obtained by Spud on the TDC. We had maneuvered for a perfect shot."

The forward torpedo tubes were flooded down and the outer doors were opened. Cutter summoned McGregor to give the final order to fire. But the captain was late in coming up to the conning tower. And when McGregor finally arrived, said Lieutenant Budding, who was standing next to the plotting table, "he decided that because the target was on a steady course, he would turn the boat away for a stern tube shot."

Cutter was befuddled. "The Captain took one look through the periscope and ordered, 'Left full rudder, all ahead two-thirds speed'. I said, 'What is that for, Captain?' He replied that he wanted to give the after room some practice. I couldn't believe it. By God, we opened out at six knots. By the time we fired four torpedoes, the range was over a mile. Too far in view of the fact that our steam torpedoes left big wakes, easily seen from the target." The ship predictably evaded the torpedoes easily.

Knowing he missed, the captain shouted, "Right full rudder. All ahead full. Make ready the bow tubes." It took fourteen minutes to make the turn, during which the enemy ship making fifteen knots pulled further away while showing only its narrow stern to the *Seahorse*. In desperation, McGregor ordered low speed settings for the torpedoes so their range could be extended. He gave the order to fire four more torpedoes. All missed.

When submarine force commanders at Pearl Harbor got the news, they ordered McGregor to terminate the patrol and head for Midway. Though directed to shell a phosphate plant on the island of Anguar en route, the captain was unable to find the island.

Cutter, bitter with disappointment, had counted thirty-one enemy ships that the *Seahorse* could have attacked during its two months at sea but had not done so because of the captain's temerity. The thought of tankers, freighters, and troop transports reaching port unhindered to reinforce Japanese frontline positions was unthinkable. "With that well-trained crew and all those torpedoes and nothing happened. Terrible," he anguished. "I felt a very grave responsibility. We had to get results when we went out there, because we were the only offensive thing we had at that time. We were the only ones out in the Far Pacific."

On the voyage home Cutter remained outwardly loyal and abiding. McGregor asked him not to write the patrol report, the normal responsibility of an executive officer. Rather, the captain said he'd do it. "McGregor said to me, in one of his more candid moments, that it would take a Philadelphia lawyer to prepare this patrol report. He clearly meant that it was going to be difficult to write the report honestly and not have him, personally, come out looking like an inept combat skipper."

Cutter could contain himself no longer. In frustration, he accused the captain of undermining the patrol. McGregor retaliated by relieving Cutter and making Lindon acting executive. "The captain did it in a nice way, really," said Cutter. "He said, 'You just stay in your room, Slade. Let Spud get some training; he will do the navigating'. But, in effect, he relieved me of all duty. The crew knew it. It was a very difficult situation, and I felt very depressed."

McGregor also privately drafted an unsatisfactory fitness report on Cutter in an attempt to deflect personal criticism from higher-ups. He urged the Navy to reassign Slade to the academy's athletic program for the duration of the war. Cutter, suspecting such a move, wrote his own account of the patrol, citing McGregor's lack of aggressiveness—a bold move because the missive could be viewed as an act of insubordination with severe consequences.

In a letter to his wife, Cutter was downcast. "When I think of seeing those bastards going by the *Seahorse* like trolley cars and then think of what we did about it—woe is me!" he wrote. "There will certainly be a change or two made—no doubt about it!"

In fact, commanders in Pearl Harbor were already debating the fate of the boat's two top officers, whose feud threatened to ruin both their careers.

13

Pangs of Conscience

THE *Seahorse* arrived at Midway on the afternoon of 27 September. Both Cutter and McGregor were on the bridge as the black boat came alongside its mooring pier. Neither man exchanged pleasantries, just the normal relay of commands as the big diesels shut down to mark the end of a 13,651-mile voyage. The reception was unceremonious as a gangplank was put over to the boat. A radioman came aboard, climbed to the bridge, and handed a dispatch to the captain. McGregor studied the contents, frowned, passed it to Cutter, and abruptly went below without uttering a word. It was the worst possible news for McGregor— a summary dismissal as commander by direct order of Lockwood. The vice admiral was so angry at the submarine's performance that he would not authorize a combat insignia award for the just completed war patrol. He also was determined to make an example of the captain: Commanders of Pacific submarines henceforth would be aggressive—or else.

Thoroughly humiliated, McGregor stayed aboard, preferring not to go up to the officers' club nor to the island hotel where officers off patrol bunked. "It was more than a little embarrassing," Slade said of his intermittent encounters with McGregor in the submarine's compartments. "He was upset about the whole thing and said practically nothing." Cutter thought better of putting the ex-skipper on report.

Rather, he tore up the letter he composed on the way to Midway. Then, three days later, in a surprise move by Lockwood, Cutter was promoted to commanding officer of the *Seahorse*.

There was no ritualistic change of command as was the usual practice. But several skippers from other boats joined him at the officers' club to toast the occasion with martinis. Among them was "Dusty" Dornin, who had just arrived after his first war patrol as captain of the *Trigger* (SS-237). Despite several torpedo duds, the submarine turned in spectacular results: four ships sunk, including two oil tankers in the East China Sea. Though Cutter and Dornin had much to celebrate, the business of war and the fact that both submarines would soon return to combat lurked in the background. Lockwood was especially anxious to put *Seahorse* back in action, confident the new skipper would atone for the disappointing first patrol. Slade was just as eager. "Boy, oh boy," he noted in a letter to his wife. "All I want is fuel, fish, and provisions, and to get going. To hell with this recuperation business."

There were few diversions for crewmen relaxing between patrols at Midway, a Navy fortress twenty-two hundred miles from Japan and twelve hundred miles northwest of Hawaii. Before the war, the two square miles of sand dunes dotted by clumps of tall palm trees served as a refueling stop for Pan American Airlines' luxurious China Clipper service. A large, ramshackle hotel, built by Pan Am, had been converted to officers' quarters and was sarcastically christened the "Gooneyville Lodge" in reference to the ungainly albatrosses that nested in vast numbers on Midway. Liberty for sailors meant playing cards, football, and volleyball, drinking beer and whiskey, and watching the antics of drunken gooneys that were addicted to beer. At night, wedge-tailed shearwaters, which the sailors dubbed "moaning birds," wailed incessantly from tunneled sand nests. It reminded the men of how lonely Midway was. There were no women on Midway. The last one left when Pan Am suspended operations at the start of the war.

Cutter faced a vexing problem in his first few days as captain: crewmen were wary that he had something to prove. McGregor's characterization of Cutter as a "reckless hooligan" on the *Pompano* made them nervous. Joseph McGrievy, chief of the boat and the go-between among the officers and enlisted men, tried to ameliorate the situation by stressing Cutter's proven record. "It's a good thing *Seahorse* is being refitted at Midway," he later told the new captain. "Had the refit been back in the States, half the crew would go over the hill."

Cutter tried to resolve the situation by being open and honest. He offered every man a chance to transfer off if he so chose, no questions asked. Only one accepted. McGrievy helped persuade the rest to give the captain a chance. To build unity, the captain joined the crew in baseball and football games against the crews of other submarines during the refit. Slade, of course, played with characteristic abandon. That style became clear to the executive officer of the *Trigger* during a makeshift football game at the Gooneyville Lodge. "Someone issued a challenge: a billiard ball took the place of a football, and the game ended with a forward pass nearly thrown through one of the Gooneyville Lodge's lightly built walls," recalled Lt. Edward L. Beach. "What I remember most about that game is not who won but the set of bruises I carried for a week afterward in trying to tackle Slade Cutter. He nearly crushed me when I unwisely tried to keep him from making a touchdown with a red-and-white billiard ball. One does not lightly tackle an All-American tackle, even in a friendly way."

Though the crew of *Seahorse* was competent, Cutter believed he needed someone to bring a fighting spirit to the vessel: an extrovert, the kind of officer who could break the ice and put a little fun into the war patrol, but would be imperturbable in combat. Someone like Ralph Pleatman.

The word on Midway was that the *Pompano*'s former assistant TDC operator was miserable since being assigned to a relief crew at Pearl. Cutter viewed him as ideal because of his tactical skill, unbridled enthusiasm, love of practical jokes, and ability to connect with crewmen through off-color humor at difficult times. Foremost, Pleatman exuded a burning desire to strike hard at the Japanese. Because the boat had openings for two officers, Pleatman could easily be one of them. The problem was how to get him.

Opportunity arrived in a surprise visit by Vice Admiral Lockwood. Cutter was playing a spirited game of beer-and-baseball with his crew when a messenger summoned him to the base library. He had no idea that "Uncle Charlie" was inside. "I was sweaty, dirty, and dressed in shorts when I appeared before the admiral," said Cutter. "After offering me congratulations upon getting my command, he asked if there was anything he could do for me. I seized the opportunity and said I'd like to have Ralph Pleatman for one patrol." Lockwood said he would arrange it.

The next day, the admiral met with his submarine captains, torpedo officers, and chief torpedomen to convince them that problems with the firing mechanisms of their torpedoes had been resolved. In tests ordered by Lockwood, in which live torpedoes were fired at various angles into a submerged Hawaiian cliff, divers discovered that one was a dud. Its warhead split open on impact. Big chunks of TNT littered the seabed. An examination proved the firing pin was too heavy and became jammed in its guides when hitting the target at a perpendicular angle; the pin never reached the torpedo's detonation cap. The problem was tracked back to a cost-cutting decision before the war to convert the pins from more expensive but lighter copper to steel. Lockwood had a lighter prototype tooled at Pearl Harbor from the wreckage of a Japanese Zero. It solved the problem. New firing pins were thereafter installed in all torpedoes. The first shipment of corrected torpedoes was loaded aboard *Seahorse* and *Trigger*. With this boost to morale, Lockwood bid his men good luck and abruptly flew back to Pearl.

TWO DAYS LATER, as Cutter slept in his hotel room, the door flew open at dawn and a glowering Ralph Pleatman walked in. He flung his briefcase, hitting the captain squarely in the chest, and shouted, "You son of a bitch!"

"What the hell's wrong?" Slade stammered, shaking off his slumber. Pleatman explained he had gotten married and received orders to return to the States for assignment to new construction. That would have assured him plenty of time to be with his bride. Lockwood's orders to fly instead to Midway spoiled everything. Cutter empathized with Pleatman, saying he had no way of knowing. Slade brought Pleatman up to date about events on the *Seahorse,* how McGregor had driven a wedge between him and the crew, and how he needed Pleatman's unique leadership skills to heal the breach—just for one patrol. With that, the officer broke into a broad grin and apologized.

Initially, some officers were resentful of the close relationship between Cutter and Pleatman. Cutter put him in the upper bunk in his *Seahorse* stateroom though he was the least senior officer aboard. The captain also appointed him TDC operator, a post that should have gone to the diving officer. "Spud" Lindon instead moved down to plotting officer. That technically placed him under Pleatman, a move that did not sit well with Lindon. But he soon got over it as Pleatman demonstrated his mathematical genius and lightning-like reflexes at the targeting computer. His irrepressible personality and disdain for the Japanese soon rallied the crew to his side. In terms of enemy action, his favorite expression was "Fuck 'em, let's go!" Cutter worried that such profanity might grate on the crew, especially the twenty-one rookies assigned to the boat out of submarine school. So he took Pleatman aside, saying "Look Ralph, you can't say 'fuck 'em' in front of the enlisted men like that." Taken aback, Pleatman replied, "Then I can say 'fuke 'em,' goddamn it." To which the captain conceded, "Okay, you can say 'fuke 'em.'" That then soon became the signature expression in the boat.

As Cutter prepared for a new war patrol, the *Pompano* was due to arrive at the base. There were many friends aboard, among them his former skipper, Willis Thomas, and Thomas McGrath, who had moved up to executive officer when Slade left the boat. For three weeks, ComSubPac sent daily messages for the submarine to report its position. But there was no answer. By 15 October, the boat was listed as overdue and presumably lost off the east coast of Honshu. Later intelligence revealed it had torpedoed and sunk two cargo ships before striking a mine and exploding in late September with the loss of the entire crew.

Cutter wrote home to inform his wife so she could help Thomas's widow when the Navy officially informed her of the presumed death of her husband. "Franny was able to console her and be with her and so on. As for me, I didn't vicariously put myself in the position of Thomas at all. It didn't affect me too much. We all thought we'd probably not survive the war. By then, we had lost so many subs."

The death toll had in fact increased. Five submarines—the *Pompano*,

Grayling (SS-209), *Cisco* (SS-290), *Dorado* (SS-248), and *Wahoo*, skippered by "Mush" Morton—were lost while the *Seahorse* was being refitted at Midway. The Japanese had become more adept at antisubmarine warfare; in addition, U.S. submarines began venturing into shallower, mine-filled waters around Japan where they were more vulnerable. Still, Cutter had no doubt the United States would win the war by the sheer power of its industrial might. "Even if they get us before the war is over, we're so far ahead of the Japanese now they'll never catch up," he told a war correspondent for the Associated Press. The reporter, awestruck by the former All-American football and boxing hero, described him as "a fighting giant. . . . a blonde, easy moving chunk of brawn weighing 225 pounds."

As the refit came to an end, training exercises began around Midway. Cutter drilled his eighty-man crew as he would a football team. "Sports makes you offensive minded. That's the big thing," he explained. "I trained my *Seahorse* crew the same way I did my battleship *Idaho* football team years before. On each training period we would start with the individual and the fundamentals, then on to department training, then molding all departments into a team for surface gunfire and another team for torpedo battle stations. The important thing was to develop in each man self-confidence and confidence in his team." Diving, surfacing, engaging in mock attacks—all operations were carefully timed and improved on through incessant practice. "You've got four lookouts, two officers of the deck, the captain—a lot of people on deck. We would sound the diving alarm, and we would be under in fifty seconds, and everybody would be below. Now that takes teamwork," explained Cutter. "When they go down the hatch, they don't just go down the ladder; they jump down, and the guy who jumps first better get the hell out of the way, because another guy is coming down on top of him."

Unlike other captains, Cutter believed in diving quickly to great depth, a practice that startled Rear Adm. George Crawford, who was aboard as an observer during the training exercises. *Seahorse* junior officer Frank Fisher was practicing as the diving officer at the time. "When we dived," said Fisher, "I said, 'Full dive on the bow planes, twenty degrees down angle.' The admiral looked down at me from the conning tower hatch and said, 'Ensign, every other submarine dives with an 8-degree down angle. Why do you have to be different?' I said, 'Aye, aye sir, 8-degrees down angle.' Slade immediately leaned over the conning tower hatch and said, 'Make that a 25-degree down angle.' I guess the admiral then knew that Slade Cutter was in command of his boat, and so did the crew."

The intensity of the training sessions was broken by Pleatman, who saw an opportunity to pull a practical joke on the skipper. On a quiet afternoon, Pleatman was the officer of the deck and bellowed, "Captain to the bridge! Captain to the bridge!" Cutter, who was relaxing in his stateroom, came charging out, bounded through the control room, and climbed swiftly up the ladder through the conning tower to the bridge. There, he found Pleatman standing with a stopwatch in his hand. "That was pretty good, Captain, but I think if you really try, you ought to be able to knock a couple seconds off your time." Cutter, who had a well-developed sense of humor, roared, as did the crew.

With the training period complete, the *Seahorse* cast off on the afternoon of 20 October 1943 to mark the beginning of the submarine's second war patrol—a mission that was to last through mid-December. Cutter's orders were to head for the East China Sea to patrol enemy shipping lanes west of Nagasaki. The submarine was to replace other submarines finishing up their patrols.

It took eight days to make the solitary transit, during which time Cutter maintained the rigorous practice schedule all the way out. Finally, he passed word over the loud speaker system, "From now on, any battle stations will be the real thing." A cheer went up.

Closing on the southern tip of Japan, the boat faced great danger because of the possibility of attack by land-based bombers in daylight hours. Thus the *Seahorse* generally remained submerged in the daytime, giving the crew a chance to sleep. A skeleton watch was established, making periodic radar, sonar, and periscope sightings as the boat drifted along. At dusk, the submarine would resurface and the crew would come alive to begin the search for enemy vessels. The living routine, by then, was upside down. Crewmen ate breakfast in three shifts at sundown and dinner at sunup when the tension of surface patrol ended—a routine called "reversa" in the undersea fleet. As captain, Cutter typically got two hours of sleep in a twenty-four-hour cycle. He drank thirty cups of coffee a day and became a chain-smoker. He also used Benzedrine supplied by the Navy to stay awake at critical moments. "I could sleep some in the daytime, not very much, but some. At night, never," said Cutter. "I don't think others did either." All of this took a toll. He began chewing white aluminum hydroxide tablets to treat a burning sensation in his stomach.

On the morning of 29 October, the boat made its first radar contact. It was a trawler several hundred miles off the southwestern Japanese coast. The vessel was like many family-owned fishing boats manned by Chinese and Korean fishermen. For several hours, he and his officers debated the pros and cons of making an attack. On the one hand, there was no evidence of a radio antenna or guns that would reveal a military purpose. On the other hand, the 150-ton ship probably was supplying food to Japanese troops. Still, attacking a defenseless vessel was against Cutter's moral fiber and he resisted. "Finally Pleatman came down to the wardroom with our operational order," said Cutter. "And the first paragraph said, 'You shall attack all enemy ships encountered with gunfire or torpedoes.' *You shall*—imperative. And Pleatman said, 'You've got to do it, Captain.'" Grudgingly, the captain conceded, bowing to the gun crew's eagerness for action.

The submarine surfaced and began pummeling the fishing vessel with the boat's deck cannon. Its point-detonating fuses went off when they hit anything, even the cloth of a sail. Round after round over fifty minutes left the ship aflame from stem to stern. It was little more than target practice. There was no return fire. Nine crewmen escaped the slaughter by diving overboard. The murderous assault sickened Cutter as the *Seahorse* continued on its way. But he noticed a marked change in the attitude of his crew. "They became very aggressive and they enjoyed it. They were all nineteen to twenty-four years of age. A game. It was a game to them." The captain, on the other hand, could not shake a sense of shame for setting the survivors adrift in the ocean with no hope of rescue.

The next day, the submarine made contact with yet another unarmed fishing vessel. From periscope depth, Cutter counted seven young crewmen working a fishing net that extended for miles. He drew the *Seahorse* away to make a high periscope search for a more suitable target. But there were no targets to be found, and the submarine made its way back in accordance with orders. At 1655 it burst from the surf, frightening the fishermen who fled across the forecastle, as if preparing to resist. Taking no chances, the *Seahorse* holed the stern with cannon fire. Then, Lieutenant Pleatman and three armed crewmen paddled over in a rubber boat and climbed aboard. They scooped up charts, publications, logs, and other materials in the crew's quarters where survivors hid in the forward hold. "It was a bunch of kids, maybe fourteen- and fifteen-year-old boys, scrambling to get underneath the blankets. I mean, it was just pitiful. They were half scared to death," said Cutter. Pleatman and his companions completed their quick search and abandoned the doomed trawler. As the *Seahorse* pulled away, Cutter's concern deepened. The confiscated material included a photograph of one sailor's family and virtual proof the trawler was no more than a fishing boat.

The next day, the submarine encountered a third fishing boat and surfaced only 740 yards away. This time, the ship attempted to ram the *Seahorse,* which blasted it with gunfire, leaving it ablaze and sinking. A half-dozen crewmen jumped overboard and grabbed hold of lines trailing after the trawler as it moved away and sank. That night a storm came up. Cutter thought of those men and how there was no way in the world they could have survived. The succession of massacres ultimately broke his will. "It was just too much, and I said to the officers, 'Goddamn it, I'm not going to do this anymore.'"

As it turned out, there would be little time to dwell on the issue. Six hours later, the *Seahorse* made radar contact with a sizable convoy outbound from Nagasaki, the industrial heartland of Japan. At least seventeen targets, probably more, were counted on the submarine's oscilloscope. Cutter posted McGrievy on the bridge as the submarine moved in on a clear, moonless night. The chief of the boat had extraordinary night vision—"like a cat," boasted the captain. McGrievy soon sighted southbound troop transports, oil tankers, and freighters led by destroyers and smaller, more maneuverable *Chidori*-class patrol boats, specifically designed to locate submarines with sophisticated sonar and listening gear, and loaded with copious supplies of depth charges. Cutter maneuvered the *Seahorse* to the head of the convoy where the boat flooded down at 0315 on 1 November, Slade's thirty-first birthday. Cutter was peering through the periscope to check off the final bearings for an attack on a closing freighter when sound operator Roy Hoffman reported a vessel bearing toward the submarine from the opposite direction. The captain swung the periscope around just in time to see the bow of a fast-moving destroyer on a collision course. "Take her deep! Down scope!" he shouted.

The submarine nosed steeply under as Hoffman counted down the approach. Cutter braced, believing the warship would ram the conning tower or at least clip the periscope sheers. It just missed. Amazingly, no depth charges fell; the ship had not detected the *Seahorse*.

Cutter wasted no time. He brought the submarine back to the surface for an end-around to get in front of the convoy a second time. It took two hours. At 0505, the *Seahorse* submerged again in attack position. Radar confirmed seventeen ships approaching from the north. Escorts were in tight to the main body, protecting what Cutter made out through the periscope to be a large tanker, a passenger liner, and two large freighters. Two patrol craft broke away from the edge of the convoy toward the *Seahorse*'s position, keeping the Americans from attacking as the convoy passed. Persistent depth charges over the horizon finally drew off the *Chidori* escorts, allowing the *Seahorse* to surface at 1345.

Over the next six hours, the submarine followed the patrol boats back to the convoy. Then under cover of darkness at 2200, Cutter moved in for a high-speed surface attack. The quartermaster on the bridge reported four orange flashes to the rear of the convoy, and the distant "thump" of sustained depth charges was clearly audible to crewmen in the *Seahorse*. The radar operator also reported enemy ships scattering from an apparent attack by another submarine. Though the convoy picked up speed, it did not alter course, obviously unaware of the *Seahorse*'s presence on the surface ahead. Cutter ordered more speed. The submarine raced into the middle of the convoy, hidden by darkness. The four diesels in the engine room roared at ear-splitting levels, powering the submarine toward the targets. Dodging the escorts, Cutter took aim at the port bow of a large freighter led by a smaller one. On the bridge and in the conning tower, the action was frenetic. "The adrenaline starts flowing and the mouth gets dry, and you really think fast," said Cutter, who remained in the conning tower with the fire control party.

With the TDC plotting the courses of the two ships and feeding telemetry to torpedoes in the forward firing tubes to set their gyroscopes automatically, Cutter gave the order to fire at the larger target at 0046. Simultaneously, he turned the submarine toward the smaller vessel just as radar reported what appeared to be a second ship, possibly a destroyer, just beyond the target. Cutter hesitated, fearful the destroyer would pounce on the *Seahorse* before it could evade attack. As a precaution, he decided to go around the ship to check for the escort and sink it first. Moments later, all three torpedoes fired at the first target exploded, splitting it in two and sending a powerful shock wave rolling across the ocean. Cutter dashed up the ladder to the bridge to see for himself. "It was a great satisfaction to see the first torpedo we fired explode on a ninety track, and see that ship break up in two and go down," said Cutter. The stern of the 2,852-ton *Yawata Maru* broke free and sank. Momentarily, the bow rose high, then slid beneath the waves.

The *Seahorse* circled to the other side of the second target only to discover that the radar blip was a mirage. The delay allowed the second target to escape. Visibly agitated, Cutter shifted his attention to two approaching freighters. Though patrol boats escorted them, no one saw the *Seahorse* coming. Cutter, riveted to the TDC, kept an eye on the radar scope tracking the escorts in relation to the boat. The officer of the deck on the bridge fed targeting coordinates to Pleatman. Six torpedoes were armed and ready, three for each target. Cutter repeated the order to fire six times. The torpedoes exited the boat in the heavy "whoosh" of compressed air, causing the submarine to shudder. Moments later an explosion rocked the first target, followed by a secondary explosion that illuminated its stern. Two other torpedoes struck the second target with catastrophic damage. With massive tears in its side, the 5,859-ton *Ume Maru* capsized within seven minutes. The spectacle enthralled those on the *Seahorse* bridge until they saw patrol boats speeding toward them. Cutter ordered more speed and outdistanced the slower *Chidori*s, which were dropping depth charges randomly and slowing to pick up survivors. Capitalizing on the panic that gripped the convoy, Cutter abruptly turned back to finish off the first target, which was lying dead in the water. As he positioned the *Seahorse* for a final salvo, a terrific explosion engulfed the 7,089-ton naval transport *Chihaya Maru,* causing it to disintegrate and sink.

Cutter did not sleep throughout the forty-four-hour engagement. Coffee, cigarettes, and Benzedrine kept him awake. During a lull in the action, he exuberantly passed through all the boat's compartments, complimenting the ecstatic crew while explaining in detail what had been accomplished: Three enemy ships sunk in twenty-four hours. He sought the input of every man aboard. He sat with them in the mess hall to relive the attacks, to get their suggestions on strategy. "I wanted them to feel that they all played a role, which is an important part of leadership," Cutter said.

The boat's success erased all doubt about the captain's ability. The fact the boat had accomplished so much without serious counterattack also gave crewmen confidence in their skipper's unusual tactics—diving deep quickly, passing beneath survivors of torpedoed ships, and staying on the surface to maximize the boat's speed whenever possible.

As soon as the *Seahorse* cleared the area, Cutter radioed ComSubPac. Two other submarines also reported attacking the same convoy. The *Halibut* (SS-232) claimed one ship sunk and Dornin on *Trigger* claimed three, the same count as *Seahorse*. Dornin and Cutter broadcast their results at roughly the same time, confusing the command as to who sank what. Making light of the possibility that each man was claiming the same ships, a junior officer radioed back, "The first liar doesn't have a chance." Cutter was incensed at the implication that he had fudged the attack. "Of course every boat in the sub fleet read every other boat's messages, so we were being called liars in front of the entire sub fleet. Goddamn, that made me mad! So I fired off a dispatch back to SubPac telling them that we were on the surface when we fired. We saw our torpedoes hit the targets and saw the ships sink." The following night at Pearl, Lockwood chastised the officer who sent the message. He also sent apologies to Dornin and Cutter. The exchange, humoring other skippers at sea, led to the myth that Cutter and Dornin were in competition and mad at one another.

Over the next ten days, the *Seahorse* continued its patrol in the South China Sea, looking for ships coming and going from Formosa, Nagasaki, and Shanghai. Numerous sightings of fishing boats were made but Cutter let them pass. There were no other contacts until the night of 13 November. Under a full moon, lookouts spotted faint columns of smoke on the horizon but the submarine was unable to intercept the ships. Two days later, the *Seahorse* entered a heavy fog. Lookouts discerned a slow-moving ship as the submarine bore toward it, setting up for an attack from the bow tubes. At the last moment with the submarine closing fast, the fog lifted to reveal the hulk of a torpedoed ship sitting high on a jagged coral reef. The *Seahorse* made an emergency turn toward deep water, barely missing the reef and certain disaster.

Early on the morning of 17 November, lookouts again sighted smoke on the horizon. The *Seahorse* moved in to investigate. Though visibility was poor and the boat's radar was malfunctioning, lookouts made out a convoy of two medium-sized freighters with two escorts. One of them, a destroyer, turned and raced toward the *Seahorse*. The boat went deep as the destroyer plowed past without dropping depth charges. Back at periscope depth, Cutter was in perfect position to torpedo one of the freighters. But the target inexplicably turned away and began speeding up. Something was wrong. Simultaneously, the sound operator on *Seahorse* reported the destroyer turning back toward the submarine, its sonar locking onto the submarine. Every eight seconds, the warship bounced a metallic ping off the hull. Cutter made for the depths in hopes of finding a thermal layer under which the submarine might hide. The *Seahorse* could find no such layer, however, and it dropped below four hundred feet and began silent running. The splash of depth charges on the surface was clearly audible to those in the conning tower. For more than an hour, explosions rocked the ocean, but the depth charges missed the boat. As the submarine tried to clear the area, four very close blasts bracketed the boat. Light bulbs shattered and men had to cling to whatever they could find to keep from falling. But there were neither leaks nor damage to equipment aboard, a testament to the boat's careful construction. At 0630, nearly four hours after the attack began, the destroyer sped away. Cutter brought the boat up for a periscope search an hour later, only to discover an airplane circling the destroyer, angling back toward the *Seahorse*. The warship sped up, slowed down, and sometimes stopped, all the while listening for the submarine. Four hours later, it abandoned the search.

At dusk, the *Seahorse* surfaced in a stormy sea. Soon a Japanese aircraft passed low over the bow, dropping a flare—not a bomb, fortunately—as the submarine made an emergency dive. The *Seahorse* resurfaced and battled typhoon conditions for the next two days. Another airplane came out of a low cloud and caught the *Seahorse* on the surface. The submarine barely got under when two bombs hit the water, exploding close aboard. "He shook the daylights out of us but the old *Horse* thought nothing of it. What a ship!" Cutter later noted in a letter to his wife.

On 20 November, Cutter moved up to the rocky southern coastline off Nagasaki where he thought ships might be hiding. Initially, only a couple of two-masted sailing ships and some fishing vessels were encountered. But shortly after 0100 on 22 November, the *Seahorse* made radar contact with a convoy of three small freighters led by two destroyers making nine knots. From a range of 1,830 yards, Cutter fired a spread of four torpedoes. Two hit the largest target, sinking the 3,322-ton freighter *Daishu Maru*. A destroyer charged toward the submarine as the boat dove to three hundred feet, Cutter barking, "Rig for depth charge! Rig for silent running!" The warship rumbled over, dropping thirteen extremely heavy depth charges. But they were off target and did no damage. Cutter brought the submarine back to periscope depth and observed the destroyer searching unsuccessfully for the *Seahorse* as survivors of the freighter were plucked from the sea. At 0418, two hours after attacking the ship, the *Seahorse* surfaced and cleared the area.

For the next two days there were no sightings. But on 26 November at 1045, the submarine encountered a northbound convoy of eight large ships headed for Nagasaki. Cutter stayed on the track submerged until nightfall when the *Seahorse* surfaced and set out in pursuit. Among the targets were two large tankers and a freighter, all in a column traveling with three destroyer escorts. There was no moon to silhouette the ships, but the air was clear. As the *Seahorse* closed, the destroyers kept ranging back and forth, getting in the way every time the *Seahorse* neared attack position. At 2250, the situation was looking desperate because the convoy was nearing its destination. Either an attack would have to be made soon or the *Seahorse* would lose its advantage. Cutter decided to gamble on a high-speed surface attack. He knew the Navy rated tankers between battleships and cruisers in importance. "I was just about nuts with frustration so I put all engines on at full power and simply went right on in and to hell with the escorts," said Cutter. "We decided to go in as far as we could at maximum speed and start shooting. We would fire our last three torpedoes in the forward torpedo room at the leading tanker and swing the boat around and launch four other torpedoes from the after torpedo room at the second tanker." Budding, by far the most aggressive officer on the boat, who had made a habit of egging Cutter on in combat, did not think the captain could pull it off this time. He urged him to abandon the attack. With one of the escorts a mere fifteen hundred yards away, even Pleatman gulped. "Five dollars, you don't get away with it, Captain." Cutter could not be dissuaded.

He knew from Hoffman, his sonar operator, that the destroyer was heading away from the submarine. The *Seahorse* roared undetected toward the tankers at fifteen knots. The submarine left a phosphorescent wake. Cutter was amazed the destroyer lookouts did not see it. At 3,750 yards from the lead target, the captain gave the order to fire. Three torpedoes left the boat in quick succession. Swinging the boat around, Cutter postponed the order to fire the stern torpedoes because the range was too great. Moments later, two of the three initial torpedoes exploded against a four-thousand-ton unidentified tanker, shattering it. The destroyer charged toward the submarine, but then swerved away, confused as to where the *Seahorse* was. Cutter pushed the advantage, reversed course and raced toward the second, larger tanker, now desperately trying to make a getaway with a cargo of volatile gasoline. Too late: four torpedoes surged toward the target. Cutter scrambled to the bridge where he and others looked back in darkness. Three minutes later, two torpedoes struck home with dull thuds as a destroyer came around the stern of the tanker to defend it. Below decks in the *Seahorse,* the crew heard the impact. "There was cheering from below, so I knew we hit him and then fingers of flame erupted the whole length of that ship," said Cutter. "Red flames came out, and all of a sudden it went up in one huge mushroom of flame. It was an explosion the likes of which few men have ever seen. The mushroom reached at least three thousand feet high and persisted for several seconds, changing color from a dull orange to a brilliant blue-white. The area was as bright as day."

McGrievy, on the bridge with Cutter, was astounded. "It was the most spectacular explosion I've ever seen," he said. "The light from the explosion was bright enough to read a newspaper by." The bridge party could feel the heat from forty-seven hundred yards away. Men below deck were so startled that they thought a bomb had been dropped very close to the submarine. Pieces of the 7,309-ton *San Ramon Maru* fell from the sky in a wide radius. The destroyer near the tanker lost propulsion and came to a dead halt, scorched by the blast that killed crewmen topside.

The *Seahorse* hauled away, certain there were no survivors. "The next thing I knew Pleatman's in the conning tower with a five-dollar bill to pay his debt," said Cutter. The captain made a note in the submarine's log that "unlike the rest of *Seahorse*'s victims which had gone down, this tanker went up."

Because the submarine was running low on fuel, the captain decided to turn back for home. Only four torpedoes remained, all in the stern torpedo room. If the boat were lucky, the *Seahorse* might engage another convoy en route. Three days later, on 30 November, the *Seahorse*'s luck continued when three medium-sized freighters accompanied by two destroyers lumbered into view.

The convoy zigzagged radically every few minutes to foil attack. At sundown, the *Seahorse* surfaced and pulled ahead, Cutter determined to use his last four torpedoes. But the convoy continued to change course radically, making an attack difficult, especially from the stern torpedo room, because the boat would have to make an approach, then turn 180 degrees to launch the torpedoes. To complicate matters, the submarine's radar malfunctioned. A game of cat and mouse ensued for several hours. Each time Cutter got in position to fire, the targets would zig, forcing the captain to obtain a new setup. An hour before midnight, Cutter had again attained attack position and vowed to "nail them on the next zig," no matter what. However, the plan again went awry.

Currie was on the bridge with eighteen-year-old lookout James Reardon. Currie, a slow-talking southerner known as Speed, verbally fed data on the speed and range of the targets through the hatch to Cutter in the conning tower near the TDC manned by Pleatman. "We could see the Japs on deck going about their business as we made our way through the convoy and escorts," recounted Reardon. "Suddenly we were spotted.

I could see them run to their guns and open fire on us. The skipper yelled up to Speed to let him know if they started getting too close to us and he would dive. They didn't call Currie "Speed" because he did anything fast, including talking. I didn't think he would ever get the word to the captain to dive. I was damn close to yelling 'dive' myself. I thought the first shot was close enough!"

Projectiles began falling all around the boat, exploding as they hit the surface. The first detonated three hundred yards to starboard. Some landed astern and others to the port side of the accelerating submarine. Depth charges also exploded, none close enough to alter Cutter's determination to press the attack. Cutter was fully engaged, consumed with the determination to strike. "I was so damned mad at that convoy that the officers and men on the bridge and in the conning tower suffered," Cutter later wrote his wife. "If we had only had some torpedoes in the bow tubes, we would have annihilated them. We got sighted because we had to maneuver so radically to fire from the stern that they saw our wake."

The convoy changed course slightly but did not separate. Finally, at midnight, Cutter attained position for an attack from thirty-seven hundred yards on the lead freighter and gave the order to fire the boat's last four torpedoes. One blew up prematurely, fifty seconds after leaving the boat. The explosion drew the attention of the entire convoy. "All hell broke lose," Cutter noted in his patrol log. The ships began discharging depth charges and firing deck guns haphazardly. Detonations could be heard in every direction. Meanwhile, two brilliant flashes were seen in the direction of the target six minutes after the torpedoes were fired. However, in the commotion of so many blasts, no one could be sure the freighter had been hit.

The *Seahorse*, out of torpedoes and low on ammunition, submerged and headed for Pearl. Cutter credited the ship's success to Pleatman. "He was magnificent. He was just as aggressive as hell and he supported everything I wanted him to do—tremendous help," the captain confided. The crew was so taken with Pleatman that the quartermasters prepared a special pennant in his honor to be flown from the periscope on arrival in Pearl.

On 7 December 1943, the second anniversary of the Japanese attack on Pearl Harbor, the *Seahorse* arrived in Midway to refuel, then proceeded to Hawaii. Five days later the submarine made a triumphant entrance into Pearl Harbor, its periscope fully extended with its victory pennant flying high and reading, "Fuke 'em!" A large party of admirals and other officers greeted the submarine at the base. Lockwood came aboard to offer congratulations.

As promised, Pleatman got his wish. He was detached to return to the States for new construction and his bride. Cutter was proud of what had been accomplished on the patrol. Nevertheless, he continued to be haunted by the destruction of the three fishing vessels. "Sinking transports was so impersonal," he said. "You knew hundreds of people were killed. But you're firing a torpedo and you don't see it and you don't think of it. But that gun action. I didn't like it."

At the submarine base, Cutter bumped into his first skipper, Robert Rice, whom he had served with briefly on the S-30 at the Academy. He now was commander of his own fleet boat. Cutter asked what he did when he ran into fishing trawlers in enemy waters. "I let them alone," Rice replied. Later Lockwood and Capt. Richard Voge, combat operations officer, summoned Cutter to a conference to discuss the just-completed war patrol. He brought up his reticence about sinking trawlers. "Admiral, I sank three of these things out there with gunfire. And jeez, it was just murder," Cutter said. "We went aboard one before we sank it, and there were fifteen- and sixteen-year-old kids aboard. So what would you do?"

"Slade, let your conscience be your guide," replied Lockwood.

"Well," replied Cutter, "I'm not going to attack them any more."

Lockwood shifted the discussion to assessing the sterling results of the *Seahorse*'s second war patrol. In fifty-three days spanning 11,873 miles, the boat had posted the best record of combined tonnage and number of ships sunk in the entire war. Two oil tankers, one transport, three freighters, and three trawlers now lay on the ocean bottom. Another 4,816-ton freighter was damaged or sunk. The patrol would earn Cutter a Navy Cross. It also established him as a fearless and brilliant strategist, putting him in the top ranks of U.S. submarine captains. As tradition dictated, Captain Voge allowed skippers coming off successful runs to choose their next assignment. Cutter suggested a return to Palau. "The *Seahorse* has unfinished business down there," he said. "I want to go back."

"Okay," replied the captain, "you can go."

14

The Chase

A T ITS MOORING at Pearl, the *Seahorse* was primarily manned by a relief crew during the refit, giving veterans a chance to unwind at the Royal Hawaiian where they celebrated their astounding success. To show his appreciation, Cutter suggested a luau. "In order to have a luau, you have to have a pig, and pigs weren't readily available," he said. "But my Japanese landlord, Kuneo Ota, from when Fran and I lived in Honolulu, had a lot of contacts. So I went to Kuneo and asked him if he could get me a pig. He got me one, a good-sized pig. And we made arrangements to have a fine luau."

Crewmen dug a hole on the beach some distance from the hotel, built a fire, and put the pig on the coals. They covered it with stones and tea leaves and allowed it to cook for at least twenty-four hours. Back at the hotel, just-arrived crewmen from the *Trigger* heard about the luau. Skipper Dornin thought one pig could easily feed the crews of two submarines. "How about cutting me in on this?" he asked Slade when he saw him. Without a second thought, Cutter agreed to share the largesse.

Thus the crews—about 160 enlisted men and officers—convened on the beach and started drinking while waiting for the pork to finish cooking. "We should have known better than to set up a joint party between rival submarines," said Lieutenant Beach, the *Trigger*'s executive officer.

"With booze only too plentiful, wisecracks were endemic and fights certain."

It was not long before inebriated crewmen began arguing as to which submarine was better. "Dusty was a great leader, and he had his guys thinking that they were the best in the world, and they were—next to the *Seahorse*," said Cutter. The bragging became belligerent when a drunken *Trigger* sailor, the boat's chief petty officer and Beach's navigating quarter-master, approached boyish Lieutenant (j.g) Budding and slapped his fingers on his collar. "You were just along for the ride," he chortled, upbraiding the officer. Slade overheard the insult and was furious. The captain demanded the quartermaster be reprimanded on the spot. A *Seahorse* sailor toddled over and took a swing at the offending *Trigger* rate. The result was a wild melee.

"Dusty and I tried to stop it," said Cutter of the ensuing chaos. "All my officers pitched in and so did theirs, to break up the fight." The shore patrol, alerted to the altercation, responded with two tractor-trailers outfitted with wire mesh cages. The MPs put the *Seahorse* sailors in one cage and the *Trigger* sailors in the other and drove them back to the hotel. "End of luau," said Cutter. "No pig. I never even saw the pig. I don't know what happened to the pig. Somebody had pork. But it wasn't the *Trigger* or the *Seahorse*."

The next day, Dornin was embarrassed by what had happened. He ordered Beach to do whatever was necessary to heal the breach. "He directed me to see that my quartermaster was reduced in rating, boiled in oil, put on bread and water for a year, buried somewhere where he could do no further harm and in general made to ponder the error of his ways." Beach demurred, blaming war pressures and booze for the ruckus. Dornin agreed to downgrade the punishment to a paper reprimand—as long as Cutter went along. Beach went to the *Seahorse* skipper's room at the hotel to apologize. Slade was still angry, but the lieutenant managed to win Cutter's concession to a reprimand. The captain added, "If I never see that man again, any time, anywhere, I will forget the whole thing." Beach agreed to do his best to make that happen.

With that, the lieutenant heaved a deep sigh of relief. "I was actually getting to my feet to depart when the door to our hotel room was flung open—and there stood my chief quartermaster, swaying slightly under the influence, announcing loudly that he had heard we were in there talking about him! It was instant disaster. For the second time in my life, I had to physically tackle the redoubtable Slade Cutter—this time to prevent him from wreaking instant and grievous harm on my precious sailor." Beach managed to calm Cutter down by assuring him that the quartermaster would be properly punished—"a little boiling in oil," as Beach later put it.

As was the habit in the Navy, about a quarter of a submarine's crew was rotated off after a few patrols to supply trained veterans for new vessels being built at shipyards in New Hampshire, Connecticut, Pennsylvania, Wisconsin, and California. The force was expanding so rapidly that additional training facilities were established at Pearl Harbor to augment the submarine school in New London. Occasionally a new man came aboard via a different route. One such individual on the *Seahorse* was a petty officer by the name of Roland "Dutch" Reuther, formerly in the relief crew at Midway.

"He came aboard and snooped around until he found something wrong," said Cutter. "He told me our records were in terrible shape. He was referring to our personnel records maintained by my yeoman, and he was right." The yeoman was an outstanding radar and sonar operator but was indifferent to record keeping. "I went to his tiny office one time to get some stationery out of his desk and pulled the top left-hand drawer open," explained Cutter. "What I found in there were ladies' panties and bras. So I said to the yeoman, 'What in the world are these things? You don't wear these, do you?' 'Well,' he says, 'those are just trophies of my conquests. I always take a pair of panties or a bra or something.' That's the kind of guy he was."

Cutter allowed a degree of informality aboard the submarine where close ties existed between the enlisted men and the officers. "You thought of them as brothers, doing a job," said the captain. The men could dress down for comfort while on patrol. It was not unusual for them to wear skivvies when it was hot. The captain had two rules that were inviolate: no beards (for sanitary reasons) and no deviation from absolute adherence to the chain of command (even when the boat was in port). The captain made a point of the latter during the refit.

"One morning, a second class machinist's mate brought up a man from the engine room. He told him to do something, and this fireman told him to go to hell. So my reaction to that was, 'Follow me!' I didn't know what I was going to do with him 'til I got up on deck. I might have thrown him in the water. I was really whizzed off." The captain looked astern of *Seahorse* and saw amphibious landing craft lined up for the invasion of Kwajalein (in the Marshall Islands). "Everybody knew that amphibious landings were rough. So I looked at those LSTs [Landing Ship Tanks] and they had one with the number 1014 on its side. I said, 'You're going on that. That's your next billet!' And with that I went up to the force personnel officer of the base and asked him to order the man to the LST. And that's where he went."

While the refit continued, *Seahorse* sailors discovered to their amazement that new submarines launched in Wisconsin were outfitted with slot machines. They were donated to the crews by the Manitowoc Police Department, which had confiscated them in vice raids. Local authorities thought they would help boost morale in off-duty hours. With Cutter's permission, his crew got the Honolulu police to give them a battered slot machine from the department's evidence room. It was installed in the after battery near the *Seahorse*'s galley. The boat's fire-control technicians were given the extra duty of keeping it working. "We had an arrangement that every bit of money the slot machine made, which was considerable, was put into the ship's recreation fund," explained Spud Lindon. "This was for ship's parties and the general welfare of the crew."

The apparatus was a big hit but lived up to its reputation as a "one-armed bandit" by giving skimpy payouts. Subsequently Lindon sweetened the pot with cash from the recreation fund. The machine became a focal point during off-duty hours. The nuances of slots on other boats also became the subject of endless banter whenever submariners got together. On one of the Manitowoc submarines, the machine was so unbeatable that a sign was posted over it: "During depth charge attacks, stand under this machine. It has never been known to be hit yet!"

As December came to an end, the crew of the *Seahorse* prepared for the boat's third war patrol. The U.S. counteroffensive in the Pacific—an island-hopping campaign staged from Australia and aimed at recapturing the Philippines—was underway. The first step of that campaign was to neutralize the eastern rim of Japan's South Pacific defenses. In

November, U.S. troops had taken Bougainville in the Solomon Islands, and Tarawa and Makin in the Gilbert Islands. The next goal was Kwajalein, where the Japanese were moving reinforcements and supplies by convoy from the Palaus and Truk. The United States intended to prevent that from happening. And that depended in large part on keeping submarines on constant patrol.

Cutter met with intelligence officers and exchanged information with other submarine captains. He also devoured patrol reports as soon as they were available. "Everybody read them. I think we wrote them with that in mind—to be as helpful as we could to other people. At the officers' club we'd discuss the enemy's capability and what evasion tactics you use and how effective his antisubmarine screens were. Everybody was so honest, and everybody wanted to help everybody else. It was a joint effort throughout the submarine force—very high morale and esprit de corps. Everybody loved everybody else, and really it was a very wholesome environment. We were very proud. We were like the Marine Corps and I think for good reason."

During the refit, significant new electronics were added to the *Seahorse,* including an advanced PPI (plan position indicator) radarscope to display the position of all ships in a convoy simultaneously, thereby giving Slade Cutter a major strategic advantage in combat.

The *Seahorse* departed Pearl on 6 January 1944 for the return voyage to Palau, more than four thousand miles away. Slade was as eager as he had ever been, wanting to show up McGregor. Two days into the mission, the boat arrived at Johnston Island, the Navy's refueling outpost southwest of Hawaii where the submarine topped off its reserves. The submarine continued on a west-southwest bearing without incident, the crew training incessantly. The unmarked submarine crossed the International Dateline on 10 January, prompting an intercom message to all compartments: "Now hear this! Today is tomorrow!" Three days later, the *Seahorse* entered enemy waters where a four-engine Japanese patrol bomber roared toward the boat. The submarine made an emergency dive, expecting an attack. However, the airplane cruised on by. For the next few days, Cutter continued westward, making no contacts. Then, on the morning of 16 January, lookouts sighted smoke on the horizon.

The *Seahorse* made a swift end around to get ahead of the target, a small freighter closely escorted by four patrol boats, raising suspicion it carried a valuable cargo. However, the tracking party in the conning tower concluded it was a Q-ship, a warship disguised as a freighter to draw submarines into a trap. Such ships had a shallow draft; torpedoes fired at them passed under without exploding, enabling the escorts to follow the wakes back to the submarine to plaster it with depth charges. Cutter decided to attack anyway, using the boat's advanced Mark XVIII electric torpedoes that left no wakes.

In virtual silence ninety feet below the surface, the *Seahorse* moved in. All four escorts were between the target and the submarine, but they were unable to pick up any trace of the undersea craft. The submarine closed to within two thousand yards to a perfect firing position. But the target zigged, throwing the torpedo data computer off, and forcing Cutter to terminate the attack rather than waste torpedoes. The *Seahorse* was in a predicament. The escorts—two ahead, two astern—were within six hundred yards—just six lengths of the submarine. The "ping" of sonar transmitters could be heard all around the boat. There was also a mysterious clicking at four-second intervals. Worried, Cutter took the boat deep to clear the area. But one of the escorts dropped back as the rest continued ahead with the freighter. The submarine-killer began circling and lowered a listening device into the ocean where it picked up the muffled sound of the *Seahorse* descending. The Japanese captain switched on his sonar gear and quickly obtained a hard fix on the submarine. The escort bore in and began lobbing depth charges. The first exploded close without warning, driving the boat wildly downward. The sledgehammer blast knocked crewmen to their knees. Then another explosion. And a third, closer. A fourth, very close. A fifth. And a sixth, a blockbuster that left ventilation pipes vibrating. The pressure hull and superstructure groaned.

The escort captain could have inflicted mortal damage had he pressed the attack. Instead, he broke off prematurely and returned to the convoy, allowing the submarine a second chance. As soon as it was safe, Cutter and the *Seahorse* rose from the depths, determined to wreak havoc.

After dark, the captain reestablished radar contact. On the surface and charging, he closed on the target. Executive Officer Currie and

Lieutenant Lindon were posted on the bridge with McGrievy and two other enlisted men as battle lookouts. McGrievy made visual contact and Currie lined up the ship on the bridge TBT, a bracket that held binoculars and manually fed targeting data to those in the conning tower. The open hatch connecting the bridge to the conning tower emitted a red glow from down below where Cutter, Budding, and others studied the telemetry from radar and the TBT. At 2010 from a range of twenty-four hundred yards, Cutter gave the order to fire four conventional torpedoes in quick succession from forward bow tubes. The first two hit within a second of one another near the ship's engine room, proving it was not a Q-ship. The third exploded under the bridge, blowing it completely off the ship. The 784-ton *Nikko Maru* split in two and quickly sank, its true purpose and cargo never to be known. The escorts milled about in circles, dropping random depth charges, uncertain of where the submarine was. Cutter, navigating between them, snaked his way back to the open ocean and continued westward toward Palau.

The captain set a course for Fais Island to bombard the phosphate plant that the *Seahorse* had been unable to find when McGregor was in command. On surfacing in the early afternoon, lookouts noticed a considerable oil slick trailing the submarine. But seas were too rough for anyone to venture on deck to look for the source. Fearful of enemy bombers seeing the slick, the *Seahorse* dove, only to face a worse calamity: The main induction piping began flooding. The tubes, three feet across and among the largest openings in the hull, fed air to the diesels during surface propulsion. Hydraulic seals should have closed over them automatically as the submarine began its descent. However, seawater inexplicably began to pour into the engine rooms, threatening to swamp the boat. The alarm was sounded to "Take her up!" and "Blow all ballast!" With the precision gained from frequent rehearsals for such emergencies, the crew released compressed air into the ballast tanks girdling the pressure hull, bringing the *Seahorse* quickly back to the surface where pumps drained the bilges. When the weather broke, sailors scrambled over the deck to discover the gasket on the main induction valve dislodged in two places. Crewmen cemented the gasket back in place; others discovered a cap on the forward refueling line had worked loose during the depth charging, causing the oil leak. With repairs made, the *Seahorse* continued on its way, arriving off Fais Island on 19 January.

While making a careful periscope reconnaissance, Cutter noticed a heavily camouflaged artillery muzzle silhouetted against the sky. He moved the submarine in closer and through the periscope photographed the gun for later analysis. Because the phosphate plant looked abandoned, he decided not to waste ammunition bombarding it. Instead he made for Palau, three hundred miles to the southwest.

Less than a day later, an "Ultra" dispatch from SubComPac redirected the *Seahorse* further south to intercept an enemy convoy ferrying military supplies from Wewak, the northern port of New Guinea, to Palau. Cryptographers had broken the Japanese military code to reveal when a vessel left port, what route it was taking, its destination, and estimated time of arrival. Allied listening posts strung around the Pacific gathered Japanese radio signals and relayed them to code-breaking stations in Pearl Harbor, Washington, D.C., and Melbourne, Australia. Once the intelligence was deciphered (the "Ultra"-secret of the war), it was rebroadcast to all U.S. submarines on war patrol. Right on schedule at 1312 on 21 January, the mast tops of two ships came into view. However, passing squalls made it difficult to keep the ships in view. So Cutter made a high speed end around based on guesswork about the convoy's course.

He guessed correctly. At 1617, the submarine dived and waited in ambush. Through the periscope, Cutter identified two large freighters, their decks piled with cargo. The vessels, escorted by three destroyers, zigzagged independently of one another, making it impossible for the *Seahorse* to attack both from a single setup. Thus, Cutter decided to wait for dark and make a high-speed surface radar approach, allowing the submarine more maneuverability. The boat surfaced at 1900 and closed on the largest target, the 3,156-ton Army transport *Ikoma Maru*. At a range of twenty-eight hundred yards, Cutter fired three torpedoes from the forward tubes. He then turned the boat slightly in the direction of the smaller 3,021-ton cargo hauler *Yasukuni Maru* as the first two torpedoes exploded against the *Ikoma*. Twenty seconds later there was an unexpected third explosion. The *Seahorse*'s last torpedo intended for the *Ikoma* hit the *Yasukuni*. Both stopped dead in the water.

Sailors on the two ships, desperate to avoid a second salvo, ran to deck guns, and began pumping shells in all directions in a vain attempt to hit the unseen *Seahorse*, remaining motionless on the surface at a safe distance. Two escorts had left the scene, apparently unaware the ships had been hit. That left a single destroyer to motor back and forth between them, the larger of which was settling in the water on an even keel.

After twenty minutes, Cutter decided to fire two conventional torpedoes at the *Ikoma* from a distance of thirty-six hundred yards. Amazingly, both missed. Cutter thought it was a fluke. He took the submarine in closer and launched two more torpedoes. Again, both missed. The captain suspected the forward TBT had been knocked out of alignment in the depth charge attack days earlier. That indeed proved to be the case and was corrected in time for a fourth attack, this time using wakeless electric torpedoes fired from the stern. Lookouts noticed the smaller *Yasukuni* sinking stern first just as Cutter fired. Two minutes later a fireball erupted abaft of the *Ikoma*'s smoke stack. Brilliantly illuminated by the inferno, the ship seemed to leap upwards as the second torpedo hit forward of the bridge, shattering the freighter, and leaving barrels of petroleum bobbing in a sea of burning gasoline. Petroleum drums periodically exploded in showers of fiery debris. Cutter passed through the submarine's compartments, urging groups of seamen to go to the bridge to view the carnage. Some had never before witnessed such a spectacle and they appreciated the opportunity.

The submarine resumed its patrol of the shipping lane between Palau and Wewak. On 24 January, the boat submerged at dawn and began an approach to Malakal Passage through which ships passed to reach Palau. The *Seahorse* took up a twenty-four-hour vigil outside the strait. Frequent sightings of destroyers, patrol boats, sampans, and aircraft kept the crew alert—especially after the surface radar unit crashed. The conning tower soon became littered with radar parts as technicians attempted to fix the equipment. "I was very anxious for this thing to get fixed because we needed it," said Cutter. "I kept coming up to the conning tower and asking Hoffman, the thirty-three-year-old operator, how he was doing. Finally he said to me, 'For Christ's sake, captain, get out of here! I'll let you know when it's fixed.' So I graciously as possible went below. I almost said, 'Aye, aye, sir!'"

It took another day before the radar was back in commission. Hopes soared at dawn on 27 January when the masts of a large ship appeared coming through the pass. But it turned out to be a hospital ship, so Cutter let it pass. Early in the afternoon of 28 January, the *Seahorse* sighted three patrol boats making a concerted antisubmarine sweep off the entrance to the passage. All three were using echo ranging in a thorough, three-hour search for submarines. Two hours later, telltale columns of smoke appeared in the direction of Palau. Steaming out of Malakal Passage were three large freighters flanked by five escorts: two on the port side, two starboard, and one astern. Three were echo ranging. Aircraft flew overhead.

Cutter, who had been sleeping, was summoned to the conning tower. Dressed in pajamas, he charged up the conning tower ladder from the control room. This was the moment he had been waiting for. Redemption for that pitiful first patrol under McGregor was at hand. As darkness fell, the *Seahorse* surfaced and began a high-speed end around. It took about an hour before the sharp night vision of McGrievy located the oncoming ships. The convoy seemed to know the submarine was out there, initiating a battle of wits. Through the night, the *Seahorse* made repeated attempts to attack the freighters. But each time, evasive zigzagging by the targets foiled Cutter's meticulous setups for an attack. The destroyers also routinely managed to get between the submarine and the targets. "We were making high speed, and there were indications that the escorts were using sound bearings to keep on the bearing line between us and the targets. It was too accurately done to have been a series of coincidences," noted the captain with mounting frustration.

With dawn edging the horizon, Cutter broke off the attack and raced ahead of the convoy for a submerged attack later that morning. But that too was stymied, this time by island-based bombers, making it impossible for Cutter to get in on the targets. Furious, Cutter vowed in the ship's log that "we are determined to get them tonight." The captain had been awake for twenty-four hours, chain-smoking and drinking cup after cup of coffee. Still in his pajamas, he remained riveted to the submarine's electronics and plotting table.

At 1807, the boat's engines roared to life as the submarine surfaced and surged ahead at flank speed toward the convoy's last bearing. An hour and a half later, radar contact was reestablished. It took another two and a half hours to make the run around as the moon set. But like the previous night, the destroyers kept getting in the way. "Each time we approached our firing position, there would be an escort right between us and the target, whereupon we would open out and look for another opening," the captain sighed.

He kept trying. That perseverance finally gave him a momentary advantage in the predawn hours. The targeted vessel changed course, throwing its two escorts far off its port beam. "This was the chance we had been waiting for for two nights," Cutter noted. "It now developed into a race between *Seahorse* and the escorts as to who would arrive in position first."

The destroyers charged, trying to close the gap. But the submarine had the speed and distance advantage. The *Seahorse* bore in on the freighter. At a range of twenty-six hundred yards, Cutter fired three torpedoes, then broke off the approach. Those on the bridge watched as the first two exploded, setting the ship afire. The third blew the stern off. The ship rose by the bow, silhouetted by a furious gasoline fire. In eight minutes, the 2,747-ton Army freighter *Toko Maru* disappeared.

One down.

Cutter turned his attention to the remaining two ships which had sailed away. A sound head lowered below the boat was unable to relocate them. Lookouts sighted a destroyer on the dim horizon however. The submarine, remaining out of sight, followed it in hopes it would lead it back to the convoy—which it did three hours later. Inexplicably, the ships were heading back to the site of the sinking, perhaps making a run back to Palau. Aircraft maintained position over the convoy throughout the day, keeping the submarine from surfacing. But the sonar pinging of destroyers leading the slow-moving freighters allowed the submerged boat to follow the general track of the ships.

At dusk, the convoy commander tried a new tactic by setting a trap. In the twilight, one of the destroyers dropped far behind the convoy, then came charging back. The escort skipper hoped to catch the *Seahorse* surfacing against a rising moon. Cutter, however, caught a break when Hoffman, on sound, picked up the faint approach of the submarine-killer. The *Seahorse* stayed down and the escort passed over harmlessly.

Cutter had been awake for forty-eight hours and was wired, now using Benzedrine to stay awake. Resurfacing, he ordered a tenacious search for the convoy that had slipped away. Fifteen hours later the boat reestablished contact. Again, Cutter was stymied by overhead aircraft. The boat remained submerged until evening when it surfaced for another end around.

The captain, his pajamas soaked by perspiration, still commanded the action in the conning tower. He had been awake seventy-two hours. The entire crew was exhausted and edgy as the *Seahorse* finally achieved attack position on one of the two remaining ships. Then the radar failed. Without it, the whereabouts of the destroyers was anybody's guess. Cutter ordered the sound head lowered beneath the submarine. It confirmed the presence of two submarine-killers nearby. The radar blinked back on in time to identify a third. Then it went out again.

On the bridge, lookouts made visual contact with one freighter because of its size. However, the escorts were too small to be seen in the darkness. Sound could only produce a general bearing. Tense moments passed. Cutter cursed the radar. The tracking party waited. Nine minutes passed. Suddenly the oscilloscope blinked back on, showing the precise position of all convoy vessels.

Cutter resumed the approach and, at nineteen minutes past midnight, fired four torpedoes from the stern tubes. All missed when the target changed course. Explosions at the end of their runs alerted the entire convoy to the renewed presence of the *Seahorse.* It took another hour for Cutter to set up another approach; at 0200 he launched two more torpedoes from the forward tubes. Again the target zigged, avoiding the missiles. Cutter chastised himself for not being more patient. "All hands were exhausted after a chase of eighty hours, and we were probably too anxious to get it over with," he said. Succeeding now depended on the boat's last two torpedoes, two Mark XVIIIs. A risky change of strategy was necessary, however, because the torpedoes were in the stern tubes. In the predawn hours, Cutter maneuvered the boat to within ten thousand yards, then submerged, pointing the stern toward the oncoming vessel. The tracking party, meanwhile, maintained a constant radar fix on the target. The ship changed course as the *Seahorse* backed in closer. Three destroyers echo ranged nearby, one of them only eight hundred yards off the submarine's starboard quarter. Cutter risked detection by raising the periscope to aim at the ship in the dark. He brought McGrievy down from the bridge to man the periscope and fire when ready. The target more than filled the periscope's field at a range of 1,050 yards. "We had to swing the periscope to the right to see stars beyond his bow end, then back it down a bit and fire," said Cutter. "The same procedure was followed for the second shot aimed forward of the stern."

It took twenty-four seconds between firings. One destroyer was so close that Cutter had to take evasive action. "We went ahead standard speed with left full rudder and started deep to avoid possible damage to the periscope from a collision," he said. A depth charge exploded above the *Seahorse,* sending water rushing through the superstructure. Moments later, two heavy explosions rocked the target, now beset by numerous secondary explosions. "They sounded like strings of Chinese firecrackers, and indicate either ammunition or gasoline drums going off," Cutter noted in the ship's log.

The submerged *Seahorse* passed near the sinking ship and then moved away out of range of the destroyers. Twenty minutes passed. Another heavy explosion was heard in the direction of the target. It was the sound of the 4,004-ton freighter *Toei Maru* imploding as it headed for the bottom. Cutter brought the submarine to periscope depth to take a look and at 0443 surfaced to witness a mass of gasoline-fueled flames with drums still exploding on the surface. "It was very light in the East, but the attention of the escorts was directed to rescue work. We could see them moving around, silhouetted against the fire as we went out to dive," said Cutter.

The crew was jubilant but utterly drained. The six hundred-mile chase—the longest sustained pursuit of an enemy convoy in the war— had taken eighty-two hours and thirty-three minutes. It lasted from 1719 on 28 January—when the *Seahorse* first sighted the Japanese convoy—until 0352 on 1 February when Cutter sank the last target. "I was in pajamas when I was called to the conning tower, and I was in pajamas when it was all over. God, they must have smelled," Cutter said. "It was a long, hard thing, and you just stick with it, but it leaves a mark on you." To him and every man aboard, it was worth it. The attacks had deprived Japan of fuel and arms that might have cost U.S. lives.

Out of torpedoes, there was nothing more for the *Seahorse* to do but return to Pearl. "Boy, I was exhausted," said Cutter. "We dove and went down to two hundred feet and leveled off, and everybody was secured except the bare watch just to keep the submarine going. I went into the wardroom, and a guy by the name of Frank Royal Fisher, the junior grade lieutenant, was sitting in there and said, 'How about a game of acey-deucy, Captain?' I started to play but I couldn't think about acey-deucy. And the pharmacist's mate came in and wanted to know how I felt, and I said, 'I don't feel very good. I can't relax and cannot sleep.'"

Medic Newton Karisch left the wardroom and returned with a pint of Old Crow whiskey. Cutter finished it in short order. "But it didn't do me a bit of good. I didn't get the least bit sleepy." So Karisch gave the captain sleeping pills. But they also did no good. Cutter began pacing the ship. Karisch was scared. "Captain, no more of this," he demanded. "Try to go to sleep."

Cutter returned to his quarters, lay down, and fell asleep—but only for an hour and a half.

"I woke up with a terrible, terrible headache. I couldn't sit down. I walked back and forth, back and forth in the narrow passageway from the control room to the forward torpedo room, back and forth, back and forth, and I was just beside myself." Luckily, the combination of sleeplessness, booze, and sedatives did not have fatal consequences. Finally, the captain fell into a deep sleep.

With the crew looking forward to a triumphant return to Pearl, the boat was diverted to Wake Island. The *Seahorse*'s mission was to stand off the island and rescue any aviators who had to bail out or crash land during bombing raids. The boat arrived on 7 February. At midnight every night for a week, B-24 Liberators roared in over the submarine to bomb enemy entrenchments, then flew back to their base. None were shot down, nor did any aviators need to ditch for other reasons. Thus on 12 February, SubComPac released the boat for the journey home.

Four days later, at noon on 16 February, the *Seahorse* arrived at the submarine base in Pearl Harbor to a noisy welcome home. Admiral

Lockwood and Captain Voge were among those welcoming the crew dockside. For sinking five ships during the forty-six-day patrol, Cutter earned a Gold Star in lieu of another Navy Cross. Since he took command, his tally stood at eleven ships sunk in just two patrols. Lockwood was ecstatic. "For the second time in succession, the *Seahorse* carried out an aggressive and successful patrol. All approaches were made after careful study of the situation and were followed by determined, extremely well-planned and executed attacks."

There was little time for the captain and his crew to relax and enjoy their accomplishments, however. Planning was already underway for a mission that was more dangerous than any before, one that those at the very top of the undersea command thought the submarine might not survive.

15

Ordeal off Saipan

THE EXHAUSTED crew of the *Seahorse* had endured strenuous action and psychological terror on two consecutive missions. Yet there would only be a few weeks of relaxation in Honolulu before another harrowing run to support the U.S. offensive in the South Pacific.

In the first half of 1944, the island-hopping campaign had stepped up in intensity. Troops had landed in Kwajalein in January, and an Allied attack on the Admiralties was imminent. An invasion of Hollandia was planned for April followed by a concerted effort in June to capture the key Japanese strongholds of Saipan, Tinian, and Guam in the Northern Mariana Islands.

For Cutter, the danger of his next assignment became apparent when Lockwood summoned him to a strategy meeting at the submarine base. The vice admiral explained that the *Seahorse* was to travel thirty-three hundred nautical miles to Saipan where it was to draw off antisubmarine units, thereby allowing the *Greenling* (SS-213) to sneak underwater demolition experts onto the southern coast of the island to see if there were any mines or underwater obstacles to oppose an U.S. amphibious landing set for May or June. In effect, the *Seahorse* was to be a decoy in exceedingly hazardous circumstances. "The last submarine that had gone there was driven off by relentless anti-sub activity. So I knew it would be difficult," explained Cutter. "Dick O'Kane, commander of the *Tang* [SS-306], had been sent there, and he had a bad time. They drove him off and kept him away. He was with a wolf pack; there was not just Dick alone. There were two other submarines."

Both sides in the war considered Saipan pivotal because of its proximity to Tokyo, thirteen hundred miles to the northwest. If the United States could seize it, the island's airfield and that on Tinian could be used by new long-range B-29 bombers to launch sustained bombing strikes against Japan for the first time. Lockwood cast the *Seahorse*'s mission as an opportunity because there would be abundant enemy targets for Cutter to go after. However, that was not the boat's primary purpose. "We're going to land in Saipan and Tinian," the admiral explained. "You've got to stay in there because we've got to draw these ASW [anti-submarine warfare] forces off so the *Greenling* can go in. So you stay there and attack. Make yourself known.

"And one other thing, Slade," Lockwood said, pausing for emphasis. "You will not be taken prisoner."

Cutter, of course, had no such intention. He and Franny had agreed on that early in the war. "We heard terrible stories, and I guess it was just about as bad as we heard—what the Japs were doing to prisoners." Still, to hear Lockwood's imperative was chilling.

During the three weeks that the *Seahorse* was in dry dock, the relief crew loaded the submarine entirely with Mark XVIII electric torpedoes at the captain's request. Though they were slower, they were wakeless and thus, when fired, would not betray the submarine's location to what were considered Japan's best submarine-killing forces.

On the morning of 16 March, the *Seahorse,* in company with the *Harder* (SS-257), left Pearl Harbor for its fourth war patrol, a voyage expected to stretch into May. Cutter noticed that the top ten feet of the *Harder*'s periscope sheers were painted a vivid pink. The Navy had been trying different color schemes in order to better camouflage its boats, depending on whether they operated in the tropics or more northern climes. Normally, the Navy used black, gray, and tan. But pink? Lt. Cdr. Sam Dealey of the *Harder* insisted that it better reflected the color of the water around it, thus making the periscope less visible to the naked eye when raised above the surface in daylight. Using pigments stored aboard *Seahorse*, Cutter decided to follow Dealey's lead.

For ten days, the vessels headed west, practicing attack approaches on each other and proving conclusively that radar could locate the periscope of a submerged vessel if it was extended above the ocean surface just a few feet—a frightening prospect if Japan acquired radar.

On the evening of 26 March, the submarines separated; the *Harder* headed for the Caroline Islands while Cutter set a course for Saipan. The next morning, the *Seahorse*'s SD (ship detection) radar, also designed to detect low-flying aircraft, failed. Less than two hours later, the officer of the deck sighted a twin-engine bomber approaching and sounded the diving alarm. The airplane dropped three bombs, all of which missed as the boat went deep. The *Seahorse* stayed down for two hours so technicians could repair the radar. The submarine resurfaced just after noon and stayed up for five hours. The lookouts were enjoying a spectacular tropical sunset when an officer using the periscope to scan the path of the sun with a polarizing filter noticed the feather of a periscope wake where the lookouts could not see it. It disappeared before radar could get a fix. Cutter ordered evasive course changes but remained on the surface to maximize the boat's speed. Twice radar contact was made with the mystery submarine's periscope. Finally at sunset the *Seahorse* pulled away.

The next few days passed without incident. In the predawn hours before the boat dived each day, Cutter was the last off the bridge. He would take one long last look up at stars in the sky all the way down to the horizon where the pale glow of sunrise reached toward the heavens. In his moment of solitude as the noisy diesels shut down in preparation for the dive, he thought of Franny and Annie thousands of miles away. And he wondered if he would ever see them again.

On 31 March, Cutter received an Ultra from ComSubPac. A Japanese carrier task force was en route to Saipan from the north. "All I knew was that the dope we got was good," said Cutter. "I didn't know where it came from, and I didn't care, as long as they kept giving it to us."

As the *Seahorse* moved north to intercept the convoy, the submarine's radar operator reported interference on the boat's frequency. Cutter changed course to investigate. He could see the faint shape of a vessel approaching at ten knots, and ordered battle stations while opening the outer torpedo tube doors for a possible torpedo attack. The target began maneuvering in a large circle. The *Seahorse* responded by doing the same. "Both of us were like a couple of tomcats, waiting to see who was going to pounce on whom first," said Cutter. "For some reason I held off, even though there were supposed to be no other American ships within several hundred miles of us."

The captain was finally able to see the silhouette of the target as it passed against the western horizon at sunset. It was a submarine and it began blinking Morse code: "Come on over. Speed five knots. Sam."

Cutter was astounded. "It was Sam Loomis in the *Stingray* [SS-186]. He had received the same Ultra, and since the hunting had been poor in his area, he came down into my bailiwick to form an unofficial wolfpack, knowing that I was there. We pulled alongside *Stingray*, and using a megaphone, the two of us decided on a plan of attack."

Cutter, of course, was glad to see his old friend. Loomis had been a superb executive officer in the *Snook* (SS-279) before taking command of the *Stingray*. Making his first patrol as captain, he sank a four-thousand-ton freighter before heading south to meet Cutter. "There are some people who are smart who just can't achieve academically," said Cutter of his former academy roommate who had struggled in school. "You run into these people. Loomis was one of them."

The two submarines glided through calm seas, running on batteries so that the two captains could converse more easily. "You took one hell of a chance coming into my area as you did," Cutter said.

A grinning Loomis replied, " I knew you wouldn't fire until you had identified the target."

"You have more confidence in my self-control than I do," said Cutter. "I think that the good Lord had more than a little to do with it."

Unable to locate the enemy convoy, the two submarines separated, the *Seahorse* continuing on to Saipan where two days later lookouts sighted ships at anchor in the broad harbor of Tanapag, the principal town on the west coast of the fourteen-mile-long island. A looping coral reef more than five miles long enclosed the anchorage. Tanapag sat on a coastal plain fanning out to the west from a 1,554-foot-high volcanic ridge stretching north-south down the center of Saipan and bisecting its five-mile width. A large Japanese immigrant population had inhabited the island for decades, farming terraced hillsides and plateaus.

For a few days the *Seahorse* lingered offshore undetected. Cutter scrubbed a planned attack on an inbound convoy when the ships snuggled up to the reef and entered the anchorage through an uncharted channel. Opportunity arose again on the mid-afternoon of 7 April when three large freighters escorted by two destroyers and high-flying aircraft emerged from the harbor en route to Guam 135 miles south. The *Seahorse* followed submerged until nightfall when it surfaced under a full moon and clear skies.

Cutter had every intention of announcing his presence. The submarine made an end around and positioned itself dead ahead of the convoy at midnight as the ships neared Guam. The musical chime of the general alarm set crewmen running for battle stations as the submarine headed into the center of the convoy. Soon the chirping of sonar revealed the approach of the destroyers. Cutter skillfully avoided contact, sliding in the darkness between them. The officer of the deck barked out bearing, range, and angle on the bow to the targeted lead freighter. In the conning tower, Cutter prepared to shoot three Mark XVIIIs at the closest target twelve hundred yards away, then swing the submarine around to launch three more at a second target at twice the distance.

"Bearing—mark! Three five four!" shouted the captain. "Fire one! Fire two! Fire three!" The *Seahorse* shuddered as blasts of compressed air sent the torpedoes on their way from forward tubes.

"Fire four! Fire five! Fire six!"

One minute passed. Then the sharp crack of three explosions. Cheers from the lower compartments were heard in the conning tower. Two minutes later, there were more explosions in the direction of the second target: simultaneously, there was a tremendous explosion from the first target. Those on the bridge witnessed a brilliant mass of flames shoot high into the air as debris fell in a cascade around the 6,583-ton ammunition ship *Aratama Maru*. The second target, the 1,915-ton *Kizugawa Maru*, also was aflame but remained on an even keel.

In the conning tower, sound-operator Hoffman reported the destroyers picking up speed and bearing toward the submarine. The *Seahorse* dove steeply, veering to starboard. But it could not go deep because of shallow coastal waters between the destroyers and Guam, seven miles away. A steady barrage of depth charges bracketed the submarine. For three hours twenty-eight explosions ripped the depths as Cutter attempted to work away from Guam. "The escorts naturally anticipated this, and forced us to parallel the coast for a considerable distance," the captain noted in the patrol log. Finally there was a lapse. The *Seahorse* found a route between the destroyers and vanished. The boat later surfaced before dawn and headed toward Saipan, putting its stern to the *Kizugawa Maru,* enveloped in flames and aground off Guam.

After a daylong voyage, the boat resumed its patrol off Tanapag where enemy airplanes harassed the submarine day and night, forcing frequent dives. On the late afternoon of 9 April, lookouts noticed smoke from an in-bound convoy. The *Seahorse* closed on the surface at flank speed until enemy airplanes drove it under. Cutter moved in submerged and, looking through the periscope, couldn't believe his eyes. It was the largest convoy he had ever seen—at least fifteen to twenty merchant ships led by four full-sized destroyers pinging the ocean depths but unable to detect the *Seahorse.*

In the captain's field of vision were four ships, overlapping one another. He selected a large freighter and fired three torpedoes, but they missed when the convoy made an unexpected course change. Cutter fired a fourth on a new bearing but it also missed. Only three minutes had elapsed. The captain raised the scope, took a split-second look, aimed, and fired from very close range. Two more torpedoes sped from the forward tubes. Two explosions staggered the freighter, bringing it to a dead halt.

Hoffman reported destroyers heading for the *Seahorse.* And something else: a torpedo making a circular run, putting it on a collision course with the submarine. "Take her deep!" shouted Cutter. The submarine dipped at a 40-degree down angle, peeling off to the port side. Crewmen clutched tables, ladders, pipes, anything to keep their footing during an elevator-like ride into the depths. Their hearts were in their throats. Hoffman counted down. Those in the conning tower braced for impact as the Mark XVIII scooted past with an audible whine. It just missed. Twice more it circled at a safe distance before finally running out of fuel.

Cutter, relieved yet puzzled that no depth charges had been dropped, brought the boat to periscope depth only to encounter a charging destroyer. "Rig for depth charge attack!" Cutter bellowed, as the boat dove quickly, stern first. The crew smothered anything that made noise: air conditioning, hydraulic steering mechanisms, motors and relays. Planesmen and helmsmen shifted to hand control. The sound of the onrushing destroyer spread a pall of apprehension. Frozen men stared at anything but into another man's eyes as the sound became louder. No one said anything above a whisper. The warship passed, its engines fading astern. Then the barely audible splash of a depth charge canister, followed by a sharp click and the sledgehammer blow of the explosion. The boat shook wildly as it passed two hundred feet. Lights went out. Cork insulation and paint chips floated loose. The hull buckled ominously. Depth charges fell from all directions from all four destroyers. It was five minutes of utter terror for the *Seahorse,* descending rapidly with a steep up angle.

The submarine passed four hundred feet. Three blasts from below the boat startled the captain. For the first time in his experience, the depth-charge indicator—a box in the control room with lights linked to microphones in the bow, stern, starboard, port, overhead, and hull—lit up simultaneously. But the *Seahorse* persevered, reaching the safety of six hundred feet.

During a lull, the *Seahorse* rose to periscope depth to discover that the stricken 4,667-ton naval transport *Mimasaka Maru* was still in one piece. Because no one was attempting to tow the ship, Cutter decided there was time to move to the northwest, surface out of sight in order to get a partial battery charge, then brave another destroyer counterattack to administer a coup de grâce before daybreak. By the time the *Seahorse* returned, however, there was flotsam everywhere: proof the ship had sunk. Life rafts, part of a deckhouse, crates, boxes, wooden buckets, and cylindrical gasoline tanks for aircraft floated in a massive oil slick stretching to the horizon.

The *Seahorse* continued its patrol off Tanapag where enemy aircraft and warships pressed the hunt for the submarine. "It was during a period of full moon, and we'd get on the surface and they had aircraft up there with radar," said Cutter. "But their radar apparently was not directional. They would fly in circles and would go whichever way the range decreased. They didn't know exactly where we were. They would be circling us, gradually closing the range. I knew where they were and we'd follow them until they started coming in too close and then we'd dive. They would call destroyers over but they wouldn't know where we were and we were always able to get away by heading away at ninety degrees. But we had to dive all the time. We couldn't get a full battery charge. And that's not a good situation. You're always worrying about the state of your battery and whether you would need it during depth charging."

Cutter was especially worried about the mental state of his executive officer, Lieutenant Currie. Like several other crewmen, he showed signs of great stress. "As the navigator, he couldn't plot his position, his hands were shaking so bad," said Cutter. "He was a fine officer but it had just been too much—the constant contact with the enemy ASW forces and the large number of depth charges we got earlier. So I had to relieve him of all duty to get him to rest."

Days of near-constant pinging by destroyers kept everybody on edge. "I'll never forget seeing the dining table and nobody ever sitting down to eat. Nobody was hungry, too uptight," said Cutter. The captain did his best to keep the crew in the various compartments informed. But there was not time in the hectic moments of attack and counterattack. "I always felt awfully sorry for the guys below who didn't know what was going on. We knew what was going on in the conning tower. We knew where the destroyers were; we knew when they were making a run; and we knew when to expect them. We knew when they passed overhead up there across our bow; we knew the charges were coming down. And we would take evasive action before they had a chance to get down there."

As Vice Admiral Lockwood and Captain Voge had hoped, the *Seahorse* played the role of decoy to perfection. The boat had created major havoc off Saipan, distracting the enemy and allowing the *Greenling* to go in undetected to scout the south beach to assure it was adequate for the planned invasion.

At dawn on 11 April, Cutter took the submarine to deep submergence and remained there for twelve hours. Just a skeleton crew stood watch as the others, including the captain, crashed in their bunks. The day passed peacefully for everyone except Hoffman who, with earphones strapped to his head, listened in the conning tower for any enemy approach. Destroyers and other patrol craft crisscrossed the ocean three hundred feet overhead, sending out constant sonar pings that seemed almost musical but after a while agitating. Hoffman got so annoyed that he decided that if he had to endure it, why not the whole crew? So he hatched a practical joke near the end of the sleep period. The periscope was housed in a cylindrical well. To keep the periscope from fogging, the ventilation system passed through the well, keeping the moisture content down. The ventilation duct tended to project sound—throughout the ship. So Hoffman turned the gain up to maximum and dropped his earphones into the well. "I'll tell you, he got everybody up, including the captain, in one hell of a hurry," said Cutter. "It sounded like a destroyer was right outside the hull." Crewmen staggered out of their bunks, as did Cutter, who raced through the control room and up the ladder to the conning tower. Hoffman grinned down at him maniacally, dangling his headphones. "Some sense of humor," smoldered the captain, ordering Hoffman not to do it again.

ComSubPac informed the *Seahorse* that bombing raids on Saipan were planned for 14 April and ComSubPac wanted Cutter to stand by to rescue aviators if necessary. The captain was not happy. He knew Tanapag harbor was packed with ships about to depart. Yet because of lifeguard duty, the *Seahorse* would not be in position to attack them. The submarine took up its station early on 14 April and waited several hours until another radio intercept announced the raids had been postponed. Cutter used the opportunity to head for the harbor in hopes of getting there in time. Unfortunately, he was too late. A large convoy had disappeared over the horizon. The *Seahorse,* unable to surface in daylight because of the risk of being bombed by shore patrol aircraft, had no chance of catching up. Nevertheless, a Japanese cruiser, a large tanker, and a few freighters remained in the harbor. As much as he wanted to venture inside, Cutter knew it would be suicidal in such shallow water. Therefore, he waited several days until Easter Sunday morning—when the *Seahorse*'s luck changed in the most unexpected way.

At dawn, the boat submerged fifteen miles west of Tanapag and proceeded slowly toward the harbor while mapping the irregular ocean floor. Lieutenant Lindon was on the attack periscope raised twelve feet above the surface, triangulating the submarine's position by sighting the smokestack of a sugar mill on Saipan, a lighthouse, and a cliff. Cutter, having just finished eating, climbed into the conning tower with a cup of coffee in hand and relieved the lookout on the wide-angle search periscope. The captain made a slow rotation, his arms draped over the periscope handles, looking for ships or airplanes. In making the 360-degree sweep, the blurry smudge passed by. He backed up the periscope and steadied the eyepiece. It was a submarine, a large rising sun emblazoned on its conning tower. The submarine, its deck crowded with lookouts, was making ten knots toward the harbor. "The captain was steering a constant helm zig plan, and we were lucky enough to be in the right spot to catch him as he was starting back from the end of his right zig," said Cutter who passed word to the rest of the crew. Lieutenant Budding produced a TDC firing solution as the forward torpedo doors were lowered. At midmorning, Cutter fired two torpedoes from sixteen hundred yards away. The first hit the target's forward torpedo room two minutes later, producing a more violent explosion than any previous torpedo attack. *Seahorse* crewmen thought at first a bomb had been dropped on them. The blast was so powerful it lifted deck plates and violently shook the bulkheads of the *Seahorse*, scattering orange peels, wrapping papers, and other sorts of trash that had been stowed there by yard workers during the refit.

No one on *Seahorse* doubted the Japanese submarine, the I-174, had been destroyed. But there was no jubilation. Rather, gloom settled over the crew. "It was the only sinking to my knowledge where no cheers came to the conning tower from below," Cutter said later. "After the hit, all of us thought, 'But for the grace of God, that could have been *Seahorse*.'"

For one crewman, the attack was a shattering experience. He was an eighteen-year-old who had been on the relief crew at Pearl and had begged Cutter to allow him to go out with the *Seahorse* so he could qualify for a combat pin. "He was an only child. His mother was a widow who sent me a letter saying he was her whole life. She didn't want him to go out in the submarine and she wanted me to take him off. I got the boy in my cabin and we talked very confidentially, and I showed him the letter. I let him read it, and I said, 'Now you can get off. I'll transfer you back to the relief crew.' Well, he broke down and cried. He wanted to go that bad, so we took him out. But I was worried about him. And when we hit that submarine, this kid absolutely went to pieces, screamed and fell to the deck worrying about his mother and he was out of it." The pharmacist's mate gave him a sedative, and at Cutter's direction, knocked him out with additional sleeping tablets every time the submarine went into action for the rest of the patrol.

For the next few days, the *Seahorse* remained offshore. An attempt to overtake an outbound freighter led by a destroyer failed. But on 26 April, lookouts sighted smoke from a convoy of three large freighters, a small cargo hauler, a destroyer, and three smaller escorts. The ships were moving slowly, which enabled Cutter to follow submerged for ten hours. At sunset, the boat rose from the depths and raced ahead, the captain hoping to attack around midnight. The submarine dived ahead of the enemy ships and headed in, stern first. The escorts were pinging steadily, and Hoffman on sound reported the destroyer had speeded up and seemed to have a fix on the submarine. Cutter swung the periscope around to get a momentary glimpse of the submarine-killer. He had to work fast, directing the sonar operator to send a single electronic ping toward the target to confirm the accuracy of the TDC firing solution. Simultaneously Hoffman reported the destroyer nearly on top of them. Cutter could wait no longer. "Fire seven! Fire eight! Fire nine! Fire ten!" The torpedoes left the stern tubes in a convulsive shudder of compressed air. The destroyer now "looked as big as a battleship" in the periscope, according to Cutter. At the last moment, however, it changed course and moved off. Moments later the first torpedo hit its target forward of the bridge, followed by a second hit below the bridge and a third aft. The 5,244-ton naval transport *Akikawa Maru*, loaded with bauxite ore, sank stern first as the *Seahorse* headed deep. The escorts dropped depth charges as the submarine moved under the track of the freighter and escaped.

The boat surfaced later and, in accordance with orders, headed for Satawan Island where it was needed for lifeguard duty. ComSubPac directed the submarine into a "safe-conduct lane," a path of travel where U.S. aviators were under orders not to attack submarines. Cutter did not take any chances. He posted eight lookouts and two officers on the bridge. As the submarine neared Satawan after a two-day voyage, the large number of U.S. carrier-based airplanes in the area made Cutter nervous. So he took the further measure of having crewmen pin a large U.S. flag to the deck, making it clearly visible to aviators. Unfortunately, that was not enough.

A U.S. B-24 Liberator came out of the sun, crossing the *Seahorse*'s bow from port to starboard at two hundred feet. The lookouts looked up in surprise. "I saw two bombs drop out of the open bomb bay doors," said Henry Bouley, a torpedoman serving as the forward lookout. The explosives detonated on impact with the ocean, barely missing. Lt. F. R. Fisher, officer of the deck, instinctively reached for a flare gun and fired a recognition flare as the bomber circled for a second run. The pilot, a former classmate of Cutter, saw the flare just in time as the submarine dived. A smoke rocket fired from submergence also warned him off.

In the control room, Cutter was furious. How could an airplane get in and drop its bombs before the diving alarm had been sounded? "God, I was upset about that. Fisher came down and, boy, I gave him the business, 'What in the hell are you doing up there with that watch, sleeping?! How in the world did he get in on you?'"

With the danger over, the *Seahorse* resurfaced, with the lookouts on doubly high alert. Cutter stood watch with them. It was not long before another Liberator at twenty thousand feet worked around to the sun and then banked in an apparent attack approach. Cutter took no chances and dived. "Goddamn B-24s!" he shouted as he went below. The boat remained submerged while Cutter drafted a dispatch to Pearl Harbor complaining bitterly of not being provided safe passage. However, he accepted responsibility for the submarine not being alert to the first Liberator. "*Seahorse* is to blame. The watch was asleep," he concluded, a decision he would come to rue.

With no further interference, the submarine arrived safely off

Satawan for the strike by U.S. forces. Submerged, the *Seahorse* closed to within thirty-five hundred yards of the island at noon on 30 April. Cutter got close enough to see newly constructed buildings around a makeshift airfield. After a brief reconnaissance, he drew the submarine away as three U.S. dive-bombers zeroed in on the base. "The first plane was on fire as it came out of its dive," said Cutter who watched through the periscope. "It got back up to its original altitude, with the fire out and a faint wisp of white smoke trailing behind. The plane appeared to be under control, and was making very high speed. After maintaining level flight for about thirty seconds, it went into a straight shallow glide and failed to come out. It crashed about one thousand yards astern and blew up. Flame and pieces of the plane were contained in the splash, and it was all over for the crew."

Later, the *Seahorse* surfaced and set up a voice radio watch for aviators who needed help. But only the single airplane was lost in the conflict. The submarine remained fifteen miles offshore through the night and into the next day, waiting for a portion of a carrier task force that was bombing Truk. Shortly after noon on 1 May, nine U.S. cruisers and eight destroyers came into view. The submarine exchanged recognition signals with them and then, as Cutter put it, "we took station in a front row seat for the show. It was a good one."

The warships plastered Satawan with cannon fire, setting off numerous fires. Eight more dive-bombers joined in, as did float planes launched by the cruisers. During the attack, the commanding officer of the cruiser *Louisville* radioed Cutter to ask if the *Seahorse* needed any supplies. The skipper replied there was a critical coffee shortage. The *Louisville* directed the submarine to come alongside to accept the transfer of coffee, ice cream, and fresh vegetables. Cutter was duly impressed. "We consider it Democracy working at its best when a task force flagship will call a submarine alongside and transfer non-essentials during an engagement," he noted in the ship's log.

The rest of the day, the *Seahorse* crew listened in on voice transmissions between the *Tang* and airplanes engaged in the bombing of Truk. In the course of several hours the submarine rescued a record twenty-two aviators.

With the *Seahorse* short on fuel and the crew in need of some well-deserved rest, ComSubPac transferred control of the submarine to the Southwest Pacific command based in Brisbane, Australia, and ordered Cutter to head for the subcontinent for a refit, which was a boost to morale. En route, the captain decided to take a shortcut across a corner of the prescribed sea-lane for the *Seahorse.* It would cut the travel time substantially. However, it put the submarine in a free-fire zone where it could be attacked by Allied forces at will. To protect against that, Cutter urged the lookouts not to lose their concentration. It was not long before a B-24 zeroed in on the submarine. This time the lookouts broadcast the alert in plenty of time, allowing the *Seahorse* to dive and escape. The bomber circled for an hour and a half before the pilot gave up and left the scene. The submarine resurfaced, with the crew giddy in anticipation of an early arrival in Australia. What they did not realize, however, was the pilot alerted the Australian command that a suspected U.S. submarine was in the free-fire zone. Soon orders arrived from General Douglas MacArthur's headquarters in Brisbane, directing the submarine to return to the safety lane and remain there. Worse, the *Seahorse* was to maintain a speed of no more than twelve knots the rest of the way. That meant it would arrive later than if Cutter had remained in the protective lane from the start.

As it turned out, these orders were lucky for the *Seahorse.* The Japanese Navy had surmised that Americans were building up their forces in New Guinea for the invasion of the Marianas. As a result, it deployed a scouting line of six submarines to watch for any sign of the invasion force once it left New Guinea. Thanks to Ultra, the precise location of the submarines was known—in the free-fire zone that the *Seahorse* had just vacated. A hunter-killer team of U.S. destroyers was dispatched to clear it out. One of the destroyer escorts, the *England,* located and destroyed five of the six submarines in a twelve-day period.

The *Seahorse* reached Milne Bay in New Guinea on 7 May where it refueled, then continued on to Brisbane, thirteen hundred miles further south. The boat ended its fourth war patrol the morning of 11 May 1944, mooring at Brisbane's naval base on the eastern seaboard of Australia. Captain Cutter and the *Seahorse* had accomplished all that

ComSubPac had envisioned. The boat's fifty-five-day patrol spanned 12,639 miles. Five torpedo attacks had destroyed four freighters and a submarine. Cutter earned another Gold Star in lieu of his third Navy Cross—a record that further enhanced his fame and made the *Seahorse* a submarine superstar having sunk sixteen ships in three patrols.

But some aboard wanted off. They were fearful of the *Seahorse*'s upcoming fifth war patrol and the superstition among submariners that the fifth brought bad luck.

Down Under

THE DECISION by ComSubPac to send the *Seahorse* to Brisbane for refit could not have come at a better time. One officer and many enlisted men had near breakdowns during the Saipan mission. Others remained on edge and in desperate need of relief from their ordeal. For the weary submariners, Brisbane's distractions were much needed as they began two weeks of liberty. In the 1940s, the city had found a niche in tourism as the gateway to the Great Barrier Reef to the north and the pristine beaches of the Gold Coast to the south. Sixty miles west, the misty blue mountains of the Great Dividing Range separated the narrow coastal plain and its sugar plantations from the barrens of the Outback that span the continent. The city was a sprawling panoply of factories, stockyards, and red-tiled or tin-roofed houses on wooden piles fanning out in a wide valley through which the Brisbane River wound past wharves and the city's coveted colonial-style homes with long verandas. White, red, orange, and purple blooms of native bougainvillea vines and tropical vegetation of all kinds embroidered the city, which was crisscrossed by trams and streetcars. Originally established by the British as a penal colony, Brisbane later flourished as immigrant settlers developed Queensland's natural resources, particularly coal, gold, silver, lead, and zinc. World War II pumped a new source of wealth into the economy and transformed Brisbane into an arsenal for the war effort. Brisbane was headquarters of both the Army and Navy in the southwest Pacific. A sizable submarine facility had grown up at the city's New Farm Wharf on the river. A dozen undersea boats at a time were tied up alongside the tenders *Sperry* and *Holland.* Nearby barracks housed relief crews spelling those coming in off patrol.

Sailors off the submarines poured into the streets of the capital, joining a raucous crowd at bars and hotels that made Brisbane the "New Orleans of the Down Under." Hard partying, horseplay, and rivalry among seamen, aviators, Marines, and Army troops frequently ended in street brawls. Vice Admiral Arthur "Chips" Carpender, Commander Naval Forces Southwest Pacific, was sufficiently worried about the potential for submariners getting into trouble that he created two rest camps for them some distance from Brisbane—one at Coolangatta, seventy-five miles south of the city at the southern end of the Gold Coast; the other in the mountains at Toowoomba, in the Darling Downs wheat belt, on the western slopes of the Great Dividing Range. Carpender also leased houses in Brisbane for commanding officers, plus cottages for subordinate officers on a particularly beautiful stretch of the Gold Coast known as Surfer's Paradise about thirty miles south of Brisbane.

Cutter checked in at Harwood House, a sprawling, two-story wood-frame home leased from one of Brisbane's leading families. Meanwhile, the other *Seahorse* officers headed for Surfer's Paradise as the enlisted men embarked for Coolangatta further down the Gold Coast.

The natural rivalry between Navy sailors and Army soldiers in Brisbane was exacerbated by feuding between Carpender and General MacArthur, supreme commander of all forces in the southwest Pacific. "A very childish situation existed between these two senior officers," said Cutter. "They didn't want to cooperate with each other. It was a kind of messy affair."

The rift began in the summer of 1942 when the general learned the Navy was planning the first major counteroffensive of the war at Guadalcanal and the Army would have little or no involvement. Furious, MacArthur accused the Navy of trying to usurp control of the war, "the role of the Army being subsidiary and consisting largely of placing its forces at the disposal and under command of Navy or Marine officers," as he put it. The dispute resulted in a compromise arranged in an icy summit in Washington between Army Chief of Staff George Catlett Marshall and Admiral Ernest King, commander in chief of the U.S. Fleet. The two agreed on a two-pronged strategy: The Navy would fight an island-hopping campaign skirting the Philippines to the east while MacArthur's forces moved against New Guinea, Rabaul, New Britain, and eventually the Philippines to the west. The two branches would join in the Philippines for the final thrust at Japan.

Despite the pact, Navy brass, including Carpender, were hostile to the general from that point forward. MacArthur, elevated to supreme commander of Southwest Pacific forces, did no favors for the Navy. The most overt symbol of this in Brisbane was the fact that no Navy officers were allowed inside the Lennon, the city's largest hotel and MacArthur's headquarters. Military police enforced the ban at the entrance to the hotel's popular nightclub.

During his stay at Harwood, Cutter and the other submarine commanders frequently pulled outlandish pranks on each other. Slade and Lt. Cdr. Bladen D. Claggett, just off of the *Dace*, were at the center of the capers, one of which went to extraordinary lengths: "An engineering officer who was in charge of the refit was staying at Harwood House. His name was Stanley 'Shorty' Nichols and he had a drinking problem," explained Cutter. "Well, Shorty, Claggett, and I took on a load of beer and we were pretty bombed. Shorty fell into a deep sleep after passing out. We had a cigarette lighter, and we lit the hair on his chest, and it started burning. The way it works, it fizzles like a fuse until it burns down to the saucer of the pore where it goes out. Shorty'd wake up and scratch it. Then we'd light it in another place, and he'd scratch again. Finally he woke up. He said, 'Ah, you want to play, huh?' With that, he was wide awake, and we didn't go to bed the rest of the night; he wouldn't let us. We were absolutely exhausted. But it was a lot of fun."

The next night, co-conspirators Cutter and Claggett noticed that Claggett's executive officer, Lt. William G. Holman, had fallen asleep. "He had a very hairy chest so we lit him up. He was scratching and scratching, but he never woke up and we burned almost all of the hair off his chest. Looking back on it, how can reasonably mature people in their early thirties do such things?" chuckled Cutter, whose name became a curse with Holman's wife after she found out after the war why her husband's chest had so many burn marks on it.

During the refit, the two skippers lined up a couple dates for a night on the town and headed for the Lennon. "We didn't know about this barring of Navy officers," said Cutter. "So we got down there and there were two MPs at the door. One of them said, 'You can't go in, only Army personnel, unless you are the guest of an Army officer.' This Army captain, or first lieutenant, came up and heard it, and said, 'These gentlemen are my guests,' and with that he took us in and left us. We felt real good about beating the system."

To those on liberty, Brisbane offered plenty of female companionship which led to a sort of amnesia among crewmen in regard to wives back home. Many Australian women were either war widows or separated from their boyfriends and husbands fighting for the British overseas. "I think the wives back home in the United States knew about it, and I think most understood the thing," said Cutter in reference to his crewmen-turned-geographical-bachelors.

Many Australian troops returning home resented the Americans. Dell Brooks, *Seahorse* yeoman, encountered that resentment in a theater in Brisbane showing Walt Disney's 1942 animated classic, *Bambi.* In one segment, Bambi cries out, "Mommy, mommy where are you?" From the balcony came a voice, "She's out with some damn Yank; where do you think she's at?"

On a Sunday morning, Cutter decided to make an unannounced visit to Surfer's Paradise to see how his officers were doing. A narrow road from Brisbane led to the Gold Coast, then rambled down the shore through a string of small beach towns. The cottages for the officers were exotic, built on the edge of the white, sandy beach. "I got there and most of the officers were still asleep. One of them was in bed with a gal who was the housekeeper. When one submarine's gang moved out and another moved in, there they were. They kept the house clean, they were lovers, they cooked for them—it was beautiful, a real good setup. This one officer on the submarine who was a very, very proper man, married to a very proper girl, he was the one in bed with this girl, and I couldn't believe my eyes. He said, 'Hey, Captain, come on in.' I went in and there he was in bed with this gal, and on the dresser was a picture of an Australian soldier." The photo was of the woman's husband who was fighting Germans in North Africa.

To Cutter, the housekeeper and the *Seahorse* officer simply were two cases of loneliness encountering each other on a romantic beach. The relationship would last only as long as the officer remained at the cottage. Said Cutter, "When you went back to the ship, that was it."

As liberty came to an end, Cutter arranged for an officers' party in town. Among those attending was McGrievy, who had been promoted to ship's ensign. After a heavy night of drinking, he staggered back to New Farm Wharf, intent on crashing in his cramped bunk—known as the Goat's Locker—in the forward battery compartment. The bunk was confined, not only because it was shorter than normal, but it also was restricted on the overhead by the curve of the hull. Because of his five-foot, seven-inch stature, McGrievy could endure the tight quarters. However, on the way through the submarine, he passed Cutter's unoccupied cabin nearby and was attracted to the wide-open bunk with twin fans blowing cool air over it. Figuring the skipper would stay ashore that night, McGrievy thought "what the hell" and lay down on the bed and went to sleep. He awoke with a start the next morning. Leaping to his feet, he made his way topside, evading Cutter who was in the control room. On deck, the ensign chain-smoked a dozen cigarettes while trying to think of an excuse. Unable to think of anything plausible, he went below to apologize. The skipper, towering a half-foot over his ensign and outweighing him by fifty pounds, abruptly cut him off. "Good morning. McGrievy," he growled. "The last time I saw you, you were deep in the sleep of booze. Do you know that I slept in your bunk? Goddamn you! Every time I turned over, I hit my head on those lockers on the overhead. But you looked like you needed my bed worse than I did, so I didn't want to disturb you."

It was this sort of good humor that endeared Cutter to his men. They idolized him, a sentiment shared by his mentor, Admiral Lockwood, back in Pearl. The admiral extolled Slade's aggressiveness and his uncanny ability to find and sink enemy freighters and tankers. Lockwood mused in his diary that if asked, Cutter probably could find enemy ships inside Pearl Harbor.

As the month of May wound down, the refit came to an end and the crew returned to the submarine to get it ready for another war patrol. "Everybody was very serious; all the foolishness stopped," said Cutter. The Navy's system of refitting submarines ensured that the work was done properly. About 20 percent of every returning submarine's crew—those who had made three patrols—were transferred off, many joining the relief crew for several months to give them an extended break from combat. Similarly, new sailors assigned to the boat came from long stints in the relief crew. "They were motivated because they were going out on the sub," explained Cutter. "And the ones being transferred off were interested in the refit because a lot of their pals were going back out. We got marvelous work, really."

A few crewmen were untouchables when it came to transfers. One was Hoffman, the boat's sonar operator. "I wouldn't go to sea without him; he was my eyes and ears through the sonar," said Cutter. "He would always say when we were clear to surface. The tendency was to be on the conservative side, but not Hoffman. When he thought it was safe, he would say so, and we would go on his word."

The business of training the reconstituted crew and checking all the submarine's complicated systems took about two weeks. The one diversion allowed by Cutter was taking visitors out on training dives in the river channel. Among the VIPs was the Army first lieutenant who vouched for Cutter and Claggett and their dates so they could get inside the nightclub at the Lennon. "It was the only time he had ever been in a submarine," said Cutter. "Some of the boys had met some Army nurses and we took them out too. We had a good time, a lot of fun."

Meanwhile, at Pearl Harbor, Voge, Lockwood, and the submarine command plotted out the *Seahorse*'s next war patrol. The boat would proceed to the Philippines to attack ships on the east coast, then head west into the South China Sea below Taiwan, seeking more action before returning home to Pearl via Midway. The initial objective was to proceed to Surigao Strait north of Mindanao in the Philippines. There, the *Seahorse* was to join Lt. Cdr. Ben Oakley in the *Growler* (SS-215) to guard the eastern entrance of the strait. The two skippers were to be on the lookout for Japanese Admiral Jisaburo Ozawa's carrier-battleship fleet based in Tawi Tawi on the western side of the Philippines, and to report the position of any portion of that fleet that ventured through the strait to try and thwart the Navy's imminent invasion of Saipan and Guam. The submarines also were to attack those warships.

There was no question the *Seahorse*'s patrol sector would be another tough one. There would be many targets but they would be closely guarded by Japanese ASW vessels. In addition, more than half the torpedoes that the *Seahorse* would be carrying would be conventional steam-driven weapons that left a heavy wake, unlike the electric torpedoes that Cutter much preferred.

Slade was cognizant of the odds against him after three patrols on the *Pompano* and four on the *Seahorse*. The challenge for him was to fight the temptation to let down his guard, to become overconfident. "In the end you get too confident," he said. "Statistically our skippers and their boats were lost on the first patrol or the fifth. On the first, skippers lacked experience but when you made your fifth patrol, you became careless, you had lost respect for the enemy. You are really a little neurotic by then because of the strain. You don't give a damn; you get so cocky. You lose perspective and don't give the enemy any credit. That's foolish."

Cutter was hardly a foolish man. He avoided tangling with enemy destroyers if at all possible. He considered Dealey in *Harder* a risk taker. "When you start going after destroyers, firing down-the-throat shots at twelve hundred or fifteen hundred yards, you are going to get it," he said of Dealey's habit of attacking a charging escort. "In my opinion, it is much better to let them go and knock off a merchantman or a tanker or something that will hurt the enemy a lot more than sinking that destroyer." The primary aim had always been to strangle Japanese commerce. And by June 1944, the undersea offensive was extracting a grievous toll on Japan. Submarines had torpedoed and sunk more than three hundred enemy vessels in the first six months of 1944, bringing the total since the war began to 819 ships. Sinkings now were outpacing Japan's ability to replace lost vessels.

As the time for departure drew near, Cutter was upset that the relief crew painted the *Seahorse* black. Admiral Carpender believed black was a better camouflage for night surface attacks. Black would be adequate at night, but during daylight hours, the color would make the submarine more visible to enemy pilots. Cutter pleaded his case but the Navy turned him down.

With a departure date of 2 June, Ensign McGrievy and Ensign A. R. Anderson had not returned from a trip to Perth on the opposite side of the continent. Anderson had asked McGrievy to be the best man for his impromptu wedding to a woman from Perth whom he met in Brisbane. When McGrievy asked Cutter for permission to go, Slade had directed him to do so but with only one purpose—stop Anderson from getting married. Now, both men were overdue and Cutter could not afford to leave without them. McGrievy had the best night vision for lookout duty, and Anderson was the only one aboard who could fix the torpedo data computer if it failed. Therefore, Cutter delayed departure past nightfall.

Well past sunset, the two chagrined sailors finally reported back aboard. Cutter read the riot act to McGrievy for disobeying orders by allowing Anderson to get married. But the captain relented on further punishment and the two men returned to work.

With the crew now accounted for, the *Seahorse* cast off on the early afternoon of 3 June to begin its fifth war patrol. Girlfriends, wharf workers, and submariners attached to other boats stood alongside the sleek vessel as its diesel engines roared to life with a burst of bluish smoke aft of the conning tower. Much of the crew stood topside, exchanging good-byes with onlookers as the boat began its journey downriver to the Pacific. The vessel slid gracefully beneath a highway bridge where scores of spectators cheered wildly, "Go get 'em Yanks!" The submarine made the ten-mile transit to the Pacific, then headed north along Queensland in company with a destroyer for protection. At sunset, the destroyer turned back for Brisbane. The submarine now was on its own, bound for a week-long voyage across the Coral Sea to Seeadler Harbor in Australia's recently liberated Admiralty Islands north of New Guinea.

The boat made frequent dives and numerous battle-surfacing exercises en route. Among the practice dives was one to great depth to check the watertight seals on the many fittings and packing glands, such as those around the bow planes and other external components operated through holes in the hull. As the commander gave the order to dive, someone had forgotten to retract the Bendix log swordarm. The device was about seven feet long and shaped like a sword and extended below the keel from the forward torpedo room where it measured the speed of the boat. The velocity of water passing through a small hole in the blade gave an accurate reading. Because of sea pressure during deep dives, seamen routinely cranked the device back into the boat with a screw-like mechanism and secured the opening with a waterproof valve. But that had not been done this time and the swordarm snapped in two as the boat reached a depth of three hundred feet, leaving an open breech, Seawater roared into the torpedo room. Torpedoman Jim Reardon realized at once the danger and leaped for a ratchet-like shutoff valve. But the leak was so furious that it was impossible to grasp the handwheel.

Lieutenant Fisher, a veteran of five *Seahorse* war patrols, sounded the alarm and yelled, "Abandon the compartment!" More than a dozen men scrambled aft through the watertight door to the forward battery. "Everyone was taking off," said Reardon. "As I started to leave, Fisher grabbed me and said, 'Not you, Reardon.' We were in deep trouble. Water was filling the compartment. We were heavy forward and heading down."

One in Five?

THE ROAR of seawater reverberated in the sealed-off forward torpedo room, the *Seahorse*'s largest compartment. A thirty-foot geyser leaped from the keel, splashing against the overhead. Lieutenant Fisher rushed to the internal salvage valve and opened it to pressurize the compartment. More atmospheric pressure inside the compartment, he reasoned, would slow the leak. However, the leak did not stop: the boat was too deep and the pressure increased too slowly. The only hope of reversing the *Seahorse*'s steep descent now shifted to the control room, and Cutter barked out commands: "Blow the main ballast! Blow safety tanks! Blow bow buoyancy!"

The chief of the boat engaged every lever on the air manifold. Compressed air exploded into ballast tanks girdling the hull. The boat's dive slowed and leveled off, then took an up angle. The *Seahorse* climbed steadily upward, easing sea pressure and slowing the leak. By the time the submarine broke surface, Reardon and Fisher had reattached the hand wheel and stemmed the flood just as a seaman undogged the watertight door to the torpedo room. Radioman Hoffman leaned in and whistled. "More than three thousand gallons of seawater filled the room," he said of the pool stretching toward the bow. "It flowed all through the equipment, saturating the sound head training motors. The damage wasn't serious, but a lot of nerves were frayed."

After draining the seawater with a bilge pump, the *Seahorse* continued to Seedler Harbor, where a relief crew refueled the boat and installed a new swordarm. During the brief layover, Cutter was determined to do one other thing: repaint the hull. Using pigment and brushes stowed aboard, crewmen bent to the task of slogging a fresh coat of gray paint over the black camouflage applied in Brisbane. In defying orders, the skipper figured what ComSubPac didn't know wouldn't hurt him; Carpender, who gave the order, was not ComSubPac. Meanwhile, the *Seahorse* received its orders to set a course to the Philippines and the South China Sea. Cutter had hoped for just such an assignment in a letter to Franny from Brisbane. "I am anxious to get out and do some dirt to the Japs. . . . I hope to get a hot area. I requested that we be assigned one. I want to find a place where there are plenty of targets; get rid of my torpedoes and head for the barn—and *you!*"

The *Seahorse* embarked on 11 June. Two days later, Japanese Admiral Ozawa's First Mobile Carrier Fleet began its move from Tawi Tawi to thwart the U.S. invasion of Saipan and Guam. Nine carriers, including his flagship, four battleships, five heavy cruisers, and scores of destroyers headed west through San Bernardino Strait between Luzon and Samar. Simultaneously, two other battle groups—a strike force built around the superbattleships *Yamato* and *Musashi* commanded by Vice Adm. Matome Ugaki based in the Moluccas and a supply convoy from Davao in southern Mindanao—headed north to rendezvous with Ozawa in the Philippine Sea for the final push toward Saipan. Ozawa's intention was to concentrate more than fifty warships and nearly one thousand carrier- and island-based aircraft to vanquish the U.S. fleet "with one blow," as the admiral predicted in a message to Tokyo.

The United States did not know where the Japanese armada was—due to a radio blackout—so ComSubPac posted submarines, including the *Seahorse,* as sentries along the western approaches to the Philippine Sea. On making contact with any portion of Ozawa's combined fleet, they were to determine what course it was taking, get off a radio report, and then attack. The *Seahorse* assumed its post 150 miles east of Surigao Strait off Mindanao.

At sundown on 15 June lookouts made positive identification of Vice Admiral Ugaki's battleship force heading northeast at sixteen knots.

In accordance with orders, Hoffman tried to radio ComSubPac. But Ugaki jammed the airwaves so no U.S. submarines could report the existence of the fleet, code-named Zebra. "When Roy was finally able to get through, it was Radio Washington he raised," said the captain. "He recognized the fist [telegraphic touch] of a man that he had worked with while stationed there as a petty officer. The Japs were jamming us so bad that Hoffman and his friend on the other end disregarded the ponderous codes which the Japanese were jamming and reverted to their old peacetime signal procedures. Nobody knew them but Roy and this other guy. As soon as the Japs would catch up with his frequency, Hoffman would switch to another. They kept this up until the message was through and the Japs couldn't shut them down."

The radioman in Washington relayed the dispatch to Pearl Harbor, where an ecstatic Lockwood read:

> At 1330 zebra task force in position 10–11 north, 129–35 east. Base course 045, speed of advance 16.5. Sight contact at dusk disclosed plenty of battleships. Seahorse was astern and could not run around due to speed restrictions caused by main motor brushes. Radar indicates six ships ranges twenty-eight thousand to thirty-nine thousand yards. Cruisers and destroyers probably could not be detected at these ranges with our radar. Possible carrier plane forced us down this morning. Seahorse trailing.

The sighting initiated a steady stream of directives to the *Seahorse* from commanders in Pearl. "They wanted all sorts of information. They wanted to know types of ships, the number of ships, the course, the speed, whether they were zigzagging and all this information they wanted. And for us to maintain contact at all costs. Which we did," said Cutter.

Intelligence from the *Seahorse* and contact with Ozawa's main fleet in San Bernardino Strait by the submarine *Flying Fish* (SS-229) proved to be critical. Admiral Raymond Spruance, who was leading the invasion of the Marianas, realized Ozawa was plowing through the Philippine Sea with every available resource. Spruance subsequently postponed the invasion of Guam and redeployed his Fast Carrier Force—Task Force 58—with fifteen heavy and light carriers plus a vanguard of battleships, cruisers, and destroyers to meet Ozawa's fleet head on.

Cutter attempted to press an attack on Ugaki's battleships. However, the *Seahorse* was unable to gain on the fleet because of electrical problems with its diesel engines. At daybreak, there was no alternative but to dive to give engineers a chance to make repairs to the motors, thus losing the chance to attack. Nevertheless, the boat's intercept proved to be an important contribution to the war effort. It confirmed the position and course of Ugaki's fleet, enabling Navy planners to project where the Ozawa and Ugaki battle groups would come together on 16 June. It gave ComSubPac enough time to position more submarines in the fleet's path. As a result, the *Cavalla* (SS-244) and the *Albacore* (SS-218) were able to sink the carriers *Shokaku* and *Taiho*, respectively, on 19 June. That same day, Ozawa launched 430 aircraft from his carriers, expecting them to be augmented by more than five hundred airplanes from Guam and Saipan in a coordinated attack on Task Force 58. Fortunately for the Navy, most island-based aircraft had been destroyed by earlier U.S. raids. Spruance's task force was waiting for the rest. Shipboard antiaircraft gunfire and hundreds of airborne fighters decimated Ozawa's raiders, destroying 330 airplanes that were unable to sink a single Navy ship in what came to be known as "The Great Marianas Turkey Shoot."

Ozawa, staggered by the loss of so many airplanes and three carriers, retreated to the northwest on 20 June, conceding the Marianas to the United States. The Army's 27th Division successfully occupied Saipan by 9 July but the toll was grievous—more than twenty-nine thousand Japanese defenders dead and sixteen thousand U.S. Marines and Army soldiers dead or wounded. When the news of Saipan's fall reached Japan, a Navy adviser to Emperor Hirohito grimly announced, "Hell is on us." Prime Minister Hideki Tojo and his cabinet immediately resigned. "Saipan was really understood to be a matter of life and death," noted Vice Admiral Paul H. Wenneker, German naval attaché to Tokyo. Likewise Admiral King in Washington, D.C., characterized the Battle of the Philippine Sea as "the decisive battle of the war." Japan's worst fears soon came to fruition: New B-29 superbombers began using Saipan's airstrip for sustained bombing strikes against Japanese cities.

For Cutter, there was heartening news about an old friend in the battle for Saipan. During Task Force 58's strikes against the island in the week before the big sea battle, only one submarine was able to get close enough to the island to rescue downed U.S. aviators. It was Sam Loomis in *Stingray* who rescued five pilots. In one instance, he went in submerged, ran up the periscope, had an aviator in a life raft tie a lanyard to the periscope, and then towed him out of range of island artillery until the boat could surface to take him below.

On 22 June, Lockwood directed Cutter to rendezvous with the *Growler* and the *Bang* (SS-385) on the shipping lanes in Luzon Strait north of the Philippines. The conquest of the Marianas allowed ComSubPac to concentrate on Japan's major supply routes in the South China and East China Seas. Many convoys passed through the Luzon Strait, a natural bottleneck between Taiwan and the Philippines. Troops, armament, oil, and other resources flowed through the strait on a regular basis. Lockwood and Voge believed the best way to strangle the lifeline was to send packs of submarines into the strait. *Bang, Growler,* and *Seahorse* would lead the way.

The *Seahorse* exchanged recognition signals with the *Growler* at midnight on 24 June. The two continued north in tandem, finally locating the *Bang* the next evening in the strait. While the three submarines lay to under the cover of darkness, Cutter and Captain Ben Oakley in *Growler* paddled over to *Bang* in rubber boats to plan strategy with Captain A. R. Gallaher, the *Bang*'s skipper, who, as senior officer, was serving as commander. It was agreed that any submarine making contact was to radio an alert to the others so all could attack simultaneously—a tactic borrowed from German U-boat strategy in the North Atlantic. The boats then fanned out through the two-hundred-mile-wide strait.

Two days passed with no contacts. Then shortly after midnight on 27 June, the *Seahorse* encountered five large ships escorted by five destroyers heading northwest toward Taiwan at twelve knots. Cutter chose not to broadcast the sighting to the other two submarines, believing they were too far away to help. At 0358, three hours after the initial contact, the *Seahorse* dived ahead of the convoy. Working beneath the escorts, Cutter brought the submarine within two thousand yards of the largest target, a tanker. Making a quick periscope sweep, the captain noticed that three freighters were closely bunched in another direction. He gambled by firing all six forward torpedo tubes—two at the freighters in hopes of hitting one or two vessels, and four at the prize, the fully loaded tanker.

Thirty seconds later a fireball erupted on the side of the tanker forward of its bridge. "It was a beautiful hit, producing a huge sheet of flame and setting the ship on fire," said Cutter. Both torpedoes aimed at the freighters also hit home, damaging two.

The destroyers reacted by jettisoning depth charges haphazardly. None exploded anywhere near the *Seahorse,* which was already making for the deep. The boat stayed down for more than an hour before returning to periscope depth. Flames and heavy black smoke marked the spot where the tanker had gone under. Nearby, a medium-sized freighter listed about 20 degrees to port with decks almost awash, while another struggled to stay afloat with a small port list and down slightly by the stern. A destroyer stood by the latter as aircraft provided cover during rescue operations.

Cutter decided to wait, to see what happened. An hour later, he took another look but could only count a single damaged freighter, the 870-ton frigate *Etorofu,* now underway and escorted by a destroyer. The second freighter, the 6,385-ton transport *Ussuri Maru,* had escaped, only to be sunk later by a U.S. bomber. Chasing the *Etorofu* was out of the question because the ship was too close to the minefields of Taiwan.

The sinking of the 5,135-ton tanker *Medan Maru* and the hits on the freighters energized the *Seahorse* crew. Cutter had expected congratulations from Gallaher when the submarine rendezvoused with *Bang* on the early morning of 26 June. Instead, the commander was angry. The *Bang* had seen the fire from the tanker. Gallaher believed he could have helped *Seahorse* annihilate the convoy had Cutter followed the agreed-upon plan to alert the other two submarines. The *Seahorse* captain, feeling humiliated, went aboard the *Bang* where he convinced Gallaher that even though he had seen the burning tanker, the vessel was forty miles away. There was no way the *Bang* could have arrived in time.

The two submarines resumed their mission as a two-submarine patrol after the *Growler,* low on fuel, departed for Midway. On the afternoon of 29 June, the *Bang* attacked a convoy of three enemy ships after sending a report to Cutter (who did not receive it). Gallaher fired ten torpedoes and believed he had damaged two freighters.

For the next four days, the *Seahorse* continued on a course prescribed by Gallaher farther west into the East China Sea. There were no enemy sightings. However, a seaman fell down the hatch during a dive, deeply gashing his leg and requiring six sutures. And Robert Holmes, the forward lookout, was injured by flying fish. The submarine encountered a school of them, gliding from the tops of high waves. "I was smacked hard: head on!" said Holmes. "The binoculars were driven into my eye sockets. As a result, I sported two severely blackened eyes."

The hunt continued until sundown on 3 July when lookouts sighted smoke on the horizon. In bright moonlight, the *Seahorse* identified five ships, heavily laden with Japanese troops, barrels of gasoline, tanks, and other armament. The convoy bore northwest toward the Chinese coast. After radioing the *Bang*, the *Seahorse* made an end around, pulling ahead of the ships an hour before dawn. Coming to periscope depth, the submarine eased in, slipping beneath the lead destroyer, which was plumbing the depths with sonar to no avail. "As he was the loudest of the pingers, our faith in the characteristic inefficiency of Jap sound operators in making contact prior to a submarine's attack was not shaken," Cutter noted derisively in the patrol diary.

With Lieutenant Budding at the TDC and Hoffman on sonar, the captain came to periscope depth between two target vessels. He fired two electric torpedoes at one target from the stern tubes from a "can't miss" distance of 560 yards, then launched a single steam torpedo at the lead vessel in a "point of aim" attack. The first torpedo exploded, ripping a fatal hole in the initial target. When the conventional torpedo missed, Cutter fired a second and third salvo from the bow tubes. Three hit the target and destroyed it.

As the convoy scattered, a destroyer raced toward the submarine's position. Cutter saw it at the last moment and ordered a quick dive. The *Seahorse* dove rapidly to four hundred feet. Inexplicably, the warship passed just astern without dropping any depth charges, apparently having no idea of where the submarine was. Hoffman reported many explosions in the general direction of both targets above. Soon the tearing, screeching sound of compartments collapsing from the pressure of seawater was audible to the entire crew. The 2,232-ton *Gyoyu Maru* had vanished with its cargo.

Forty minutes later the submarine came to periscope depth. The first target—the 2,186-ton freighter *Nitto Maru*—was barely afloat and cloaked in heavy smoke. Cutter considered putting another torpedo into the crippled ship, but decided it was unnecessary. Instead, the *Seahorse* surfaced out of sight and set out after the three remaining ships in the convoy.

After a long chase, lookouts sighted the dim outline of the targets on the edge of a rainsquall. Because the convoy seemed to be making for the safe haven of coastal waters off Taiwan, Cutter defied Japanese aircraft all morning by remaining on the surface to maximize the *Seahorse*'s speed in an end around. In so doing, the lookouts witnessed an airplane cavorting over the convoy, the pilot too absorbed in joyriding to notice the *Seahorse* looping around the ships.

About noon, the *Seahorse* moved into an attack position and submerged. A single destroyer patrolled across the bow of the lead ship in a column of three. The rest of the escorts had fallen back, apparently chasing a school of fish, which they mistook for a submarine. Cutter easily eluded the lead destroyer before passing beneath the convoy's rusty, four-thousand-ton flagship. Japanese troops by the scores were topside on a deck piled with cargo under brown tarpaulins. The irregular shapes indicated the probability of tanks. Attracting even more interest through the periscope were two oncoming ships crammed with troops and military supplies. The *Seahorse* passed beneath the second ship, a large, modern vessel, apparently diesel-driven. With the stern torpedo tubes now pointed at the target, Cutter brought the boat back to periscope depth to view the transport. "Troops were packed tight on the fantail and sitting up on the canvas-covered deck cargo," he noted. "Every bit of deck space appeared to be utilized. Soldiers were sitting tight around the fantail with their legs dangling over the side. It was a fascinating picture."

With a perfect setup attained at thirty-seven minutes past noon, Cutter fired three steam-driven torpedoes from the bow tubes. After a brief course correction, he launched three electric torpedoes at the larger diesel-powered ship. Through the periscope, Cutter observed troops on the diesel transport pointing toward the wakes of the steam torpedoes converging on the lagging, 1,506-ton transport *Kyodo Maru No. 29*. Seconds later, they hit in succession, destroying the ship. Without the warning of a telltale wake, two of the three electric torpedoes destroyed the seventy-five-hundred-ton unidentified troop transport.

For the *Seahorse's* fire control party, the attack was stunning for its precision, putting five out of six torpedoes into the targets and sinking two ships. A sense of euphoria and invincibility pervaded the *Seahorse* officers and crew, certain that they had dealt a serious blow to the Japanese war effort by shipwrecking thousands of enemy soldiers along with their equipment. Now all that remained was to slip away from the destroyer as the submarine had done so easily so many times in the past. But this time Cutter blundered.

The *Seahorse* carried *pillenwerfers:* shells developed by the Germans that could be launched from a submarine's distress rocket tube in the after torpedo room. These decoys were intended to trick sonar operators on surface ships into believing they had made contact with a submarine, drawing them off and masking a getaway by the real submarine. "They would effervesce and create a stream of bubbles that became a stationary target for active sonar," explained Cutter. "I had been carrying these things for two patrols and never used them. Now I became careless. So I said, 'Let's fire one and see what happens.' We could have lost the destroyer like we normally did, but instead we showed him exactly where we were when we let go those damn pillenwerfers."

The enemy commander realized what Cutter was up to and passed through the bubble stream to quickly establish the submarine's true location. Down below, Cutter relayed urgent commands. "Down periscope! Flood negative! Rig for depth-charge attack!" The captain, lookouts, and fire control party evacuated the conning tower for the security of the control room. Flapper valves in the bulkheads and on the ventilation system were sealed. Watertight doors between compartments were closed and dogged as a precaution to prevent flooding throughout the ship. Every piece of machinery that made noise shut down. No air conditioning. No fans. Motors and relays were silenced. Planesmen and helmsmen, who controlled the submarine's motion with electric motors, shifted to hand control. Sweat poured from their faces as they strained to turn the large wheels controlling the giant fins and rudder of the submarine. But no one knew where the destroyer was; the pillenwerfers made so much noise that it was impossible to track the movement of the escort.

Cutter, aware of a cottony dryness in his mouth, realized he might have made a fatal error. He had always been so careful: aggressive, but careful through three war patrols in the *Pompano* and five in the *Seahorse* spanning nearly three years. He had become the most formidable submarine captain in the Pacific, perfecting the technique of attack and stealthy getaway. But now he was worried. Was this his "one in five"?

The destroyer skipper, with the precision of a veteran like Cutter, dropped the first of his depth charges right over the submarine. The first erupted at 150 feet, sending up a tremendous geyser of seawater. The crack of the explosion was loud and close, followed by a shock wave that staggered the boat. The second blast hit with the force of countless sledgehammers. Crewmen lost their footing, falling to the deck. Some thought the boat had been holed. Light bulbs exploded, showering the deck with shards that tinkled through the grates into the bilges.

The initial attack just missed. There was no question the destroyer was using more powerful explosives, a new generation capable of detonating as deep as five hundred feet—two hundred feet below earlier versions. The *Seahorse* sought safety below a temperature gradient, the dividing line between warm equatorial water and colder water that deflected sonar. However, the destroyer easily penetrated the zone and continued its ferocious bombardment.

Seahorse crewmen threw mattresses onto the deck plates to soak up water and oil blown into the boat and catch loosened cork and shattered glass from the boat's numerous gauges. The slightest sound might give the destroyer a more precise fix. Auxiliarymen and trim-manifold crewmen removed tools from racks to keep them from falling. Some sailors removed their shoes. Talk was in a whisper. "Maintaining silence was so important that a cough would draw dirty looks from your mates," said electrician's mate James O'Meara.

Depth charges continued to rain down around the boat. Detonation within fifty feet would be catastrophic; twenty-five feet or less, fatal. In the conning tower, Cutter knew as much as he studied the array of lamps on the depth charge indicator, lighting up with each blast to reveal whether the explosives went off fore, aft, above, below, starboard, or port. He took the *Seahorse* deeper, coming right full rudder, left full rudder, altering course repeatedly in an attempt to escape. But even at four hundred feet, the boat could not escape. Depth charges continued to go off close aboard. Three detonated below at 470 feet. They were slightly off target and unable to break the submarine's back.

Crewmen remained petrified. Their clothes were soaked by perspiration and their eyes remained fixed on the overhead as they strained to hear the splash of depth charges, the triggering click, the chirp of enemy sonar locking onto them. "It's strange how fear teaches you how to pray," said O'Meara. "You confess every screw-up you ever made. You promise God that, if you can just get back to the surface and get an engine to run, you'll be a better man the rest of your life. That old saying of there being no atheists in a foxhole also applies to a submarine under attack."

The next blasts shook the boat, as if it were caught in a terrier's jaws. Deck plates and gratings jumped and clattered. Each detonation squeezed the high-tensile steel pressure hull inward, a shaking, shuddering, whipping motion, bouncing the boat up, down, and sideways. Crewmen fell to their knees, reaching out to clutch tables, ladders, anything to regain their footing. Pipelines reverberated the length of the ship. Emergency lights flickered. An oil cap came loose, allowing precious fuel to escape. For four hours, the attack continued as sixty depth charges detonated in an attempt to destroy Cutter and his men.

Shortly before dawn, the bombardment ceased. An oil slick caused by the loosened oil cap apparently convinced the captain that the *Seahorse* was dead. Cutter used the lull to climb to periscope depth where he viewed a second destroyer joining the first and Japanese aircraft flying back and forth over the scene. The convoy's flagship, the only one to survive the encounter with the *Seahorse,* was picking up survivors. Occasionally, the destroyers dropped depth charges—just in case another submarine was in the area. Cutter contemplated one final attack. He still had four torpedoes in reserve. However, he thought better of it.

"We were pretty well beaten down and did not feel like tangling with them again," he said. After sunset, the boat surfaced to recharge nearly depleted batteries, to air out the compartments and make repairs that included tightening the fuel cap that had come loose. Cutter got off a radio dispatch to the *Bang* and ComSubPac, reporting the attack and the submarine's brush with disaster. The *Seahorse* remained on station another day until the evening of 5 July when the captain received orders to return to Hawaii. Rear Admiral John H. "Babe" Brown, deputy commander of the Submarines Pacific Fleet, had decided Cutter needed a break. Thus, the submarine began the long, uneventful voyage home at daybreak on 6 July.

En route, there was not much to do in off-duty hours but share idle talk, play acey-deucey, read and reread letters from family and girlfriends back home, write new letters, play the shipboard slot machine, sleep, and eat. The men, tongue in cheek, dreamed up a "Top Ten" to distinguish the *Seahorse* from other boats: "Only sub in fleet known to leave the exec topside twice during dives on same patrol. . . . Crew set record for leaving boat and lining up for beer at Midway. . . . Record set by four lookouts getting down the hatch when bombed and strafed by our own B-24 bomber. . . . All-time record for wearing the same skivvies for an entire patrol set by Jim O'Meara. . . . Sleeping arrangements are such that you recognize friends by smell." The monotony made crewmen like O'Meara contemplate the "obvious" differences between husky torpedomen and slightly built electricians aboard. "Why are all torpedomen so ugly?" he mused. "Torpedomen have nicknames such as Crash, Killer, Grunt, or Beans. Most electricians are called by their given names. One must wonder if torpedomen were ugly at birth? Is it something in the genes? Would it then be possible to look in the crib of a newborn and predict a dismal future of an adult life in an after torpedo room? What a terrible thing for a new mother to contemplate. The other great mystery to me is, with all their ugliness and lack of social graces, why do they always end up with the prettiest women?"

Cutter, to break the tedium, sponsored an essay contest on "Why I'm Fighting This War" and "Why I Joined the Submarine Service." Third-class electrician's mate Gerhard Nelson was a winner: "When I graduated from high school I tried to get a job in a defense plant but got bypassed into the commissary department, making about three dollars a week less than it cost me to live. I had three female ex-school teachers for bosses, so I got a good taste of what the U.S.A. would be like if the Japs won— so here I am."

As the submarine neared Midway on 14 July, the boat's chief engineer calculated the *Seahorse* would run out of fuel if it did not slow down. Initially, Cutter decided to reduce speed. But later, when fresh calculations showed the boat most certainly would not arrive before the harbor closed for the night, the captain put all four engines back on line. The chief engineer objected, warning that a worse fate than not arriving in time awaited the *Seahorse*—running out of gas at sea and being towed into port! But Cutter's good fortune smiled again. The submarine arrived just before sunset and sailed to its berth triumphantly. At the mooring, the boat's fuel tanks were bone dry. All along Cutter knew something the chief engineer had not taken into consideration: The submarine had a full charge on its batteries, more than enough to power the boat the last few miles.

The submarine remained at Midway only long enough to refuel and effect minor repairs, then departed for the four-day run to Pearl Harbor. The boat arrived on the afternoon of 15 July to a clamorous reception from Lockwood and ComSubPac officers. Captain Cutter, exhausted, asked for two weeks' leave to return to the States to see his wife and daughter. Brown gave him thirty days. He also confided the *Seahorse* would begin a new patrol under Captain Charles W. "Weary" Wilkins from the Bureau of Personnel. Wilkins had made three war patrols earlier in the war on the *Narwhal* (SS-167). Wilkins had always wondered what he could do as skipper of a modern boat and he asked Lockwood for permission to make a war patrol. He got the *Seahorse*.

Cutter reluctantly accepted the decision. "Weary was wonderful and said *Seahorse* was my boat and he was only borrowing it for one run. He said he would change nothing and didn't—including taking along young Budding, whom I had promised to be exec."

In a few patrols, Cutter had become one of the great heroes of the war. But his accomplishments and those of the entire "Silent Service" remained classified and thus largely unappreciated by the general public. He and the *Seahorse* had posted an unprecedented record by sinking nearly two dozen Japanese ships, damaging many others, preparing the way for the invasion of Saipan by serving as a decoy, virtually eliminating a troop-laden convoy single-handedly in the East China Sea, and providing critical intelligence that gave the Navy the upper hand in the Battle of the Philippine Sea. On 24 July 1944, the Associated Press reported a rare honor bestowed on the *Seahorse*'s warrior skipper: "Lieutenant Commander Slade D. Cutter, 32, Vallejo, Calif., today received the Navy Cross with two gold stars—the first time in the war that Admiral Chester W. Nimitz has pinned three awards on one man in one ceremony." Cutter soon would receive a third Gold Star in lieu of another Navy Cross for his fourth patrol. He and the crew would also receive the highest honor accorded by the president of the United States, a Presidential Unit Citation.

Ahead for Cutter was a return home to his family, a reunion he yearned for. But his intention to return to the *Seahorse* was not to be. Instead, he would take another path, which would bring him to the attention of Presidents Dwight Eisenhower and John F. Kennedy. It would lead him back to the Naval Academy for war of a different sort. And it would reunite him with his former skipper, Lewis Parks, and uncover pitfalls that would prove personally disastrous. It also would not be long before the treachery of an old nemesis would be revealed—a deed that one Navy officer called "an act of moral turpitude deserving of the utmost contempt."

McGregor's Time Bomb

BEFORE HE left Hawaii for the mainland, Cutter bumped into Admiral Lockwood who wanted to talk to Slade about a matter that had gnawed at him for months. It had to do with the skipper's handling of a B-24 Liberator's bombing run on the *Seahorse* near Satawan Island during the boat's fourth war patrol. At the time, Slade accepted formal blame for his lookouts' not sighting the Army Air Forces bomber before it almost sank the *Seahorse* while the submarine was traveling in a designated safe conduct lane. "That was a gratuitous comment," snapped Lockwood. "For once we had those bastards dead to rights. They [Army Air Forces] don't brief their people. They don't have navigators that know where they are. This is what we are trying to catch them doing and stop them. And you blew it."

Of course, Lockwood did not let a bit of criticism tarnish his view of Slade as a model submarine captain. In fact, using the Cutter mold, the Navy was turning out younger, more aggressive captains who had turned the Pacific War in the United States's favor. The submarine fleet, having grown to nearly three hundred boats from an original fifty, had a stranglehold on the Japanese merchant marine, denying Tokyo the means to reinforce its armies or import raw materials to fuel its war machine.

Initially, Cutter was unhappy about his separation from the *Seahorse* in the summer of 1944. But after a reunion with Franny and six-year-old Anne in Vallejo, he felt much better. "By that time, I had accepted the new situation and was perfectly willing to remain with my family," he later said. Lockwood had no intention of returning Cutter to the *Seahorse*. Crewmen coming off the boat confessed nervousness about going back out with the skipper. His practice of crossing right under destroyers to get at convoy ships invited trouble, as well as his much-professed disdain for the accuracy of Japanese sonar. Many feared the captain's luck had run its course. As even he later conceded, "Submariners didn't want to stick with somebody who had been at it too long."

Lockwood eased any resentment Slade might have had by giving him a new mission: Relocate to the picturesque New England coastal city of Portsmouth, New Hampshire, to assume command of a new submarine. Slade would handpick its first crew, and best of all, his wife would christen the vessel, the *Requin* (SS-481). The keel for the new *Tench*-class submarine took shape on 24 August 1944 in one of the mammoth shipbuilding barns in Portsmouth. Numerous submarines were either under construction or in for overhaul at the base, one of the nation's most storied shipyards. It dated back to colonial days when the British needed pine trees for the masts of its dreadnoughts. Trees from the White Mountains, fifty miles west of Portsmouth, provided those masts. Lumberjacks felled the trees and rode them down the Piscataqua River to the city where they were packed aboard ships for shipment to England. A fledgling island shipyard sprang up between Portsmouth and the Maine shore, eventually becoming the Navy's first government yard three miles inland from the Atlantic. During the Revolutionary War, Navy hero John Paul Jones lived in the city while his ship, the *Ranger*, was constructed. By the twentieth century, the shipyard was converted to a submarine base, launching the nation's first government-built submersible, the L-8, in 1917.

While work on the *Requin* proceeded, the Cutters made their cross-country move, briefly stopping in the late summer at the submarine school in New London where Slade joined the staff of Commander Submarines, U.S. Atlantic Fleet, to screen crewmen for new submarines.

Whenever he got a *Seahorse* veteran coming through, he put him on the *Requin.* He also tapped the top submarine school graduates for his new boat.

The Cutters relocated to Portsmouth in the fall as work on the *Requin* neared completion. Slade had hoped to inspect his new boat. But the shipyard commander, Capt. Clifford R. Roper, an ex-submariner and former skipper of the cruiser *New Orleans,* stopped him dead in his tracks. Roper was aware of Cutter's reputation among workers in Pearl Harbor as a perfectionist and chronic complainer. "Slade, your ship will be commissioned in April, and I don't want to see you until then," Roper bristled. "You stay out of the yard. We'll build the ship, and you take it away. You stay the hell out of it." "Aye, aye, Sir," replied Cutter, noting later, "That suited me fine. I simply had my executive officer oversee the work."

With his crew chosen, Cutter had time to idle away the hours. His daily routine found him heading for the base with friends to check their mail at 1000, then visit a local bar for a round of beers and lunch. The "work day" would end at 1400 when the officers returned home. "On the way, we'd pick up two-and-a-half pound lobsters for dinner. We'd party at night. Poor Franny, I kept her up all night. We were leading kind of a harum-scarum life but we were having a good time. Plus people in Portsmouth doted on us since we were war heroes."

With the splash of champagne delivered against the bow by Franny Cutter, the *Requin* was launched on New Year's Day, 1945, after which yard workers began the four-month task of installing all its complicated equipment. Cutter assumed command on 28 April. Following a series of training dives, the submarine embarked for Pearl Harbor to prepare for its first war patrol. Franny and Anne, meanwhile, moved back to the Navy base at Vallejo, their third move in less than a year.

Cutter realized the *Requin*'s role would be far different from earlier missions just by its armament: two 5-inch guns, two 40-mm guns, eight .50-caliber machine guns, and rocket launchers on the bow for 5-inch shells. "We were going to the Island of Hokkaido to bombard a base for patrol boats, which was stupid. But our submarines had little else to do. There was so little ship traffic." Nevertheless, spirits were high as the *Requin* cast off for Japan on 13 August, the day before the war ended.

Cutter got the news at 0200 on Victory in Japan Day. He walked back to the mess, pulled a cup of coffee, and sat down with his men. "I didn't feel the relief I thought I would feel because there was a nagging thing about the Russians. Isn't that strange? They were our allies, too, but somehow, for some reason, I just had this feeling about the Russians. 'It isn't over; it isn't done,' I kept saying."

Two young sailors walked in, one with tears streaming down his face. "For God's sake, what's the matter?" asked the captain. The sailor gathered himself. "I can't get a submarine combat pin," he began. "It's been two and a half years since I enlisted to get on a submarine making a war patrol, and now the war is over." The skipper, given his own ambition during the war, understood perfectly well and offered condolences. He suggested the sailor look on the bright side. "Boy, you're lucky. You're alive!" he said.

Cutter could say so with the deepest of convictions. Many of his closest friends had disappeared. They included James S. Clark, captain of the *Golet* (SS-361); David Zabriskie Jr., captain of the *Herring* (SS-233); Kenneth G. Schacht, an officer aboard the *Perch*; Joseph H. Bourland, captain of the *Runner* (SS-275); Willis M. Thomas, captain of the *Pompano*; and Cutter's best friend, Dave Connole. The two had served in *Pompano* for three and a half years. After a long stint as commander of a submarine school training boat in New London, Connole was finally given command of the *Trigger* in the winter of 1945. On his first war patrol, he and his men disappeared in the East China Sea. He left a pregnant wife and a baby he never saw. "That really got to me," said Cutter. "We knew the war was over then; it was just a matter of a very short time."

Cutter had been among those in the submarine service arguing that a U.S. invasion of Japan was unnecessary. "The submarines had sunk the Japanese merchant marine. The B-29s could fly over Japan almost at will, unopposed by fighter aircraft because they didn't have any gasoline for their aircraft. But the war would have been prolonged had the atomic bombs not been dropped. The Jap Army was still effective. Japanese politicians who might have ended the war were still afraid of the Army."

The *Requin* made its way back to Hawaii where VJ [Victory over Japan] Day celebrations swirled at Pearl and in Honolulu. Booms across the harbor prevented the submarine from entering by order of the yard commandant. "So we were off the entrance buoy to Pearl Harbor all night long with all these things going on, fireworks and lights on, and we wanted to be there," said Cutter. "That was bad enough, but when I got in and somebody told me that they had deliberately kept us out there to teach us a lesson or something, boy, that burned me up plenty."

There was nothing Cutter nor his men could do about it. How ironic, he thought. The war began for him with a Japanese dive-bomber trying to sink the *Pompano* off Oahu after the surprise attack on Pearl Harbor. The submarine could not get into Pearl that day and had to linger off the coast. Now, nearly four years later, the war ended with his new submarine off the same Hawaiian island, unable to get in.

The end of hostilities in the Pacific revealed the tremendous toll inflicted on Japan by the Navy's undersea fleet. The boats sank 5.3 million tons of enemy shipping—twelve hundred merchantmen and two hundred warships, representing 55 percent of all Japanese vessels lost. Among those sunk by submarines were a battleship, eight heavy and light carriers, three heavy cruisers, eight light cruisers, and numerous destroyers. This was accomplished by an undersea force that made up just 1.6 percent of the Navy. Fifty-two submarines and 3,505 of the 16,000 Americans who made war patrols were lost—a casualty rate of 22 percent, highest in the Navy. An audit of Japanese records after the war greatly reduced the claims of ships sunk by many skippers, an embarrassment to them and the Navy. However, Cutter's tally not only withstood scrutiny but was increased by the Joint Army-Navy Assessment Committee (JANAC), boosting his total to twenty-three ships sunk. Among 465 submarine captains who fought in the war, he finished second only to Medal of Honor winner Dick O'Kane, credited with twenty-four sinkings.

In September 1945, Cutter and the *Requin* were invited to participate in a parade celebrating the war's end on the Hudson River in New York City. In company with two other submarines, the *Requin* traversed the Panama Canal and headed into the Caribbean just as a major hurricane churned up the seaboard. Cutter decided to take a direct route to New York through the hurricane rather than around it as the other two captains chose to do. "I'd been in a typhoon in the Pacific. There's no problem, you just dive if things get bad enough. We went right through the eye of the hurricane, and not many people have done that. You get in the center and there's absolutely no wind, flat, greasy, calm. There were waterspouts all the way around the circle of this thing. It was very spectacular."

The *Requin* arrived in New York well ahead of the other submarines. Mayor Fiorello H. La Guardia invited Cutter to his office to discuss the war. In casual conversation, the mayor told of his rough ride in Long Island Sound in an old S-boat before the war, a voyage that prompted him to get Congress to give all submariners a quarter extra pay for hazardous duty. Now he asked if he could do Cutter a favor. "As a matter of fact, Mr. Mayor, you can," Slade replied. "My wife's out in California, and I want to go out and see her, and we're going to come back to the East Coast. I have the leave, but I can't get out there. No transportation. Could you arrange for air transportation?" The mayor tried but without success.

Left to his own devices, Cutter hitched a ride to nearby Floyd Bennett Field, a Navy air station, to see if any planes were going west. On arrival, he managed to secure an invitation to a birthday party for a Navy nurse. "There was a lot of booze flowing. I talked to the various pilots and two of them were taking off the next morning early."

They were flying freight to Philadelphia, Norfolk, Jacksonville, Pensacola, New Orleans, and El Paso. Because they were flying a roomy DC-3, they invited Slade along. After an uneventful, daylong flight to El Paso, Cutter looked for other connections. He found one through Capt. Howard Caldwell, Slade's former assistant football coach at Annapolis.

Caldwell and a fellow pilot intended to fly a Beechcraft to the Navy air station at Alameda, not far from Cutter's home in Vallejo. At takeoff the next morning, disaster struck. "We were about fifteen hundred feet off the runway when the engines conked out," explained Cutter. "Howard got on the wobbly pump and started pumping the gas into the gasoline line, and the engines finally caught. These two experienced aviators had taken off on the reserve tanks without any fuel in them. If we had conked out just a minute sooner, just as we got airborne, we'd have been in real trouble."

Safely in Vallejo, Slade helped Franny finish packing for their cross-country drive when a surprise visitor knocked. It was Kenneth Schacht, seemingly returned from the dead. At 126 pounds, Slade's former football teammate on the 1934 squad had dropped more than 50 pounds and contracted tuberculosis as a Japanese prisoner of war after his capture following the scuttling of the submarine *Perch* in 1942. Married to a movie star who had divorced him during the war on grounds of desertion, he planned to look her up in Hollywood. Leaving Mare Island, the Cutters visited Slade's mother in Long Beach and dropped off Schacht in Los Angeles. Eventually, they reached Key West where they moved into new quarters and enrolled Annie in a public school. When the school proved unsatisfactory, they pulled her out and enrolled her in a Catholic school on the island. School officials were stunned to learn that Annie, who was nine, had already attended twenty-six schools.

For the Cutters, that was just life in the military. There were no guarantees the family would not be uprooted again. For the moment, the *Requin* was assigned to one of two submarine squadrons in Key West. The skipper had hoped the wartime tradition of being honest in shipboard management would be perpetuated in the postwar Navy. A visit by Navy inspectors soon shattered that illusion. "Before the war, ship inspections were kind of farces," Cutter explained. "The name of the game was to bury all your problems under the rug and hope to God the inspectors don't find out about them. Well, I thought the war had changed everything. During the war we reported any problems because we wanted them cured; we wanted them corrected. Even though it might be our mistake, we wanted it fixed. I told my crew, 'This is a new ball game. Now the Navy has learned a lesson, so tell everything that's wrong. Open up the engines. Show them everything, so they can help us get our work request through the shipyard.' All these things that we told the inspectors, they wrote up as deficiencies. It sounded like we were the most derelict bunch of people in the world," said Cutter. The captain had no alternative but to swallow his pride, concluding the Navy "had reverted to what we did before."

In October 1946, Cutter was detached from *Requin* and reported to the Bureau of Naval Personnel in Washington, D.C., to run the all-Navy sports program where he managed periodic tournaments involving athletes from throughout the fleet. He volunteered for the billet on the recommendation of Capt. Edmund Taylor, former ordnance professor at the Naval Academy. "The Navy considered the Navy sports program as very important at the time," explained Cutter. "This was during the demobilization, and in those days we had the battle force and the air stations and we had teams in everything: football, basketball, boxing, wrestling, and so forth." The all-Navy program culminated each year with a tournament where champions were crowned in each of the sports. But demobilizations steadily whittled down the fleet and the athletes.

Being detached from the operational fleet did nothing to enhance his career prospects. Nevertheless, Cutter was reasonably happy. He took the Armed Forces Olympic team to London in 1948 where his athletes dominated the summer track meet, finishing one-two in the one-hundred-meter and two-hundred-meter sprints. During that period Franny gave birth to a son, Slade Jr. "She finally got her son, and she spoiled the devil out of him," said Cutter.

Slade remained in the sports program until February 1949 when he became executive officer of the submarine tender *Sperry*, the mother ship for Submarine Division 32, based in San Diego. He was now back in his element—on a ship that was in desperate need of a skilled officer. "The tenders were in terrible shape. We were getting boys in there that couldn't even see; we received one in the *Sperry* who was legally blind," said Cutter. "It was a challenge to get the ship running and to keep serving the submarines properly." Within a year, his ability to whip the crew into a cohesive unit paid off with the Battle Efficiency Pennant in competition with other tenders in the fleet. Cutter also learned how to handle a surface ship, which would come in useful later in his career.

He served in *Sperry* until July 1950 when he stepped up to commander of fifteen submarines attached to the tender. At the time, the Navy was experimenting with new ideas to enhance the value of its submarines. Some were converted into launch platforms for Regulus missiles, the forerunner of the Polaris ballistic missile. Others were fitted to carry

Marines for possible action in Cuba, then seething with civil strife. Still more submarines were equipped with air-breathing snorkels so diesel engines could be operated while submerged, giving the boats greater speed. As division commander, Cutter moved from submarine to submarine, but he considered his job superfluous. The squadron commander, Capt. Glynn R. Donaho, was the operational chief. "He told the submarines what they would do and so on," explained Cutter. "The division commander really was not a very important person. My greatest job was keeping Donaho happy, which was not an easy task."

Slade regularly was on the receiving end of criticism for minor infractions. He finally confronted Donaho after he was promoted to vice admiral. "Commodore, one of the biggest problems was that you'd never listen. I couldn't explain things. You'd eat me out, and it was unfair. And all you'd say is, 'That is all,' and then I'd have to turn and go."

"Slade," replied Donaho, "I'll tell you how it is. Under all of this I'm a very soft-hearted guy and awfully easy to be talked down, so I just don't let anybody get a chance."

At the time, Cutter had a growing sense of futility about submarine service. "I didn't feel very important. We had the same torpedoes, the same sonars, the same radars. The only difference from the war was we didn't have a mission."

In February 1951, the Navy ordered Cutter to become director of special services in the Bureau of Naval Personnel. Commanding officer of the Navy's commissaries, exchanges, and recreation funds was a deadend post that made him none too happy. That frustration worsened soon after arrival when he and Capt. John S. McCain Jr., a fellow submariner and director of the bureau's records office, were shooting the breeze over coffee. McCain asked if Cutter had ever taken a look at fitness reports in his personnel file.

"No," replied Cutter, a bit taken back. "I haven't bothered."

"I think you'd better," said McCain.

Cutter retrieved the file and was flabbergasted to find a negative report from *Seahorse* skipper Donald McGregor who had been abruptly stripped of command after the boat's first war patrol in favor of his aggressive executive officer. Slade stared at the document in disbelief.

"McGregor had recommended that I be relieved of submarine duty and be assigned to duty in connection with athletics at the Naval Academy."

The fitness report was a potential "kiss of death" in regard to future promotions in rank. It was particularly pernicious because McGregor gave his former exec a fitness rating of "barely satisfactory," scored just above 2.5. A score below that would have required the Navy to alert Slade to the report's existence and give him a chance to reply. He never thought to check his file during the war, even though he might have suspected McGregor would retaliate since he had relieved Slade of his executive duties on the way into Midway. Cutter, however, preferred to put the incident behind him to concentrate on the war.

Within the Navy, "barely satisfactory" was recognized as a means of concealing a personal attack. McCain knew as much and recommended that Cutter try and do something about it. Slade decided not to contact McGregor, still on active duty as a professor of naval science at the University of California in Berkeley. Rather, he asked the Navy for a formal review in hopes Lockwood would set the record straight. What the admiral did was compare the records of both men. He noted that Cutter sank more than twenty ships on four war patrols, whereas McGregor sank one inconsequential ship in five war patrols (in the *Gar* and the *Seahorse*). "I think the record speaks for itself," Lockwood concluded.

Cutter was disappointed because the admiral did not directly address McGregor's assessment of Cutter. "You see, those fitness reports stay in your record," said Slade. "You never look good when you take any action against what a senior has done."

Knowledge of McGregor's action rankled many submariners, particularly Lieutenant Commander Beach, the former executive officer in the *Trigger* who viewed Cutter as a gifted, hardworking, dedicated submariner. In a reminiscence, Beach termed McGregor a "villain" and "moral coward." "Using the official procedures and organs of the Navy for a personal vendetta, as [McGregor] did, is an act of moral turpitude deserving of the utmost contempt. . . . The 'barely satisfactory' report is a time bomb waiting for the next promotion board, and all the more despicable because of this."

With the report hanging over his head and ill at ease in the peacetime

Navy, Cutter was in a funk at the bureau. Lockwood had envisioned a strong undersea fleet after the war, one in which Cutter and others might find steady promotions on an admiralty track. But the mood of the country was "bring the boys home." The need for a massive fleet seemed pointless and many vessels were mothballed or sold. The result was promotions were hard to come by in what was left of the operational fleet. A proliferation of aviators and destroyer officers also dominated the Navy, making it doubly hard on submariners. Still, a man like Cutter could hardly be ignored because of his astounding war record and athletic achievements. Nevertheless, promotions continued to elude him.

Then Lewis Parks walked back into his life.

The crusty former skipper in the *Pompano* was an admiral and the Navy's Chief of Information in Washington in 1951. He invited Cutter to rejoin him as a change of pace. It would be fun, and Slade accepted. But it was hardly the position he thought it might be. Due to circumstances not of his own making, it soon would put him in conflict with a U.S. president who thought his wife had been slighted—and a senior Naval officer who dreamed of adding nuclear power to submarines.

The *Nautilus* Affair

THE MOVE to the Navy's public information office thrust Slade Cutter into one uncomfortable controversy after another. Looking back, he viewed his two years as the biggest mistake of his life. "I was completely unsuited for public information. You have to keep your mouth shut lots of times and don't say all you know and don't be frank and above-board. You've got to hedge and all that. Well, I wasn't any good at that."

Those who knew him would agree. Said Capt. Joseph Tucker, a fellow submariner, "Slade was an outstanding boxer, football player, World War II submarine skipper and an excellent Naval officer. But in the CHINFO job, I feel that he was a duck out of water. He was a little rough at times and not the smoothest guy around."

Initially, the new post was exhilarating. As Director of the Navy Office of Information, Slade became the liaison between the Navy and news services, magazines, book publishers, authors, and the motion picture industry. Cutter got to know the top officers in the Navy who frequently had him accompany them during interviews on sensitive subjects. They included successive chiefs of Naval Operations Admiral William Morrow Fechteler ("rough and ready with a tattoo on his arm") and Admiral Robert B. Carney ("brilliant speech writer"), as well as three Secretaries of the Navy—Dan A. Kimball ("a political hack"), Robert B. Anderson ("brilliant"), and Charles S. Thomas ("a great man"). Slade also became friends with some of the top journalists in Washington, including the *New York Times's* James Reston, the Baltimore *Sun's* Walter Millis, Peter Maas of *Collier's*, and Frank Reynolds, who would become news co-anchor for ABC-TV's *World News Tonight*.

Though Cutter had no experience in public relations, three assistants —Capt. Roy S. Benson, Lt. L. Edgar Prina, and Lt. Cdr. Robert A. Barracks—helped smooth the process. Prina and Barracks were seasoned newsmen who had been recalled to duty in the Korean War. "They protected me. You can't lie to the media; nobody should ever do that. But you also can't be forthright and spill your guts, so to speak, because they'll tear you apart, which happens to our presidents now and then."

Admiral Parks viewed the role of the office as protecting the good image of the Navy. Thus, with the aggressiveness he had shown as skipper of the *Pompano*, Parks tried to manipulate the news. "He created a heck of a lot of dissension. I think he helped create problems between the services in the offices of information," said Cutter, noting Parks's practice of putting out propaganda contrasting the Navy with other military branches. "He'd compare the Air Force performance with what the Navy was doing, the carrier capability versus the Air Force capability—trying to make the Navy look good at the expense of another service."

To some, Parks's zealousness went overboard when he tried to stop Hollywood producer Stanley Kramer from turning Herman Wouk's Pulitzer Prize winning novel, *The Caine Mutiny*, into a film. The Navy hated the book, centered around the *Caine*, a rusty hulk of a destroyer, manned by misfits and commanded by Captain Queeg, mentally unstable and obsessed with minor shipboard infractions. Queeg, like a paranoid Captain Bligh, verges on madness, illustrated by his habit of rolling two steel balls in his hand. A subordinate works to undermine Queeg, who panics when his ship enters a typhoon. A mutiny occurs. The aftermath, a court-martial, sets the stage for retelling the story.

Twice the Navy spurned solicitations by MGM and Twentieth Century Fox, the two most powerful studios in Hollywood. With the backing of the mid-level Columbia studio, Kramer, a feisty New Yorker and former junior officer in the Army, took his turn. He flew to Washington where a panel of stern-faced admirals gave him a frosty reception in an ornate meeting room at the Bureau of Ships, which Kramer described in his autobiography.

"Mr. Kramer," began one unidentified admiral, "are you aware that there has never been a mutiny in the U.S. Navy?"

Kramer confessed he was unaware of that. But he reminded the board that *The Caine Mutiny* was a work of fiction, to which the admirals suggested the title of any film be changed to *The Caine Incident*.

"My main purpose," responded Kramer, "is to assure you gentlemen I do not intend to produce a picture that will make the Navy look bad. I'm here to seek your help in making certain that does not happen."

"The best way to make sure that doesn't happen," replied another admiral, "is to refrain from filming the damned book."

"The damned book is a wildfire best-seller," Kramer retorted, adding the Navy's cooperation was critical to the quality of the film. If the Navy didn't help, he added, "It won't be as good for me, and it won't be as good for the Navy."

"Are you threatening us?" came the curt reply from the admiral. "Are you telling us that unless we cooperate, you'll have your script written in such a way it will make the Navy look even worse than that infernal book makes us look?"

"Not at all," Kramer replied. "The way to make the Navy look real and powerful is to show some real ships. That will impress anyone who sees the picture."

The admirals nodded, then agreed to Kramer's plan after he invited them to appoint a qualified officer as the film's technical adviser. The producer still had to get past Parks who, it was agreed, would review the script.

The admiral and Cutter were aware of rumors that Kramer was a communist sympathizer. "That made Parks particularly nervous about the film," said Cutter. The first draft of Stanley Roberts's script came in at 190 pages, which Kramer viewed as very tight. But Parks and Cutter suggested a list of changes, including a preamble at the beginning of the film, which would note there had never been a mutiny in the Navy. The weeks dragged on as Roberts kept trimming the script. Each time it was resubmitted, additional cuts and revisions were demanded. Growing impatient, the producer rushed into Cutter's office with the script whittled down to 150 pages. "This is it! Either you approve it or I'll publicize this attitude of the Navy," he said defiantly. He demanded the script be forwarded to Admiral Fechteler, Chief of Naval Operations. Parks obliged.

Fechteler, after reviewing it, wondered what all the fuss was about. "This guy Queeg is a screwball. Hell, I've known lots of oddballs as skippers in the Navy," the admiral said to Parks. "That's no valid reason. Go ahead and cooperate. I don't see where it's going to do any harm."

"So Parks said to me, 'Okay, let her go,' and that's how *The Caine Mutiny* got produced," said Cutter.

In the end, the Navy allowed Kramer to use three destroyers, three tenders, an aircraft carrier, two thousand Marines with landing barges, and free run of Naval facilities at Pearl Harbor. The movie, starring Humphrey Bogart as Captain Queeg, was released in 1954, and earned six Oscar nominations including Best Picture, Best Actor, and Best Screenplay.

Many of Cutter's day-to-day dealings in the Office of Information were with military writers seeking help in developing a story. "For instance, one day Clay Blair came to me and wanted information about LOFAR. I had never heard of LOFAR and I replied, 'What's that?'"

Blair, the Pentagon correspondent for *Time* magazine and a World War II submarine veteran, told Slade the term stood for "low-frequency acquisition and ranging," adding, "The Navy is laying a submarine cable between Bermuda and our East Coast, and the purpose of it is to provide arrays of antennae on the ocean floor that will pick up very low frequencies generated by submarines for maybe one hundred miles."

Cutter was baffled. He had regular briefings on classified material from Rear Admiral Arleigh A. Burke, Director of Strategic Plans in the office of the Chief of Naval Operations. Burke had never mentioned LOFAR. "The information was obviously leaked to Clay Blair," said Cutter. "And when I went to Admiral Burke with that, he was horrified. 'How did this happen? Where did Blair get this information?'" Cutter and his aides were suspected of the leak, but a subsequent investigation quickly exonerated them.

Though Slade experienced a baptism of fire in the LOFAR and *The Caine Mutiny* uproars, nothing prepared him for the very public ordeal that came next. The issue was the imminent launch of the *Nautilus* (SSN-571), the world's first nuclear submarine. The design of the top-secret vessel had been unveiled eight years earlier at a top-secret meeting at the Bureau of Ships in March 1946. Vice Admiral Lockwood was at that meeting, as were other ranking Naval officials, surrounded by futuristic diagrams, blueprints, and mathematical equations taped to blackboards. Dr. Phil Abelson, the young physicist who pioneered a means of harnessing uranium as a source of energy, held his audience spellbound:

> The atomic-powered submarine in this report is designed to operate at 26 knots submerged for many years. . . . The power unit requires no added fuel or oxygen, and personnel oxygen could be replenished by electrolysis or chemical methods. It should be remembered that the 26 knots proposed is merely a beginning. With better power conversion, machinery and hull design, there is no reason why the speed should not go up to approximately 40 knots using screw propellers. Beyond this speed, combining atomic power with jet propulsion may provide speeds well over 60 knots. To function offensively, this fast submarine will serve as an ideal carrier and launcher of rocketed atomic bombs.

Nuclear-powered submarines? Vessels able to stay submerged for years, travel at sixty knots, and launch rocket-powered atomic bombs? "It sounded like something out of Jules Verne's *Twenty Thousand Leagues Under the Sea*," marveled Lockwood. "What will they think of next?"

The Navy put development of such a weapon on the fast track through a special Navy research group at Oak Ridge, Tennessee, in cooperation with nuclear scientists from the Army's Manhattan Project, which had developed the atomic bomb. The man tapped to head the group was Capt. Hyman Rickover, an electronics specialist known as a tenacious, energetic perfectionist—exactly what was required for such a complicated project. The choice was unpopular among many in the Navy—and the press knew it. The captain was not the typical line officer. He was a humorless man with a long history of caustic run-ins with fellow officers.

He often ridiculed Navy customs, and he despised its cocktail party circuit. He was terse, demanding, and had a sharp tongue. But he got results, and that pleased senior officers who championed him.

Rickover achieved spectacular technical breakthroughs by spurring subordinates and contractors to the point of exhaustion. Backed by a powerful group of legislators in Congress, the captain became Chief of the Nuclear Power Division in the Bureau of Ships and Director of the Atomic Energy Commission's Naval Reactors Branch. His power extended to selecting junior officers for future nuclear submarines, which aggravated many in the Navy hierarchy. That became evident in 1953 when the Navy selection board twice overlooked him for promotion to rear admiral. By Navy rules, any officer overlooked twice had to retire. But the Senate Armed Service Committee and Navy Secretary Anderson intervened, forcing the board to promote him.

Cutter did not know Rickover personally. However, he respected his drive to succeed. He could identify with that kind of passion. Cutter supported the *Nautilus* program, as did many top submarine veterans of World War II, including Capt. Edward Beach and Capt. Elton Grenfell. Both gave Rickover crucial support in the early development stages by cutting through bureaucratic red tape that threatened to delay the project.

As the *Nautilus* neared completion, Rickover nominated Commander Eugene P. Wilkinson to be the submarine's first skipper, raising skepticism in the Bureau of Ships. Wilkinson was not an Academy man but had graduated from the University of Southern California. However, he had worked closely with Rickover in the early research on the *Nautilus* and had commanded a new *Tang*-class submarine from 1951 to 1953. The popular choice was Commander Beach, who was naval aide to President Eisenhower and a combat veteran. Beach, however, threw his support to Wilkinson, who became the Navy's "Captain Nemo."

Three weeks before the launch on 21 January 1954, *New York Times* reporter John Finney visited Cutter for a briefing on the *Nautilus*. Finney had an advance copy of a biography of Admiral Rickover by Clay Blair and thought it would be a good time to compare the nuclear submarine with diesel-driven boats. "So he asked me some questions, all of which were answered in a fact sheet that we had prepared," said Cutter. "He had all that information but he had to have a Navy spokesman say it. So he asked me these questions, and I was the Navy spokesman.

"How fast does the Nautilus go?"

"More than twenty knots."

"Depth?"

"More than four hundred feet."

"How many torpedo tubes?"

"Four."

"How many torpedo tubes in World War II submarines?"

"Ten."

"How many periscopes?"

"One."

"How many periscopes in World War II submarines?"

"Two."

As Finney narrowed the contrast, Cutter made an off-the-cuff assessment: "The Nautilus is strictly a test vehicle. I doubt if she ever will fire a shot in anger."

Finney's article, published on 5 January 1954 in the *New York Times,* followed up Cutter's statement by quoting "Navy planners" as believing the submarine was too large for stealthy attack and quick maneuverability. That was news to the public, which envisioned the atomic submarine as an advanced technology warship, not simply an extraordinarily expensive test vehicle. The report in the *New York Times,* buried deep inside the first section, attracted little notice in Washington. But the United Press International picked up the story. And a week later, the *Washington Post* decided to reprint it—on the front page. "Well, I hadn't thought much about it until the morning of 12 January when I woke up and went down to get the newspaper," said Cutter. "Right on the bottom of the front page was a column with the headline, 'A Submarine Held Unfit for Battle Now.' I told my wife, 'This is going to be a long day.' And boy, it sure was."

Telephones began to jangle all over the capital. President Eisenhower was incensed. He telephoned Defense Secretary C. E. Wilson and Atomic Energy Commissioner Lewis Strauss. The President demanded to know why a Navy spokesman would make derogatory remarks about a submarine that Eisenhower and the Navy's best submariners had endorsed, and that the First Lady would christen at the upcoming launch. "What do you mean asking my wife to sponsor this test vehicle?" the President demanded.

Wilson, feeling the heat, was in a lather. The Secretary convened a closed-door meeting. "Wilson called in a whole task force of top Pentagon personnel for a blistering, table-thumping session which started with midday lunch and ended after 6 P.M.," reported *Time* magazine a week later. "Frequently during the afternoon, Wilson tapped with thumb and forefinger on a memorandum written by Parks and Cutter which, like the United Press story, described the *Nautilus* as a 'test vehicle.'"

The *Time* story, written by Blair, described Parks as a "radish-red admiral" in defending himself and Cutter at the inquisition. Blair jumped to the conclusion that Cutter and Parks deliberately leaked the test vehicle story to disparage Rickover. The "inside dope from the Parks office," noted *Time,* was "the atomic submarine *Nautilus* is really unsuited to combat; it is too big, too expensive, too noisy; its torpedo tubes were added as an afterthought; its sonar equipment will not work at high speed; it has no safety features. . . . Veteran Pentagon newsmen recognized the story for what it was: a brassbound attempt to strike at Rear Admiral Hyman G. Rickover."

Wilson was determined to do something to redress the situation. So he issued orders for Cutter to convene a press conference in the Pentagon to announce that the *Nautilus,* contrary to earlier reports, was a submarine fully worth of combat. In the same *Time* article, Blair reported that "newsmen sniggered at [Cutter's] straight-faced efforts," prompting the captain to respond, "Well, that's the party line, anyway." The report created a national furor, setting out Cutter and Parks as enemies of Rickover and the *Nautilus* program. "The story implied the Navy was against it, and we were spokesmen for the Navy. Nothing could be further from the truth," said Cutter. "All I had done was answer questions that the *New York Times*'s guy already had the answers for. Clay Blair did me irreparable personal damage, really. I got letters from civilians. I got letters from people in the Navy. In fact, there was a standard answer written up, which was approved by Admiral Carney which was sent out to all these letter writers who said what a dumb outfit we were. You know, very derogatory. So I told Blair when he showed up at my office, 'You son of a bitch, you come to my office again, I'm going to throw you out the window.' And I was on the fourth floor. And he never came again to my office."

Carney banned all Navy personnel from talking to Blair. Cutter, meanwhile, rode out the storm. Carney was convinced neither he nor Parks had done anything out of line. Slade continued attending press conferences and showing up at major news events. But in later years, he looked back with trepidation. "I don't think there was anything positive about it," he said. "I'd be awakened all hours of the day and night. Well, one positive thing came out of it. I quit smoking and I quit drinking during the daytime. I used to have a martini at lunch."

Despite the controversy swirling around him, Cutter's career got a lift with his promotion to captain on 1 July 1954 and a transfer to the staff of Commander Submarine Force, Atlantic Fleet. He soon would find himself aboard the *Nautilus*—as the officer chosen to evaluate its performance.

New London

THE MOVE back to the operational fleet was a great relief to Cutter and it had an ironic twist: he was posted to New London, the home port of the *Nautilus*. He became assistant chief of staff to Rear Admiral Frank T. Watkins, commander submarine force, Atlantic fleet. As the submarine training officer, Slade organized and led a five-man team of former submarine skippers who evaluated submarine squadrons. "A squadron would nominate a submarine for the battle efficiency pennant within the force. Then we would put each submarine through the paces," explained Slade. The group's expertise was so acute that it unnerved many a crew, earning it the moniker "hatchet squad" within the fleet. "We knew where all the dead dogs would be hidden. But it helped the submarine force readiness very much. The thing we liked best of all was to go aboard the boat that did everything right. We reveled in that."

One such moment came during an ASW exercise in which the submarine being observed by Cutter's team would pretend to be a Soviet submarine penetrating the East Coast. The objective was for destroyers and other surface craft plus Navy aircraft to find the submarine and force it to surface. ASW forces were told only that the target was going from Montauk, on the northern tip of Long Island, down the coast to Key West.

The diesel submarine left port on a Monday and followed a rift in the ocean floor paralleling the New Jersey coast. "We hid out there for a couple of days. There were temperature gradients that made it difficult for ASW to pick us up," said Cutter. "One night a destroyer came through and ping, ping, ping. They were on us. They had us. And they sent a recognition signal, and our sonarman gave them a recognition signal back. But the destroyer kept on going instead of trying to force us up which we couldn't understand."

The rest of the way south, the submarine evaded detection and surfaced at the entrance buoy off Key West at the exact moment the exercise was to end. To the Navy, it proved how vulnerable the United States was to Soviet submarines. But Cutter revealed in his report that a destroyer made contact with the submarine off New Jersey. The escort's captain, asked to explain, categorically denied it, saying there had been no contacts en route to Newport, Rhode Island, from Philadelphia. "Well they sent the recognition signal. We had their hull number, we knew who they were," said Cutter. "I think he didn't have a well-trained crew, that he wasn't informed, that the crew just said, 'Oh, if I tell this to the captain, why, he'll stick around here and we won't get home on time.'"

While in New London, Cutter drew the coveted assignment of evaluating the fleet readiness of the *Nautilus* after its commissioning on 30 September 1954. From the moment its captain electrified the nation by reporting the atomic submarine was "underway on nuclear power," the vessel mesmerized diesel submarine veterans like Cutter. "You realize the submarine force is doomed as you know it," he said. "But you also know what is coming on."

On the boat's shakedown cruise, it traveled 1,381 miles entirely submerged in just under ninety hours—a voyage that would have taken a diesel submarine five full days. The *Nautilus*'s ability to dive to great depth and outmaneuver antisubmarine surface vessels also made it far more effective than the old diesel submarines. In terms of habitability, it was a striking contrast to World War II submarines. Each sailor had his own bunk with a foam rubber mattress. The compartments were painted with bright colors, and a nickel-a-play jukebox was hooked up to a built-in, high-fidelity sound system.

What impressed Cutter most was the speed submerged. In exercises, a fast Navy carrier could not shake the *Nautilus*, which could keep pace submerged with the carrier on the surface. Furthermore, it dodged destroyers by staying directly under the keel of the speeding carrier. "We never got picked up," said Cutter. "It was really funny." In another exercise, the submarine accompanied a convoy of amphibious ships escorted by destroyers to Bermuda and back. The *Nautilus* was to attack the ship with dummy practice torpedoes. "All we'd do is get under a convoy ship and sit there," explained Cutter. "Every once in a while Captain Wilkinson would fire a torpedo all by sound, and the *Nautilus* had good enough equipment for that. We'd fire the torpedo and watch it on our sonar scope. You'd see the torpedo go out and cross underneath the ship that we'd fired at. Well, it was just a farce in the ease that this was done. There was no way that our ASW forces at that time could do anything to a nuclear submarine. They never were able to attack us. That was the finding. It was clear to us and it was just funny—and pitiful."

After six months of trials, the *Nautilus* had met and surpassed every standard, and there was every expectation that a design for a nuclear attack submarine would revolutionize naval warfare.

During the evaluation period, the *Nautilus* was in and out of New London on an irregular basis. At one point Admiral Rickover flew in from Washington to address submarine skippers and support staff. He briskly entered the lecture hall and launched into a no-nonsense speech. He wanted to impress on the men that it was their responsibility to tell the Bureau of Ships what was needed to keep the fleet in superior shape. "If you people don't tell us what you want," Rickover concluded, "how can we provide you with what you need? You are a bunch of dopes."

The scolding caught everyone off guard including Cutter. "He insulted the hell out of everybody in that room. I got upset too because we were not that stupid." Later that night, Slade caught the 11:36 express train to Washington, D.C., to attend to business in the capital. Rickover got on as well. "The admiral, strangely I thought at the time, invited me to come into his roomette," said Cutter. "We got to talking and he was an entirely different person from what he had been earlier in the day. Finally I said, 'Admiral, why were you so obnoxious talking to us today?'

And he used my first name, 'Slade, I'll tell you. I'm a busy man and I can't afford to give my time to people who don't remember what I say and listen to me. I'll bet you one thing; you'll never forget what I said today.' And he was absolutely right. We had lots of briefings up there, and I don't remember what any of them were, but I remember that one."

The two did not discuss the *Time* magazine fiasco. (Months earlier Clay Blair, in an attempt to patch things up, hosted a small dinner party in Washington attended by Slade and Franny, Admiral Rickover, and George Hunt, Washington bureau chief of *Life* magazine.) Still, the CHINFO incident hung over Cutter. That became obvious when arrangements were being made for a press conference with *Nautilus* officers. Commander Wilkinson wanted Cutter to attend because he was familiar with the Washington press corps. But the Pentagon rejected the idea. "Word came back, 'Don't dare let him sit in on that interview.' This was because of the *Time* magazine incident," explained Cutter. "What they were afraid of was the press corps would take me apart, that they'd be on me because of the Rickover business. And they would have."

On 1 March 1956, Slade left New London for Portsmouth, Virginia, to take command of Submarine Squadron Six, a significant promotion in terms of broadening his authority. For the first time, the Navy would hold him directly accountable for the readiness of thirty submarines as well as the tender that served them. Fortunately, the quality of the skippers was excellent because most had wartime experience. Plenty of socializing also created a close bond. Franny was active in the wives' group and the couple entertained frequently at home. "It's very important to keep the wives happy and interested in what their husbands were doing, to make them feel they're part of an outfit," said Slade.

The commander of the squadron's tender, the *Orion,* was Capt. Chester W. Nimitz Jr., son of Fleet Adm. Chester W. Nimitz (who had pinned two gold stars in lieu of twin Navy Crosses on Cutter's chest after his last war patrol). Chester Nimitz Jr. was following in his father's path as a brilliant, energetic, and decisive leader.

For instance, on a training voyage, the tender was testing live torpedoes on an old landing craft. The torpedoes were of a new kind that moved in circles until onboard sonar zeroed in on the sound of the target's propellers. The torpedo was making its circular run in the direction of the LST when an unexpected ship appeared on the horizon and closed. "Chester warned the ship to stay clear but the guy kept coming," explained Cutter. "You know how he solved the problem? He got his gun crew to man a 3-inch gun and gave them a little training by firing a shot over this guy's bow. That got his attention and he changed course directly. I never would have done that. I wouldn't have the guts to do a thing like that. I'd be afraid I'd get court-martialed. I'd have kept signaling."

Despite the promise of a bright future in the Navy, Nimitz became disillusioned after twenty years of service and decided to resign. Chester Nimitz Sr., however, had the Secretary of the Navy disapprove the request, causing a bitter rift between father and son. "So the next time when Chester decided he wanted to get out," said Cutter, "he wrote to his father and showed me the letter before he sent it, to get my impression."

Slade tried to talk him out of it. "Chester, you're bound to make flag rank," he argued. "Sure," replied Nimitz, "but I'll never make five stars. Furthermore, everybody will think I made flag rank because of my dad. I don't want to follow in his shadow anymore."

The Portsmouth newspaper found out and requested an interview. "Chester's office and mine were separated by just a bulkhead with a door, and I could hear everything going on in his cabin," said Cutter. "So I heard him give this interview to the reporters, and I just cringed when I heard what he said. I knew that they were going to take Chester apart on this one because he said one of the reasons he was resigning—he was trying to help the Navy by saying this—was because he had three daughters, and he wanted to give them advantages, dancing lessons, music lessons, and he couldn't afford it. He was a captain. He couldn't afford it on his pay to give his children the advantages of schooling, and so he felt obliged to go out into civilian life and make more money."

As Cutter feared, the reporter seized on the pay issue in the subsequent feature article printed in the Sunday papers. "They played up the fact that he wasn't making enough money as a captain," said Cutter. "Here we were in a community that was largely Navy, with thousands of enlisted people and Navy yard workers who were making a heck of a lot less, and you can imagine what the letters to the editor were about the poor captain who couldn't live on his pay."

Nimitz stuck by his resignation and went on to found his own electronics firm, became wealthy, and took up golf with a passion (including lessons from Sam Snead), only to remark later to Cutter, "The hell of it is now I've got the money to play golf and do the things I couldn't afford to do while in the Navy, but now I don't have the time. Then I had the time and not the money. Now I've got the money but not the time."

By all accounts, Cutter did a superlative job managing the submarine squadron and seemed perfectly poised to move up to rear admiral. But fate intervened at a cocktail party in New London in 1956. Slade encountered an old friend, Rear Admiral Elton W. Grenfell, from the Bureau of Naval Personnel. The admiral was involved in the athletic program at Annapolis and asked Slade if he would consider becoming athletic director. Cutter did not answer at first, telling Grenfell he would think it over. Later, he discussed the idea with his wife. Both realized that Slade was destined for shore duty and that could mean being posted anywhere, perhaps Washington, which Franny dreaded. "Since I didn't know where I was going to go and Annapolis would be preferable to Washington, I decided to accept the job." Besides, he thought, Annapolis had one of the most successful college football programs going under Coach Eddie Erdelatz.

Cutter decided to accept, after which Admiral Grenfell dropped a bomb: "He told me my job would be to fire Erdelatz. That became one of the most miserable damn jobs I ever had in my life."

The War with Erdelatz

THE RETURN of football and boxing legend Slade Cutter to the Naval Academy could not have been better timed. He presided over the groundbreaking for a new football stadium on campus. And he seemed destined to energize athletic programs that had been lagging. But football was not one of them. Cutter, in fact, inherited a premier attraction. In seven years, Edward J. "Eddie" Erdelatz had rejuvenated Navy with a pro-style offense that transformed the team into one of the elite squads in the country. Recruitments were up and the future seemed bright to the former line coach of the NFL's San Francisco Forty-Niners. Erdelatz was the gridiron savior that Navy yearned for in 1950 when it turned to him to reverse a precipitous decline.

For four consecutive years after the war, varsity football was an abysmal failure. The middies won only a single game in 1946, the worst record ever despite the return of coach Tom Hamilton, who led Cutter and the 1934 squad to an 8–1 record. The following year was nearly as disastrous—1–7–1—and Hamilton stepped down. George Sauer, who succeeded him, was unable to win a single game in the 1948 season, posting a 0–8–1 record. Though he improved on that in 1949, finishing 3–5–1, Navy again lost to Army by a humiliating 38–0 score, continuing a six-game winless string against the Cadets.

The academy turned to Erdelatz the following year, hoping that his pro experience would help. But in his first year, he struggled to a 3–5–1 record. However, the middies defeated Army 14–2. It was all the more remarkable because it was the first loss by Army in twenty-eight games. Navy regressed slightly to a 2–6–1 record in 1951. But it won its last two games, including a 42–7 thumping of Army that secured Erdelatz's job. The breakthrough was the 1952 season in which Navy posted a 6–2–1 record, again beating Army 7–0. The middies proceeded to post four consecutive winning seasons. A Navy upset victory over the University of Mississippi in New Orleans's Sugar Bowl in 1955, the midshipmen's first bowl appearance since the 1923 Rose Bowl, sealed Erdelatz's ascendancy to the nation's coaching elite. With a national television audience of sixty-five million watching, Navy shut down the heavily favored Rebels by a 21–0 score, Navy's first-ever bowl victory. The triumph changed the academy's fortunes dramatically. Applications spiraled upward. "The after-effects of that game . . . convinced many of us that good Navy athletic teams are good for the Naval Academy and good for the Navy," noted Rear Admiral Walter F. Boone, school superintendent.

But there was a dark side to all this success—a growing inability to control Erdelatz, who had begun to bad-mouth the Navy while using his success to get special considerations for his players. They, in turn, had become more loyal to the coach than the institution. "If anybody played in the game for one minute, Erdelatz had it worked out so that they were excused from classes on Monday," explained Cutter. "On Wednesday they had a scouting report, and they would have it at the boathouse and they would have a steak dinner, and they would get back about 11 o'clock at night. Thursday they were no good because they hadn't had a chance to study the night before. And Friday they were gone. How in the world are you going to carry on an academic program like that without someone feeding them stuff they shouldn't have? In other words, we were heading for a scandal. Midshipmen have got to be students. One of the problems with Erdelatz was that he tried to circumvent the system, and that inevitably would lead to a cheating situation. You couldn't help it."

Certain ranking alumni, including Admiral Grenfell, had similar fears. "Joe Grenfell carried a lot of weight with the chief of the Bureau of Naval Personnel He was a very rabid Navy sports fan," said Slade. "He was all blue and gold, old Joe was. He was a submariner and a submarine skipper before I got command, and by this time he was a rear admiral. He and other interested people wanted somebody in there that had been a football player, that was recognized as having some ability, who could talk to Erdelatz."

Slade was perfectly armed to do so, unlike his predecessor, Capt. C. Elliott Loughlin, an All-American basketball player at the academy in the early 1930s. "Erdelatz would say to him, 'You are a roundballer. You don't understand the problems of football.' And therefore he had no way of controlling him," explained Cutter. "Erdelatz couldn't tell me that. I was All-America, and I had coached football and at least knew enough about it that I could tell him, 'Well, blocking and tackling wins football games still. I don't care how much the game has changed.' It had changed a lot, but the fundamentals hadn't."

Cutter's first impression of the mercurial coach was not a good one. Within days of Cutter's arrival, Erdelatz called him. "Captain, do you know that you are authorized to have the admiral's barge on Sundays if he doesn't want it?" the coach asked.

"I didn't know that," replied Slade, to which the coach added, "Well, you are. The football season is starting in two or three weeks and I would like to have one nice Sunday with them before we get into the grind. And I would like to take them and their wives out on the barge. And you and Franny go along. We would like to have you with us."

Slade checked and found out the barge was available. So he told Erdelatz that everything was set to go. "A couple days later he called and acted very embarrassed and said, 'Do you mind if you don't go? Because I think the coaches would feel more at ease, and I want them to relax and have a good time.' So I said, 'That's fine, Eddie. I don't care.' The next thing I knew a day or two later Erdelatz called me again and invited me and I thought, uh-oh, this is manipulation. I am back on the list again! So I replied, 'Thank you very much. I have other plans.'"

The two soon clashed on a variety of issues, especially the football schedule. "Every time I'd schedule anybody, Eddie would come in and raise Cain because they were too tough. Erdelatz wanted to win. If he could have played the Little Sisters of the Poor every Saturday, he'd have been very happy. But you have to make money. You don't make money playing the Little Sisters of the Poor. You make your money playing Notre Dame and Pittsburgh and Michigan, people who are going to clobber you. You know it, but you're going to draw a crowd, and you're going to get television money."

Just before the 1957 football season began, the football coach and the athletic director had a bitter falling-out. Cutter chartered a four-engine Constellation to fly the team to Massachusetts to play Boston College. There were four extra seats so Slade invited Ben Carnevale, the basketball coach, who wanted to do some recruiting in the Boston area. Erdelatz was irate. "He can't go. You can't mix football and basketball," he told Cutter.

"What the hell," replied Slade. "He isn't coaching anybody on the flight."

Early the next morning, Erdelatz called (and awakened) assistant athletic director Edgar "Rip" Miller, and tried to convince him to "uninvite" Carnevale. But Erdelatz got nowhere with Miller, who was Cutter's buddy, and Carnevale made the trip. "It was a very distasteful thing," Cutter said of Erdelatz's meddling. "We all sat in the forward cabin; the team sat aft. Everything was downhill from there on."

Despite the friction, Erdelatz delivered another winning season. In fact, the 1957 campaign was one of his best. The middies went 8–1–1 including a 14–0 victory over Army and a berth in the Cotton Bowl in Dallas, Texas, where Navy beat Rice 20–7.

Though the conflict with Erdelatz was on the front burner, Cutter dealt aggressively with other sports at the academy. He and Miller shook things up. They fired the wrestling coach and hired Edwin C. Peery, a national intercollegiate wrestling champion from the University of Pittsburgh, who turned the middies into winners. Cutter and Miller also replaced the lacrosse coach with plebe coach Willis P. Bilderback—who promptly led the team to successive national titles. Cutter, approaching his job as if he were the commander of a submarine on war patrol, next took aim at crew.

The sport was costly in terms of equipment and transportation. In

Cutter's mind, Navy's inability to rack up victories did not justify the expense. He and Miller viewed the team and the coach as elitist, unwilling to put in the practice time needed to succeed in competition. "The players would get excused from dress parades on Wednesday and I wouldn't see them out in the river. They'd be over at the boathouse sunbathing," explained Cutter who fired the coach. That created a problem because no other crew coaches in the East wanted the job. Cutter discovered they were a tight-knit eastern fraternity that wouldn't betray a fallen brother. So Cutter looked elsewhere and found his man in Rusty Callow, crew coach at the University of California who brought in a regimen of strenuous training that scullers at Annapolis did not like. But within a single year, the middies won the coveted Poughkeepsie Regatta on the Hudson River.

Throughout this period, Cutter always spoke his mind. He did not care about ruffling feelings. His blunt, sometimes off-the-cuff, honesty tended to get him into trouble, as it did at a press luncheon hosted by basketball coach Carnevale. "We were sitting at card tables in the field house, right on the basketball floor, and Carnevale was giving this spiel about the basketball team," recalled Slade. "As I was talking during lunch, I said, 'You know, these whistle blowers are making a sissy sport out of basketball. The referees blow the whistle all the time. The kids just can't do anything out there—this personal foul business.' The next day, in the papers, it came out, 'Cutter says basketball is a sissy sport.' The superintendent wanted to know about that and so did a lot of other people. Oh, boy! And that was after I had been on public information duty for two years, and I hadn't learned." Afterwards, a friend advised Cutter, "If somebody could put a clothespin on your mouth, you'd be a hell of a lot better off."

Though the troubles with Erdelatz had died down during the off-season, they reasserted themselves as the 1958 football season approached. Cutter's concern heightened on learning that out of twenty-one graduating football lettermen, only one was going into the line of the Navy. "All the rest tendered their resignations or went into the Supply Corps. They couldn't care less about the Navy," said Cutter, who was convinced Erdelatz's cynicism was responsible. It had gotten back to Slade that the coach even had disparaged Rear Admiral William R. Smedberg III, the new school superintendent, calling him a "fool." Enraged, Cutter informed the admiral. "We've got to fire this guy," said Cutter. "He is disloyal to you. He is disloyal to the academy. He's turning the midshipmen against the Navy."

Smedberg, however, was unwilling to take a stand against such a successful coach. Cutter was stymied. Erdelatz used his success and his ability to turn on the charm to great advantage. "I may have seemed cruel towards Eddie, but I actually felt sorry for him because he was quite personable. I didn't know what to do. I even went to the head psychologist at the Naval Academy to get his advice. He was a football fan and he said Erdelatz was psychotic because outside of football season, he acted normally. But he was a basket case during the season."

With Cutter continuing to apply pressure, he learned that Erdelatz secretly took his coaching staff to Texas A&M University for a visit under the assumption he had a job lined up through one of the boosters, an oil millionaire. But when he got there, the school president turned him down. The coach returned to Annapolis crestfallen. Slade went right to Smedberg.

"Now is the time to get rid of him, because he did not get my permission to approach Texas A&M," he argued to the superintendent.

"Oh no, you can't do that, Slade," replied the admiral. "He beat Army this year. Look at his record. The graduates wouldn't take it."

"They would if you let the word out on the reason for it. They certainly would," pleaded Cutter. But Smedberg refused to budge. In fact, he did just the opposite by publicly embarrassing Cutter by not inviting him to his private quarters at the annual football banquet as tradition dictated. "I wondered what the heck was going on? I wasn't invited up, and neither was Rip. By golly, when it came time for dinner, down the stairway from their quarters came the Superintendent and Mrs. Smedberg and Erdelatz and [his wife] Agnes. He had had Erdelatz up there and not Rip and me. This was really bad, because Erdelatz became absolutely arrogant after that. I couldn't control him at all."

Through the spring football practice and into the new season, the coach had his way, even after Rear Admiral Charles L. Melson replaced

Smedberg in June 1958. Cutter continued to try to clamp down. He especially would not allow football players to miss class, causing Erdelatz to
call Cutter "a son of a bitch who was trying to destroy the football program" in off-the-record comments to wire service reporters—who leaked
the news to Slade. Despite the friction, Erdelatz again led Navy to a
winning season, a 6–3 record including a 20–14 victory over Michigan.
But he lost by a 40–20 margin to Notre Dame and 22–6 to Army in the
last two games of the season.

Something had to give—and it appeared it would be Cutter. During
the winter of 1959, he was in Norfolk, Virginia, attending a lecture at
the Armed Forces Staff College when he got a telephone call from the
Chief of Naval Personnel. "Slade," began Vice Admiral Harold P. Smith,
"if you don't care for your career, I do. You are due for a sea command,
and you should figure on leaving this summer."

Cutter thought Erdelatz had gotten to someone in the Bureau of
Naval Personnel. "It seemed strange to me. No one had been transferred
as athletic director in less than three years in that job." So he sought out
Admiral Smith in Washington to explain the Erdelatz matter. The coach,
Slade predicted, "will be absolutely unmanageable if I get out of here.
He will say he got me fired, which I think is true. I strongly recommend
that you do not transfer me until Erdelatz is gone—or let me finish out
my three years." Nothing more was said and the transfer was put on hold.

As spring football practice got underway, Erdelatz agitated over the
administration not giving him the free rein of previous years. At a Lions
Club breakfast in Annapolis, he knocked the academy and Admiral Melson. John T. Cox, director of the academy's public information office,
was at the meeting and made a full report to Cutter. Slade promptly confronted Erdelatz, who denied everything. But later a Lions Club member confirmed Cox's account. "He was really shocked by it," said Cutter.
"This time I called Eddie on the phone, and I said, 'Eddie, I know you
told me you didn't do it, but I got another report from another source,
a member of the club there. It is the very same thing, and I have to
believe it.'

"'I'm sick and tired of this bullshit!' Erdelatz blurted. He hung up.

"Well, I sat there for two or three minutes and cooled off. I called back to have him come up to the office, and his secretary said, 'Mr. Erdelatz has gone to Baltimore.'" Cutter went to Wayne Hardin, the fiery offensive backfield coach under Erdelatz, who had been at the breakfast and confirmed what the coach had said. Hardin also identified a number of other coaches at the breakfast, and they too confirmed what happened. "So I went over to see Melson right then. I said, 'Admiral, I want to fire Erdelatz.' He didn't even ask why. He said, 'It's your decision. Call a meeting of the board and see if they approve.'"

Cutter quickly convened the four-member athletic control board—Capt. William F. Bringle, president of the board and the athletic association; Capt. Joseph E. Dougherty, head of the foreign languages department; Capt. Kenneth G. Schacht, head of the department of Seamanship and Navigation; and Capt. John Victor Smith, academic aide to the superintendent. Bringle called in the witnesses and asked each, "Do you consider Mr. Erdelatz a good influence on the midshipmen?" Each replied no, then described how Erdelatz talked negatively about the Navy and the superintendent. The board subsequently voted to fire him and he was dismissed on the spot. With Cutter's endorsement, Hardin moved up to head coach.

Slade wanted the academy to go public with exactly why Erdelatz had been ousted. "But all those details were taken out of my hands. It was handled at the level of the Secretary of the Navy. The decision was made that it would appear as a resignation. The idea was to avoid any bad public relations for the Navy. I think that having it appear that he resigned, none of the alumni would blame us or blame the academy."

Newsweek magazine announced the departure in an article, "Sinking the Navy?" It reported that Erdelatz had been unhappy with shifts in Naval Academy football policy and may have been pressured to leave. Among the changes cited were football players being required to attend regular classes, being given less free time for evening football meetings, and not being allowed to leave Annapolis until Friday afternoons for out-of-town games. "When Academy officials ignored his objections," the magazine reported, "he reluctantly decided to resign."

For Cutter, the mission to fire Erdelatz had been achieved. It was just a few months later that he, too, was "fired." Orders arrived transferring him to sea duty. The academy, to Cutter's dismay, soon ousted his crew coach, though he had won the Poughkeepsie Trophy. "Those who won the regatta in those days were given the prestige of coaching the Olympic crew in an Olympic year. We expected our man to coach the 1960 Olympic crew," said Cutter. "But the Eastern crew fraternity was not about to permit a Western upstart that honor. They blackballed him. He was not coach of the Olympic crew. The next thing I knew, they fired him."

Nevertheless, Cutter could look back at many achievements. The new football stadium was dedicated before his departure. The wrestling and lacrosse teams continued to thrive. And the football program took off under Hardin. In his seven-year reign as head coach, he only had one losing season. He beat Army five consecutive years and posted 9–1 records in both 1960 and 1963, culminating in respective Orange and Cotton Bowl appearances. His teams included two of the most famous players ever to put on a Navy helmet—halfback Joe Bellino and quarterback Roger Staubach, each of whom won college football's top award, the Heisman Trophy. "I'm proud of those situations I was in because they were all successful," said Cutter. "Sentiment didn't enter into it. I wanted to get the best man, and I didn't care too much how he would fit in politically or socially at the Naval Academy or with the other coaches."

As for Erdelatz, he was hired as the first head coach of the Oakland Raiders in the new American Football League. After posting a 6–6 record the first year, he was abruptly fired after losing the first two games of the 1961 season by 50–0 and 44–0 scores.

Cutter returned to the admiralty track that would lead to command of a cruiser. At first, however, it seemed to him that he was being penalized by being given command of an oil tanker that was considered a dumping ground for Navy misfits.

22

In the Zone

SLADE CUTTER had expected one thing and got quite another when he arrived to take command of the *Neosho* (AO-143). The oiler was considered a state-of-the-art Navy oil tanker. Commissioned in 1954 and named after an ironclad monitor that patrolled the Mississippi River during the Civil War, it was the first of a new class that maximized speed and cargo capacity. Manned by 240 enlisted men and a dozen officers, it was unique in its ability to refuel warships while underway. Based in Norfolk, it regularly serviced the Navy's Second Fleet and was deployed annually for four months to the Mediterranean to refuel the Sixth Fleet.

Slade's first impression of the *Neosho* was not a good one. It looked like a rust-bucket, especially alongside a similar-sized, exquisitely maintained Exxon tanker with only a forty-man crew. What disturbed the new skipper most was the caliber of the crew. "You've got to have pretty sharp people on a cruiser. In destroyers you've got to have hard working people to count upon. And if they don't produce, why, you transfer them off and they just filter on down and finally get to the service force. And they go to the *Neosho*." Cutter considered refusing to take command unless the ship was brought up to minimum standards. But the man he was relieving was a friend whom he did not want to embarrass nor hurt professionally.

Things were as bad as they seemed. "On my first Atlantic crossing, we couldn't make any fresh water aboard," Slade explained. "So I went down to the engine room to look at the evaporators, and they were absolutely clogged with calcium deposits. I couldn't believe that the engineering officer and everybody in the chain of command in the engine room had permitted this to happen. And there was no way for me to know it until we were in trouble." Slade immediately rationed water and made for Naples, Italy, where the evaporators were dissembled and boiled to remove the calcium buildup. Even in port, if it was not one calamity, it was another. "I came back one morning and we were down by the bow. I thought, 'My God, what's happened now?' And I found out they'd flooded the forward hold with water during the night." A guilty seaman was court-martialed.

What bothered Cutter most was the cavalier attitude of his subordinates, especially three U.S. Merchant Marine Academy officers destined for high-paying jobs after their two-year Navy obligation. "They were completely disloyal to me and to my executive officer, and they didn't care if we knew it," said Cutter. That became obvious shortly after the ship got underway on the skipper's initial voyage. When he went up to the bridge, he was flabbergasted to find the ship on automatic pilot in the heavily traveled Gulf Stream. The officer of the deck was in a cabin aft of the bridge, enjoying coffee and paying no attention whatsoever to the radar scope or anything else.

With his characteristic determination to change things, Cutter demanded better. And though it was stressful, he enjoyed the challenge. "When I first took the *Neosho* to sea, I wondered whether we'd be able to get under way or stay going after we got under way, but it all worked out," he said.

In October 1960, Cutter transferred to command of the *Northampton* (CLC-1), the flagship of the Second Fleet and widely perceived as an "admiral maker" because all seven previous skippers had been promoted. "I thought I had it made," said Slade. The command ship, commissioned in 1953, had a crew of 1,153. It also had a top-secret communications group under a lieutenant who answered only to the Chief of Naval Operations. "Their command center was part of my ship but I couldn't enter it. I had a top secret clearance but I couldn't get in there," he explained. "That was strictly 'need to know,' and there was no need for me to know."

Stepping up to cruiser-type command was quite different from his experience aboard *Neosho* or in submarines. Cutter was forcibly isolated from his officers and crew. He had his own mess, and ate his meals separate from the rest of the officers who dined in the wardroom.

> Command was much more difficult than I had anticipated. I'd go through a submarine and get into everything. When the engines were being overhauled, I'd get right down there and watch it and have a personal interest in everything that went on. You get in a capital ship like the *Northampton,* and things are much different. I had a Marine orderly. I couldn't shake him. Everywhere I went, the orderly went— everywhere. And it got to be as frustrating as the dickens. I'd walk into a compartment and he would yell, 'Attention!' And everybody would snap to attention. I really hesitated to go anywhere in the ship during working hours, because everything would stop. So you feel completely detached from what's going on, and feel isolated.

The captain's role, however, was not to immerse himself in hour-by-hour practical aspects of the ship. Rather, he was to satisfy the new commander of the Second Fleet. "I saw to it that he got all he wanted, and he wanted plenty," said Cutter. "Vice Admiral Claude V. Ricketts was the most conscientious and demanding officer I've ever been with." Of primary concern to Ricketts were inadequacies in the Fleet's readiness plan for possible emergencies in Cuba or Central America. He worked his skippers overtime, bringing the plan up to snuff. Ricketts also preached a single mantra to the commanders: "You're not doing enough with your congressmen. The Congress controls the Navy. We've got to sell them on our needs." Thus, senators and congressmen often were VIPs at shipboard cocktail parties. Image was everything to the soft-spoken admiral. Every chance he had, he would try to gain a favorable opinion of the Second Fleet. "For instance, we were in Bermuda, and we had a big party there, put up all of our canvas," explained Cutter. "It was a hell of a job to get the ship all rigged. We got in full dress and put on a real fancy show, hors d'oeuvres and all that, so visitors had a good time, and the admiral invited all the right people in Bermuda because it would help the image of the U.S. Navy."

Ricketts, like Cutter, was a boxer at the Academy in the 1930s. Off the job, they got to know one another and at one point attended a testimonial in Annapolis for former boxing coach "Spike" Webb. They sat at the head table with Webb-trained boxing protégés Gene Tunney and Rocky Marciano.

Despite his off-the-job amiability, the admiral remained aloof on the job and very demanding. For example, Ricketts chastised Slade for a mishap during the docking of the *Northampton* in Norfolk. A pilot came aboard to take the conn while directing tugboats by radio. "But the tugboat had its engines in reverse, full speed astern, and he couldn't stop them, and *whammo!* He hit our bow, a tremendous thud," said Cutter. Fortunately there were no damage to the command ship. But the collision unnerved the pilot, precipitating a comedy of errors in getting the ship to its berth. The *Northampton* arrived late and Ricketts was mad. "He thought this was an abysmal performance and called me down to his cabin to express his displeasure and I agreed with him. He was correct. I always made absolutely certain that if he said, 'Get under way at 8:00 o'clock in the morning,' that when they sounded the first ding-a-ling on the eight bells at 8:00 o'clock in the morning, all lines were dropped and all back two-thirds ordered. We followed the letter of the law with him. He was a stickler for being precise. Today I'm always exactly on time, and some of it is due to Ricketts." The *Northampton* was mostly stationed in Norfolk, with little sea duty until the Bay of Pigs crisis in April 1961.

Cuban exiles, trained by the Central Intelligence Agency (CIA) and sanctioned by the former Eisenhower administration, were planning to invade Cuba to overthrow the revolutionary government of premier Fidel Castro, the target of several failed CIA assassination plots. After Eisenhower cut off diplomatic relations with Castro in January 1961, incoming President John F. Kennedy learned of the invasion plan and ultimately gave permission to proceed. He and others in his administration were careful, however, to distance themselves from the operation, saying it was exclusively a Cuban initiative against Cubans.

On 13 April, a flotilla of seven ships loaded with fourteen hundred Cubans armed and trained by the CIA cast off from Nicaragua and headed for a swampy spit of a beachhead called Bahia de Cochinos—the Bay of Pigs—on the south coast of Cuba. Seven U.S. destroyers disguised as part of the rebel force escorted the invasion force, then remained out of sight ten miles offshore. The plan was for the Cubans to march inland, incite a popular uprising, seize Havana, and install a new government. As part of the overall strategy, the United States posted two aircraft carriers south of the landing site. Identification markings on aircraft aboard the carriers were painted out and bomb cargoes were moved out of storage for imminent use.

At the time, the *Northampton* was docked in Portsmouth. Slade, unaware of the upcoming crisis, had made plans to take Franny to the hospital the next morning for a medical procedure. But that evening, Rear Admiral David L. McDonald, Commander of Carrier Division Six, ordered the *Northampton* to depart at once. "I was told to get under way within four hours. And we got the boilers up, and we went down to the Bay of Pigs to support the operation." The *Northampton* had a direct line to the White House and President Kennedy, and Robert Kennedy was in constant touch with Ricketts aboard the flagship, according to Cutter.

On Saturday, 15 April, the president flew from the White House to his Virginia retreat, Glen Ora, to monitor the invasion. Six ancient B-26 bombers supplied by the CIA to Cuban insurgents that day bombed three airfields in Cuba as a preemptive strike. The attack, designed to eliminate Castro's air force, succeeded in taking out only half the planes. Castro immediately mobilized his forces, causing Kennedy to consider calling off the landing. But he acquiesced by day's end. It was the first major foreign policy decision of his three-month-old presidency.

In the early morning hours of 17 April, the rebel landing got underway with the expectation of air cover from Navy carriers. However, the invasion was a fiasco from the outset. Landing craft were hung up on unexpected coral reefs. A parachute drop designed to secure a main road to the beach was off target. Castro's surviving aircraft decimated the troop transports with rockets, strafed the LSTs, and shot down the handful of rebel B-26s trying to provide support. Fifty-four Soviet-made tanks backed by thousands of Cuban troops surrounded the beachhead. Faced with a humiliating defeat, the exiles pleaded for help from the carriers. But fearing the U.S. role might be unmasked, President Kennedy lost his nerve and called off the intercession. General Lyman L. Lemnitzer, chairman of the Joint Chiefs of Staff, exploded. "This is criminally negligent!" he said, terming the president's action "absolutely reprehensible, almost criminal." Those in the battle fleet were just as irate. "It was a terrible thing because we spent the next five days picking people out of the water that were escaping," said Cutter. "We had the submarines go in submerged with periscopes raised to try and tow some of them out, hanging on to the periscopes until the submarine could surface. They were on boats and rafts and flotsam, whatever they could hang on to. God knows how many of them drowned. And we'd promised them support, by the U.S. Navy, and we were called off at the last minute. I'll tell you, when that article by Robert Kennedy came out in *U.S. News & World Report* blaming the Joint Chiefs of Staff for that decision, that was absolutely wrong. That decision was made in the White House. It was terrible to abandon the CIA-trained men."

The article, an interview with Kennedy, appeared in the 28 January 1963 issue of the magazine. In it, he claimed that his brother did not cancel U.S. air support of the Bay of Pigs invasion because none had ever been planned. "It's just not true," he insisted. In a discussion with Admiral McDonald months later, however, Cutter asked him about Kennedy's denial. The admiral did not address it directly but wondered aloud, "I wonder why they had us paint out everything the night before if they didn't expect us to go in the next day?"

As his first year as skipper wound down, Cutter made plans to take the *Northampton* to the Black Sea as a challenge to the Soviet Union. "We had a great trip planned to show the flag and let the Soviets know we could get in the Black Sea. We were really looking forward to that." But it was not to be.

The Navy had decided to convert the *Northampton* into a national command post. At the Norfolk Naval Shipyard, workers created shipboard quarters for President Kennedy and his family. During the conversion, the president's personal physician came aboard on important business.

"He brought a suitcase and put it in my safe," explained Cutter. "He told me I should never open it and never look inside and advised me not to tell anybody the suitcase was inside. He made a big deal about it and that really got me interested. If he hadn't said anything, I wouldn't have cared. I wouldn't have thought about it. But then the doctor went into a very top secret huddle with the ship's doctor. I wondered what was going on. President Kennedy had something wrong that I didn't know anything about. And I've often wondered what was going on there."

Slade never found out. All that was known publicly about the president's health was that he had long suffered from congenital, chronic back pain for which he received cortisone injections. His private physicians and Navy doctors, however, knew the president was seriously ill with Addison's Disease that had critically damaged the adrenal glands which controlled his immune system. Without the hormones secreted by the glands, the slightest illness, including a simple cold, could be fatal.

As a command post, the *Northampton* served as an emergency evacuation vessel whenever the First Family traveled anywhere on the East Coast. "When President Kennedy went down to Palm Beach, we went down there and stayed out of sight of land in the Gulf Stream and had his Marine helicopters aboard to go in and pick him up in case something happened," explained Cutter. The ship also tracked Kennedy north to his family compound at Hyannis Port, Massachusetts, where again the ship lurked out of sight in the Atlantic. During Cutter's service, the need never arose to send the helicopters and he subsequently never met the president.

Cutter chose to leave the *Northampton* in August 1961, less than a year into his command, to become assistant chief of staff to the Navy's Strike Force South in Italy. "A good friend of mine had had the job, and his wife had told my wife that she had loved it. Then Franny asked me to ask for it. And I did. So, of course, I got it because nobody in his right mind would want it."

The reason: It was a shore liaison in Naples for the Sixth Fleet. Rear Admiral Edward A. Hannegan was in charge and Cutter was his assistant. Navy insiders knew the assignment was a dead end. "It was really a paper outfit. And there were two unemployed people—Ned Hannegan and Cutter," said Slade. At least it was a chance to settle down with his family, to spend a couple of years of quality time with Franny and the kids. And at that point it was enough.

Cutter had not given up on becoming rear admiral. In fact, he thought he still was on the flag track and had been told as much by superiors. Nevertheless, he figured his chances were narrowing. His decision to leave the operational fleet to join the public affairs office and later become academy athletic director certainly did not garner him any points. There also was the matter of the negative fitness report from Lieutenant Commander McGregor in his personnel file. But most detrimental was the fact that years earlier, while serving in the Bureau of Personnel, he had not attended Naval War College in Newport, Rhode Island, when he could have. He and Franny had just built a home in Annapolis and did not want to lose it. Also, Franny had suffered a minor stroke and was suffering bouts of depression. Slade believed another move would be too hard on her. As an alternative, he asked that he be allowed to attend either of the two other war colleges in Washington. But the request was turned down; the slots were filled. When Cutter made it clear he would not go to Rhode Island for the ten-month program that would lead to his master's degree, his detail officer was appalled, remarking, "Do you know what you're doing, Cutter?"

For the moment, Cutter put all that out of his mind and enjoyed life in Europe. The Cutters rented half of a magnificent villa owned by a wealthy Italian marquesa and marquis who had fallen on lean times. The home was staffed by a landscaper, a laundress, and a cook (all employed by the marquis). Slade and Franny enrolled their two children in the local American school where Slade Jr. soon learned to speak fluent Italian. The Cutters also traveled extensively in Europe.

The role of the Navy office in Naples was to build morale and persuade members of the North Atlantic Treaty Organization (NATO), to which the Sixth Fleet was attached, that the station was important militarily to the United States. There were six nations in NATO at the time —France, England, Italy, Greece, Turkey, and the United States. The naval attachés of all six nations often hosted each other at dinner parties in Naples. "It was fun. I enjoyed it socially," said Cutter. "I mean, you'd be invited to three cocktail parties a night, literally. You'd go to several cocktail parties a week, and everybody felt they had to entertain." NATO brought ancient enemies together—Greece and Turkey—in a relationship that amazed the Cutters.

> The Greek officer had a wife who was really a charmer, very intelligent, young, pretty and from Athens. All these Greeks, if they wanted to survive, they had to marry a wife with money, because they were getting about eighty dollars a month. So all the Greek women married to Greek officers were the cream of the crop of all the wives in NATO. So this gal had the Turk officer and his wife, Franny and me in her house for dinner. The Turk and the Greek hardly spoke to each other. They didn't dislike each other, but one was a Greek and the other a Turk and that was enough. The Greek became a good friend of mine and I finally asked him why he didn't talk to the Turk. He said, "Look. See the medals on my chest? Every one I got is for fighting the Turks." That's all he said.

Occasionally, dignitaries passed through, including President Kennedy and Vice President Lyndon Johnson, who were a study in contrasts. Johnson made a cursory inspection of NATO troops on his visit in 1961, then waded into a crowd of local officials to shake hands, a complete contravention of protocol. "I was so ashamed," said Slade. The vice president's wife gave a talk, and then his daughter, Lucy, got up and gave a talk. It was out of place. They're nice people and all that, but it was terrible because this was a very formal, dignified thing. Later we had a briefing where NATO officers from Greece and Turkey were to give Johnson top-secret information. They had the briefing all set and he didn't show up. Instead, he went out glad-handing the Neapolitans who gathered wherever there was anything going on just because they didn't have anything else to do. Then he ducked into his limousine with his wife and daughter and drove off. There's the briefing up there and no one to brief. Terrible."

Kennedy arrived months later at the height of the Berlin Crisis during which he made his famous "Ich bin ein Berliner" speech. On arrival in Naples, the president inspected the troops as Johnson had done. "He would stop before each one. He went through the thing just very properly," said Cutter who was part of the official greeting party. "And then when NATO had the briefing, he attended. He asked every briefer a question. And he knew the answer before he asked it. He knew more than they did about their job, but he was going through the motions of making them feel good. And I'll tell you, President Kennedy almost converted me to being a Democrat, which is unthinkable. I was real proud of him."

Cutter thought his last, best chance of making rear admiral was during that first year in Naples. But that hinged on the secret proceedings of the Navy selection board in Washington that met to promote eight captains to rear admiral. Unbeknownst to Slade, Admiral James S. Russell was president of the board. He was in Naples visiting Admiral Hannegan and attended a cocktail party hosted by the Cutters. The next morning, he flew to Washington to preside over the selections. There were eight hundred captains in the zone and the board had the records of all them. Board members quickly narrowed the field to one hundred. They voted that down to sixty-four, then thirty-two, then sixteen. Slade was still in the running. In the final vote to get the number to the required eight, it came down to either Cutter or Capt. William C. Abhau, a classmate of Slade's. When Cutter had command of the *Northampton,* Abhau was skipper of the cruiser *Helena.* In debating the merits of both men, the board looked for factors that might favor one over the other. They found it in the fact Cutter had not attended war college. Abhau had. The vote was taken. Abhau got the promotion.

Admiral Russell flew back to Naples and went to see Cutter. "This was very unusual, a four-star admiral coming to my office to extend his condolences and tell me what happened," said Slade. The admiral felt badly because he realized that it most certainly was Slade's last shot. Russell wanted him to know how close the vote was and that the deciding factor was War College—not the McGregor incident, nor his days in the information office, nor his service as athletic director. The admiral took Cutter step-by-step through the tortuous process. Cutter reacted as cheerily as possible but could not contain his bitterness. "Hell, admiral," he began, "that's the way it is, and I can understand that. I should have gone to War College too. Maybe if I had, then I'd have had a master's degree in political science, and it would have made the difference."

When the news got out that Slade had not been selected, he received a letter from his old friend Lewis Parks in Washington. "You'd better get out of there," he warned. "That's no place to be if you want to be promoted. You'd better come back to the Pentagon." Slade subsequently wrote to Admiral Smedberg, the former academy superintendent and now Chief of Naval Personnel, to seek a transfer. "The admiral wrote back very frankly and bluntly, saying nobody wanted me because I was too close to retirement. So I said to myself, 'Well, forget it.' And I stayed in Europe."

Cutter remained in Naples for another year before orders arrived transferring him to Commander Naval Training Center in Great Lakes, Illinois, in what was to become one of the happiest years of his Navy career.

The center, founded in 1911 at the direction of President Theodore Roosevelt, was like a vast college campus with a large campanile at its center. It was situated on the edge of Lake Michigan abutting Chicago's northern suburbs. It was the largest training facility of its kind in the world. During Cutter's tenure, Great Lakes trained eighty-one thousand students annually, mostly enlisted men. The school had a reputation of taking great care in molding its recruits. Of course, with so many passing through, misfits were inevitable. But even they were given a second chance in the school's retraining company. In Cutter's mind, the center tried hard to round out the rough edges and, for the most part, succeeded. "The emphasis was trying to salvage people, everything we did there," he said.

As commanding officer, Slade answered to Rear Admiral Howard A. "Red" Yeager, the colorful commandant of the Ninth Naval District, who had little, if anything, to do except convene staff meetings and give speeches. A primary mission of both Admiral Yeager and Cutter was maintaining the Navy's good image in the Chicago area. As Cutter had been in Naples, Cutter and Yeager were figureheads, the public liaison from the training center. "Red was trying to make a job out of nothing," said Cutter, "and he was always asking Franny and me to entertain visitors because he didn't want to be bothered. So Franny and I would have to throw the parties. The biggest problem with Red, however, were those calls for help with the admiral's garden. He'd say, 'Slade, those goddamned rabbits were eating my cabbage.' Or, 'Slade, those goddamned rabbits are eating my lettuce. What are you going to do about it?'" Yeager's pleas were more humorous than an annoyance. The admiral and the captain, in fact, became good friends through their love of golf and bowling.

After a year at Great Lakes and with Slade closing in on mandatory retirement after thirty years of service, he decided to put in for another billet as director of the museum at the Navy Historical Center in the Washington Navy Yard. It was suggested to him by Rear Admiral Ernest M. Eller, commanding officer of the center, who believed the museum was being mismanaged and needed a strong leader. For Cutter, becoming director would allow the Navy to extend his active duty another two years. Because he and his wife yearned to retire in Annapolis, taking the job would fulfill that dream as well. The couple purchased property during a visit and had a house built in the upscale Providence section of Annapolis. Simultaneously, Slade asked to be relieved at Great Lakes on 1 July 1965 and remained on active duty as director of the museum.

The repository, located in the former Breech Mechanism Shop of the old Naval Gun Factory, was packed haphazardly with rare Navy relics from all the nation's wars—from the Revolutionary War period through the Mexican-American War of 1846, the Civil War, the Spanish-American War, World War I, World War II, and the Korean War. Ship models, uniforms, ordnance, photographs, fine art, and military equipment abounded. Among the artifacts were Admiral Dewey's uniform, sword, and personal effects from the Spanish-American War, and the hut and equipment used on Rear Adm. Richard Byrd's exploration of the South Pole.

Cutter immediately set to work organizing the collection, bringing it out of mothballs, and planning the layout. An F4U-4 Corsair fighter plane and a Japanese Ohka bomber were suspended from rafters over the exhibits, many of them interactive. For instance, visitors could look through two working submarine periscopes, or stand on the recreated bridge of a Navy destroyer.

"My job was to coordinate the efforts of everybody, keep them happy, and get funds for them, and arrange for the visitors coming in to see the museum, and getting the museum ready," said Cutter. He soon turned the museum into one of the capital's most user-friendly galleries.

Six months into the job the Navy asked Cutter to step aside to create a billet for an excess of active duty captains. At that point, he did not mind, because the hour-long drive in heavy traffic from Annapolis was wearing him down. So at age fifty-three, he retired near the Naval Academy that he and Franny so dearly loved. Those hopes, however, soon changed when Franny's health began to falter. Because of the climate in Annapolis, she suffered frequent asthmatic attacks, making it impossible for her to remain. To save her life, Slade sold their home and the couple moved west to Tucson, Arizona, where the arid climate allowed Franny to recover. Cutter served for six years as headmaster of the Southern Arizona School for Boys, the only such prep school in the state. In 1962, Cutter was inducted as a charter member of the National College Football Hall of Fame in South Bend, Indiana.

Though Franny recovered from asthma, she developed high blood pressure. She also suffered from bouts of severe depression. "I had to be with her constantly, day and night," Slade explained. "I couldn't play golf. I couldn't even go swimming in the pool outside the entrance to our apartment because she was afraid I was going to drown, and she'd come out there and try to pull me out of the water when I'd get to the end of the pool."

As Franny's health declined, the couple relocated to San Antonio, Texas, to be near their daughter Anne and her family. Franny realized the end was coming, and urged her husband to remarry once she was gone. Her fondest hope was that he would marry her lifelong best friend, Ruth McCracken Buek. All through Slade's four years at the academy, Ruth "dragged" with Slade's best friend, "Dusty" Dornin. The foursome regularly double-dated. Slade and Franny became engaged at graduation, as did Ruth and Dusty. But two years of forced separation ended their romance. Though Ruth married another Navy man, she remained close to the Cutters. They often exchanged visits, and the Cutters regularly stayed with Ruth and her family when visiting Philadelphia for the annual Army-Navy football game.

Franny died in October 1981 and was buried in Annapolis. Afterwards Slade, who had been devoted to her for fifty years, was emotionally spent and in deep grief with no intention of ever remarrying. To help buoy his spirits, Anne suggested he drive to Philadelphia in his RV and purchase tickets to the 1981 Army-Navy game. She and her husband would fly up to join him. On arrival, Slade called Ruth, then a widow of eight years, and she invited him to park his motor home at her house in Villanova. Only Anne's husband flew up from Texas. Thus, he, Slade, and Ruth went to the game, a defensive struggle that ended in a 3–3 Army-Navy tie. Afterwards, Ruth's brother invited him to a posh Christmas party at the Philadelphia Country Club. "It was a few days later, so I stayed for it. In the meantime, I'm with Ruth all the time. I really didn't have any ideas about her, any design on her. We were just good friends. At the party, we danced and had a good time."

The night before he left for Texas, Slade questioned Ruth about her views on marriage. She said she would remarry under the right circumstances. "Then will you marry me?" Slade blurted. "Yes, but not now," she replied, figuring it was too early after Franny's death. Slade suggested a kiss. "It was the first time I had ever kissed her. Her lips were all puckered up, and I've always referred to that as the 'kitchen kiss,' because Ruth is a very proper person. Well, then the next day we went out through the garage to get to the motor home and I went to kiss Ruth goodbye, and then I got a reasonable kiss out of her. I felt more encouraged."

On the trip back and for days to come, Slade called Ruth regularly. And when his daughter booked passage for him on a trip to China with the Naval Academy alumni association, he asked Ruth to go with him. She agreed—as long as they got married. Though Slade was worried about how his children would react, the two kids knew of their mother's dying wish. Besides, said his son, "What the hell are you waiting for, Dad? You're seventy years old. You don't know how much time you've got left. Go ahead and marry her." Anne agreed. "Daddy, I think it's wonderful." The wedding was held on 12 January 1982—about three months after Franny's death—in Anne's home, with the honeymoon in China. Ruth's three children and Slade's son and daughter, all of whom had shared Christmas holidays together as kids, made up the wedding party.

Through the years to come, Ruth, an energetic woman of grace and dignity, became as devoted to Slade's well-being as he had been to Franny. They made frequent road trips, Ruth doing much of the driving. Eventually they visited every state in the continental United States plus northern Mexico and Canada.

Slade could look back on an amazing journey, one in which he had left an indelible mark on the Navy as an athlete and an officer with few peers, a man of action who left an obscure farm in Illinois to become a military legend.

23

Tilghman Island

THE DRIVE from his home in Annapolis in 1999 would take little more than an hour. But for Capt. Slade Cutter, the journey was to span a lifetime.

At age eighty-nine, he and his wife crossed the four-mile Chesapeake Bay Bridge, then headed south on Route 50 in the early autumn splendor of Maryland's pastoral Eastern Shore. She was at the wheel; Slade had long ago given up driving. He had been fighting Parkinson's disease, a stubborn battle with the degenerative disorder of aging that left him bowed but unbeaten. He remained a tall, husky man who walked with a swift, forceful gait. Daily, he swam fourteen laps of the Olympic pool at his life-care residence, a regimen that kept his body as fit as possible. "Something will get me but it won't be Parkinson's," he often boasted with the defiance that once characterized his command of a submarine.

The Cutters turned off the expressway where it crossed Route 32 and followed the highway west through the center of the peninsula that gradually curves to the south to the middle of the Chesapeake where it cups the mouth of the Choptank River in the Bay Hundred region. The couple passed through St. Michaels, the touristy seaport on the north side of the peninsula, and continued west another fourteen miles to a drawbridge over Knapp's Narrows. Beyond the mechanized span lay their destination, Tilghman Island, the sleepy home to generations of oyster fishermen.

Charted in 1608, the island is just four miles long, a mile wide, and perfectly flat. Yet it is a world unto itself, with a country store, a public school, a few restaurants, inns and guest homes, a bait and tackle shop, a few curio stores, a nautical book shop, and weathered homes and cottages. Tilghman is a workingman's island where crab pots are stacked haphazardly in front yards and just about everyone has a boat dry-docked, many in need of repair. Daybreak finds inhabitants sailing forth in a handful of Skipjacks, the last commercial fleet of tall ships in North America. Everything about the island evolves from its relationship with the bay and the ebb and flow of ancient cycles of life. In the spring and again in the fall, great migratory flights of Canada geese, Atlantic brant, black ducks, mallards, scaup, and bufflehead pass through. And for a few days, millions of monarch butterflies stop to feed in their epic journey between New England and the mountains of Mexico.

Crossing the drawbridge, the Cutters turned onto Coopertown Road and followed it a few blocks to the highly regarded Tilghman Island Inn. The twenty-room, two-story resort and its ornamental gardens overlook the narrows at its junction with the Chesapeake. The setting is magical, with broad canvasses of tidal marshlands and spectacular evening sunsets over the bay. The inn's ambassadors, a large black poodle and citron crested cockatiel, greeted the Cutters as they checked in. Soon, *Seahorse* shipmates from a lifetime ago began to arrive.

Electrician's Mate Sheldon Stubbs arrived with his family from their home in Portland, Oregon. Engineer Phillip Wilson and his wife Jan came from Merced, California. Bill Budding, the boyish ensign whose father built the *Seahorse,* drove down from his home in Mystic, Connecticut, as did electrician's mate Jim McGettigan and his wife Dorothy from North Wildwood, New Jersey. Former torpedomen Roland Lehman, from Fairbanks, Arkansas, and Charles Kovach, from Anna, Illinois, arrived by mid-afternoon, as did Betty Hoffman from Mariposa, California, and Natalie Lindon from Lake Park, Florida. Betty was the widow of Roy Hoffman, Cutter's indispensable sonar man; Natalie was the widow of "Spud" Lindon, the captain's executive officer.

These veterans were among the lucky submariners who made it

through World War II. Fifty-two submarines and more than three thousand officers and enlisted men never returned from war patrols. The *Seahorse* was one of the survivors—but just barely. After Slade left for new construction in August 1944, the submarine made three more war patrols, one skippered by "Weary" Wilkins who sank a single ship, and the last two under Lt. Cdr. H. H. Greer Jr. On the seventh patrol, he and his men were driven to the bottom, 470 feet down off the coast of Japan, where they endured forty-five accurate depth charges, one of the most severe beatings inflicted on any U.S. submarine. Yet the boat made it back home safely with no casualties. After the war, the Navy mothballed the submarine until it was sold in 1968 for $51,461 to an Oregon firm.

At the Tilghman Island Inn, Slade and Ruth Cutter basked in a late afternoon sun on the inn's tiki deck as boat traffic sputtered past within feet of them on Knapp's Narrows. Beyond, white egrets floated over the dreamy marshlands, a sanctuary for blue herons, ospreys, loons, and mallards that cavorted in gentle breezes. Slade, easing into a deck chair, talked of his retirement and his years with Ruth. Now, in the tranquility of the Tilghman Island Inn, they exuded love for one another. "A second wife can never replace the first one, nor can the second husband replace the first one," Slade reflected, Ruth at his side. "But they're good marriages where they're real good friends. That's the way Ruth and I are. I love her very much. I loved her before we were married. I loved her when I was married to Franny, as far as that goes—loving in the good sense of the word. And that's still our relationship. We have a lot of fun together."

In the gathering of old shipmates at the inn, poignant memories came flooding back on the expansive seaside deck. That evening the group celebrated at a banquet arranged by the owners of the inn. The veterans told old tales over a leisurely meal of Choptank oysters and Chesapeake soft-shell crabs. The grand dining was a celebration in honor of Slade Cutter, who sat at the head of the table. To a man, the veterans of the *Seahorse* believe the Navy has done their skipper a disservice by never advancing him in rank beyond captain. His achievements are the stuff of legend.

Outstanding athlete at the Naval Academy
Expert rifle marksman

Undefeated heavyweight intercollegiate boxing champion
All-American football tackle and place-kicker
Commander of two World War II submarines
Twenty-three enemy ships sunk
Four Navy Crosses
Two Silver Stars
A Bronze Star
A presidential unit citation
Nine battle stars for his submarine
Commander, Submarine Division 32
Commanding officer, Submarine Squadron Six
Commanding officer, Navy oil tanker *Neosho*
Commanding officer, command ship *Northampton*
Chief of Staff to Commander Striking Fleet, Atlantic
Commander, Great Lakes Naval Training Center

From the beginning of his career, Slade had made an impression. In the 1930s, his name conjured up awe in midshipmen who had never met him, people like Ned Beach, former Navy aide to President Eisenhower. "His was the first name we new midshipmen learned of the Navy we were now part of, and it carried fearsome inference. He was a holy terror who would rip us to bits if he caught us stepping out of line, pound us to pieces in the boxing ring, or mangle us into the mud on the football field. The tales were all we needed. They were awesome, and we believed them, every one."

Beach was never to serve with Cutter, but he got to know him during World War II. "In due course," he said, "I understood what it was about him that caused men to follow him eagerly wherever he wanted them to go. His crew idolized him, and so did everyone else who served with him, or near him." Foremost among them were the *Seahorse* veterans. "You know," said Ruth in an aside to her husband at the inn, "I think you're next to God in that crew, they think so highly of you."

Even those who couldn't make the reunion, *Seahorse* shipmates like lookout Jim O'Meara of Grants Pass, Oregon, sent regrets. "You sir," he wrote to Slade, "are a man who made waves with the Brass by doing your job as you felt it should be done. You accomplished the things you knew from experience would sink enemy ships, and you kept your men alive. You made sure they always came back from war patrol. Captain Cutter, you are a kind, humble, unheralded, brave man. This country today is badly in need of heroes. You sir, have been sadly overlooked."

Slade has always been philosophical about that, conceding it is difficult for anyone to figure out why he had not been promoted to flag rank. "I had four Navy Crosses and had been in good billets after the war. I had expected to be selected right after the war. Anybody with two or three Navy Crosses got promoted, no problem. But I believe that the Navy did the right thing. You're selected for flag rank based upon your potential as a flag officer, and that requires having been a student in one of the war colleges where you learn how to conduct yourself as a flag officer. It requires a wide basis of knowledge in a lot of different fields within the Navy. I didn't have that. I was a submariner."

Nevertheless, those who admire Slade and those familiar with the Navy's hierarchy shake their heads at the thought of all the Navy captains who had done far less in their careers and were selected. Among them was Slade's nemesis on the *Seahorse,* Commander Donald McGregor who retired as a "tombstone" rear admiral. Of the 465 U.S. submarine commanders of World War II, sixty made it to the rank of rear admiral, including Lewis Parks. A dozen made vice admiral. And three became full admirals including John Sidney McCain Jr., Commander in Chief, Pacific, who honored Slade by making him godfather to his son, future U.S. Senator John McCain whom Slade nurtured as a youth.

After the banquet, the *Seahorse* family retired for the night. The next morning the veterans boarded the *Lady Patty,* a forty-five-foot teakwood-and-brass ketch that once sailed between Hawaii and the British Virgin Islands. Craftsmen built it on a Chesapeake island in 1935, the year Slade graduated from the Naval Academy just across the bay. With the submariners topside, the twin-masted tall ship cast off, passed through the narrows, and sailed into the Choptank where Tilghman's Dogwood Harbor protected the Skipjacks including the oldest, the *Rebecca T. Ruark,* built in 1886. The *Lady Patty* cut a swath through white caps across the Choptank and into the Chesapeake. Standing amidships, Slade turned his cheek to the biting cold. He stood erect, wearing just a light jacket. His fellow submariners looked on, exhilarated to be together again at sea with their captain—like the old days when they ventured into the unknown, alone for thousands of miles where others disappeared without a trace.

Slade thought of his great-grandfather, Henry Clay Cutter, who made his own incredible journey on sailing ships from his home near Boston to the gold camps of California in 1849. That gamble earned enough to buy Slade's boyhood farm, making his life possible. In 1989, Slade and Ruth returned to what was left of the farm, sold many years earlier by the Cutter family. They visited the three-story farmhouse, still well-cared for, and the barn in back where Slade pointed to egg splatters still visible on the rafters where his brothers had hurled them in the 1920s. But across the road the verdant fields that once hugged the lazy Fox River were no more. Quarry companies had scraped the loam away to get at the underlying gravel, gouging holes and leaving piles of sterile detritus. It brought tears to Slade's eyes.

As the *Lady Patty* heeled and turned back toward the Choptank, Cutter considered the people and singular events in his early life that had such great consequence: attending the Severn dance with a date who jilted him, leaving him alone to meet his future wife Franny across the room; Paul Brown, coach of the football team at Severn School, who made Slade the football tackle who helped the lightly manned prep school become Maryland State high school champions in 1930; Navy boxing coach "Spike" Webb introducing himself by punching Slade in the stomach, and later teaching him courage, tenacity, and coolness under fire in the ring, lessons that carried over into the coming war. And Admiral Chester Nimitz Sr., whose refusal to accept Slade's resignation from the Navy after his marriage enabled Cutter to become the most formidable submarine skipper of World War II.

But beyond all these benchmarks, one single moment stood out: the day Mrs. Loomis drove up to the family farm in 1929 to suggest Slade attend the Naval Academy. Cutter still had a cherished memento from that time, a framed certificate that he'd carried with him for seventy years. It was an IOU, drawn up in Chicago for what then seemed like a king's ransom. "On demand after date for value received, I promise to pay to the order of Dudley S. Edwards six hundred dollars." It was enough money to get Slade Cutter into the Severn School. His father offered to sign it. But Edwards insisted that Slade bear the responsibility, which he did. And in his first year after graduation from the academy, he paid back in full the current interest and principal. On the reverse he had penciled in the increments: $130, $50, $5, $50, $102, $52, $6, $136, $3, $107. From that decision to attend Severn came the right man for the right time when the United States needed capable sailors to stem the enemy advance in the Pacific.

The *Lady Patty*, its sails in full bloom, bore a steady course, cradling the heroes of World War II and their beloved commander, who looked upon the kindly faces of older men he knew as teenagers. "I was the leader of a great group of young men eighteen to twenty-two years old who had volunteered for submarine duty and were eager to meet the enemy. I was thirty-one years old when I took command of the *Seahorse* and shared their enthusiasm."

A memory of childhood came into focus: "When I was a boy in Illinois, we had parades with old men who had been drummer boys in the Civil War fifty years earlier, marching with their drums and fifes and reminiscing about that war. That always meant a lot to me."

Now, squinting into the bright sunlight on the Chesapeake, his ruddy face marked by the passage of time, Capt. Slade Deville Cutter had become one of those old men. A revered warrior, fearless, determined, proud, loyal to his country and his Navy, bearing the mantle of courage passed to him as a boy from battlefield veterans of the Civil War. He carried that with him into World War II. And like the Civil War, it was a crusade.

> Everyone was eager to do his part. We knew why we were doing it—for our mothers, fathers, wives and sweethearts back home. We were a close-knit group, and every man aboard depended on his shipmates, whether they were an officer or enlisted. We didn't feel like we were heroes. We just had a job to do, and we did it as best we could, the way we were trained. It was never a one-man show, either. Everybody had an important job to do and there was very little margin for error.
>
> We sought harm's way, you know, and my crewmen wanted to do that. But they also wanted to come back. I brought them back.

The primary source of this book are many interviews conducted by the author with Slade Cutter at his home in Annapolis, at a relative's in Delran, New Jersey, and on Tilghman Island, Maryland, at a reunion of *Seahorse* veterans in 1999. The taped sessions augment biographical information drawn from Paul Stillwell, *Reminiscences of Captain Slade D. Cutter, USN (Ret.)*; Volumes I and II (Annapolis, Md.: U.S. Naval Institute Press, 1985); and Captain Pickett Lumpkin, USN Retired, *Interview with Captain Slade D. Cutter*, July 2, 1984, for the Institute of Texan Cultures Oral History Program. Also providing very useful anecdotal background is Dave Bouslog, *Maru Killer. The War Patrols of the USS Seahorse* (Sarasota, Fla.: Seahorse Books, 1996). For anyone beginning research on U.S. submarines during World War II, I recommend four studies: Clay Blair, *Silent Victory* (New York: Lippincott, 1975); Theodore Roscoe, *United States Submarine Operations in World War II* (Annapolis, Md.: U.S. Naval Institute Press, 1980); W. J. Holmes, *Underseas Victory I and II* (New York: Kensington Publishing, 1966); and Keith Wheeler, *War under the Pacific* (Alexandria, Va.: Time-Life Books, 1980).

Chapter 1. Test of Valor

My opening portrait of great peril on the *Pompano* off the coast of Japan is drawn from the submarine's third war patrol report (National Archives Microfilm Publications, 8601 Adelphi Road, College Park, Md. 20740-6001, M1752 *U.S. Submarine War Patrol Reports, 1941–45*, Fiche #659). Also insightful are Blair, *Silent Victory*; Roscoe, *United States Submarine Operations in World War II*; Stillwell, *Reminiscences*; and Lumpkin, *Interview with Captain Slade D. Cutter*. Information about coastal Japan in the area of where the *Pompano* was attacked comes from Stephanie Adler and Stephen Wolf, editors, *Fodor's Japan* (New York: Fodor's Travel Publications, 2000) and Chris Taylor, ed., *Japan* (Victoria, Australia: Lonely Planet Publications, 1997).

Chapter 2. The Man from Fox River

The story of Cutter's great grandfather during the California Gold Rush comes from Slade F. Cutter, "A Story of the Adventures of Henry Clay Cutter in the California Gold Rush" (Arlington, Mass.: Arlington Historical Society, November 28, 1927). Details of the S-4 tragedy come from my previous book,

Back from the Deep (Annapolis, Md.: U.S. Naval Institute Press, 1992) and Edwin P. Hoyt, *Submarines at War* (New York: Stein and Day, 1983). Interesting background on John Philip Sousa is found in Paul E. Bierley, *John Philip Sousa—American Phenomenon,* 2d ed. (Westerville, Ohio: Integrity Press, 1973). The history of the Fox River is drawn from Tim Palmer, *America by Rivers* (Washington, D.C.: Island Press, 1996) and R. Conrad Stein, *America the Beautiful: Illinois* (Chicago: Regensteiner Publishing, 1987).

Chapter 3. The Six-Hundred-Dollar Tryout

My taped interviews with Slade Cutter and Stillwell, *Reminiscences* provide the basis for this chapter.

Chapter 4. Severn

Background for this chapter comes from a visit to Severn School, my interview with Slade Cutter, and "The History of Severn School" on the Internet at www.severnschool.com (last accessed January 2003). Additional information is drawn from Jack Clary, *PB: The Paul Brown Story* (New York: Atheneum, 1975).

Chapter 5. Annapolis

Background on the academy comes from Jack Sweetman, *The U.S. Naval Academy: An Illustrated History,* 2d ed. (Annapolis, Md.: U.S. Naval Institute Press, 1995). The book is heavily illustrated and filled with interesting anecdotes about the academy, its history and traditions, both good and bad. Background on the sports and academic programs at Annapolis during Slade's first three years is drawn from the academy's yearbook, *The Lucky Bag, 1932–1934,* available at the Nimitz Library at the school. Information about the Cord automobile that figures in the opening vignette of this chapter is drawn from *The American Automobile: A Centenary 1893–1993* (New York: Smithmark Publishers, 1992).

Chapter 6. Whataman

My portrait of the middie training cruise to Europe in the summer of 1934 is drawn from the academy's *Lucky Bag* 1935 yearbook, available at the Nimitz Library. The yearbook provides a wealth of information about the sports programs in Cutter's fourth year. Regarding the Army-Navy game, I relied on game coverage by Lynn C. Doyle in *The Evening Bulletin,* Philadelphia, December 1 and 3, 1934, and by Edward J. Neil of the Associated Press.

Chapter 7. Turning Point

Valuable background on Navy protocol between officers comes from Vice Admiral William P. Mack and Lieutenant Commander Royal W. Connell, *Naval Ceremonies, Customs, and Traditions* (Annapolis, Md.: U.S. Naval Institute Press, 1980). Also my characterization of Captain Hyman Rickover's competitiveness aboard the battleship *New Mexico* is drawn from Norman Polmar and Thomas A. Allen, *Rickover* (New York: Simon & Schuster, 1985).

Chapter 8. Harum Scarum

My description of the submarine training school, its history, and its methods is drawn from my previous book, *Back from the Deep*. My understanding of the development of World War II submarines comes from Charles A. Lockwood, *Down to the Sea in Subs* (New York: W. W. Norton, 1967) and Larry Kimmett and Margaret Regis, *U.S. Submarines in World War II. An Illustrated History* (Kingston, Wash.: Navigator Publishing, 1996). I drew background on the growing hostility between Japan and the United States from Robert W. Love Jr., *History of the U.S. Navy*, vols. 1 and 2 (Harrisburg, Pa.: Stackpole Books, 1992) and Paul S. Dull, *A Battle History of the Imperial Japanese Navy (1941–1945)* (Annapolis, Md.: U.S. Naval Institute Press, 1978).

Chapter 9. Parks

The problems with the Hooven-Owens-Rentschler diesel engines installed in the *Pompano* and other boats are treated extensively in Blair, *Silent Victory*, and Roscoe, *United States Submarine Operations in World War II*. For anyone interested in World War II fleet submarines and their design, Richard Huble and Mark Bergin, *Inside Story: A World War Two Submarine* (New York: Peter Bedrick Books, 1991) is indispensable. In terms of the evolution of military submarines, particularly in the United States, I drew from Brayton Harris, *The Navy Times Book of Submarines: A Political, Social and Military History* (New York: Berkley Publishing Group, 1997). An historical analysis of Navy policy in regard to the Pacific is contained in Love, *History of the U.S. Navy*, vols. 1 and 2. Information about the Mare Island Naval Shipbuilding Yard is drawn from Lieutenant Commander Arnold S. Lott, *A Long Line of Ships* (Annapolis, Md.: U.S. Naval Institute Press, 1954). My portrait of Rear Admiral Lewis Parks comes from Stillwell, *Reminiscences,* my interviews with Slade Cutter, and biographical information provided by Beverly Lyall, archives technician, Nimitz Library, including an obituary, a newspaper article about the admiral, and an article about submarine warfare written by Admiral Lewis Parks ("Submarines in the War," *Army-Navy Journal,* 1942). Information about Japanese Zero fighters comes from "The Mitsubishi Zero—Zero-Sen," available at www.concentric.net/˜7Etwist/airwar/zero/ (accessed April 2002). The prelude to the attack on Pearl Harbor, seen from the submarine command's point of view, comes from Lockwood, *Down to the Sea in Subs.* The cracking of the Japanese Naval Code by U.S. cryptographers is discussed in detail in Peter Calvocoressi, *Top Secret Ultra* (New York: Pantheon, 1980). Also useful in this chapter and subsequent accounts of Cutter's seven war patrols are letters he wrote to his wife Franny.

Chapter 10. War Patrol

The cataclysmic damage done to Pearl Harbor in Japan's surprise attack and a summary of the Battle of Midway come from Dan Van der Vat, *The Pacific Campaign, World War II. The U.S.-Japanese Naval War 1941–1945* (New York: Simon & Schuster, 1991) and Harry A. Gailey, *The War in the Pacific: From Pearl Harbor to Tokyo Bay* (Novato, Calif.: Presidio Press, 1995). The core of the chapter is drawn from personal interviews with *Seahorse* veterans; Stillwell, *Reminiscences;* Bouslog, *Maru Killer;* and the first and second war patrol report of the *Pompano* (National Archives, Fiche #659).

Chapter 11. The Hooligan Boat

Problems with the depth setting and magnetic features of the Navy's heralded Mark XIV torpedoes produced one of the great scandals of the underseas war. There has been much written about the issue. For my purposes, I drew information from Love, *History of the U.S. Navy;* Roscoe, *United States Submarine Operations in World War II;* Holmes, *Underseas Victory;* Lockwood, *Down to the Sea in Subs;* Blair, *Silent Victory;* and Wheeler, *War under the Pacific.* What happened during the *Pompano's* near disastrous third war patrol comes from the formal report of its third war patrol obtained on microfiche (National Archives, Fiche #659); Stillwell, *Reminiscences;* personal interviews with Slade Cutter; and Lumpkin, *Interview with Slade D. Cutter.* Also useful is an article in *Naval History* magazine ("Parks and the *Pompano*" by Captain Slade D. Cutter, April 1987) and a particularly colorful account of the *Pompano's* first patrol written by Cutter with Don Eddy for *The American Magazine* during the war.

Chapter 12. Schism on the *Seahorse*

Most of this chapter comes from personal interviews with Slade Cutter; correspondence between Cutter and his wife Franny; Stillwell, *Reminiscences;* the formal report of the *Seahorse's* first war patrol obtained from Slade Cutter but also available on microfiche from the National Archives; Lumpkin; *Interview with Slade D. Cutter;* and Bouslog, *Maru Killer.* The discussion of the "skipper problem" comes from my previous book, *Back from the Deep;* Roscoe, *Submarine Operations in World War II;* Blair, *Silent Victory;* and Wheeler, *War under the Pacific.*

Chapter 13. Pangs of Conscience

The *Seahorse's* second war patrol report provides the basis for this chapter, as well as personal interviews; Stillwell, *Reminiscences;* Lumpkin, *Interview with Captain Slade D. Cutter;* Bouslog, *Maru Killer;* and correspondence between Captain Cutter and his wife. Love, *History of the U.S. Navy,* provides the larger view of how the *Seahorse's* mission fit into the overall military campaign in the Central Pacific.

Chapter 14. The Chase

The *Seahorse's* third war patrol report provides the core of this chapter, with embellishment through my interviews; Stillwell, *Reminiscences;* Lumpkin, *Interview with Captain Slade D. Cutter;* Roscoe, *U.S. Submarine Operations of World War II;* Blair, *Silent Victory;* and Bouslog, *Maru Killer.*

Chapter 15. Ordeal off Saipan

The *Seahorse's* fourth war patrol report provides the basis for this chapter, with supporting material from personal interviews; Stillwell, *Reminiscences;* Lumpkin, *Interview with Captain Slade D. Cutter;* and Bouslog, *Maru Killer.* I drew from Love, *History of the U.S. Navy,* and Rafael Steinberg, *Island Fighting* (New York: Time-Life Books, 1978) for overall military strategy.

Chapter 16. Down Under

My portrait of Brisbane and the feud between the Navy and the Army comes from Blair, *Silent Victory;* Roscoe, *U.S. Submarine Operations of World War II;* personal interviews with Slade Cutter; Stillwell, *Reminiscences;* Lumpkin, *Interview with Captain Slade D. Cutter;* and Bouslog, *Maru Killer.* Background on Brisbane in the 1940s is drawn from Bruce Brander et al., *Australia* (Washington, D.C.: National Geographic Society, 1968), an excellent and atmospheric narrative; Zoe Ross, *Australia. Dorling Kindersley Travel Guides* (New York: Dorling Kindersley, 2000), which includes a heavily illustrated guide to Brisbane; and Marael Johnson and Andrew Hempstead, *Australia Handbook* (Emeryville, Calif.: Avalon Travel Publishing, 2000), which provides excellent historical highlights but sparse illustrations.

Chapter 17. One in Five?

The *Seahorse's* fifth war patrol report provides the basis for this chapter, with supporting material from personal interviews; Stillwell, *Reminiscences;* Lumpkin, *Interview with Captain Slade D. Cutter;* and Bouslog, *Maru Killer.* My characterization of the Battle of the Philippine Seas comes from Blair, *Silent Victory;* Roscoe, *U.S. Submarine Operations of World War II;* Lockwood, *Down to the Sea in Subs;* and Love, *History of the U.S. Navy.*

Chapter 18. McGregor's Time Bomb

Captain Cutter's war record and awards come from his official U.S. Navy biography provided to me by Paul Stillwell. The *Seahorse* being credited with two more sinkings to bring its total to twenty-three comes from the *Seahorse* newsletter, June 2000, citing JANAC information. The final tally of the submarine offensive against Japan and the cost of that war is drawn from Blair, *Silent Victory,* and Roscoe, *U.S. Submarine Operations of World War II.* My profile of Slade's early postwar career and his discovery of a negative fitness report placed in his file by Captain McGregor comes from personal interviews and Stillwell, *Reminiscences.*

Chapter 19. The *Nautilus* Affair

My characterization of Slade's tour of duty in the Naval Information Office is drawn from personal interviews and Stillwell, *Reminiscences.* In addition, Stanley Kramer's autobiography, *A Mad Mad Mad Mad World: A Life in Hollywood* (New York: Harcourt Brace, 1997) details the producer's difficulties with the Navy in producing the motion picture, *The Caine Mutiny* (1954). The background on the development of a nuclear submarine and Admiral Rickover's role in it comes from Lockwood, *Down to the Sea in Subs;* Theodore Rockwell, *The Rickover Effect. How One Man Made a Difference* (Annapolis, Md.: U.S. Naval Institute Press, 1992); and Polmar, *Rickover.* Slade Cutter's involvement in the diesel vs. atomic subs controversy is drawn from "Atomic Submarine set for launching" (*New York Times*, January 17, 1954, 6); "Atomic Submarine only a 'test' craft" (*New York Times*, January 4, 1954, 7); "The Man in Tempo 3" (*Time*, January 11, 1954, 36); and "Full Speed Astern" (*Time*, January 18, 1954).

Chapter 20. New London

The core of this chapter is drawn from personal interviews and Stillwell, *Reminiscences*. The description of the launch of the *Nautilus* and details about its shakedown cruise are drawn from Polmar, *Rickover*, and Commander William R. Anderson and Clay Blair Jr., *Nautilus 90 North* (New York: Tab Books, 1989).

Chapter 21. The War with Erdelatz

Besides personal interviews and Stillwell, *Reminiscences*, background on Coach Erdelatz's tenure at the Naval Academy comes from Sweetman, *The U.S. Naval Academy: An Illustrated History*; and "Sinking the Navy?" (*Newsweek*, April 20, 1959) concerning Erdelatz's ouster as coach.

Chapter 22. In the Zone

Stillwell, *Reminiscences* and personal interviews with Slade Cutter provide the primary background for this chapter. In addition, I consulted the following for background on the Bay of Pigs invasion: Arthur M. Schlesinger Jr., *A Thousand Days: John F. Kennedy in the White House* (Boston: Houghton Mifflin, 1965); Thomas C. Reeves, *A Question of Character: A Life of John F. Kennedy* (New York: Dorling Kindersley, 2000), which provides an excellent discussion of the planning of the Bay of Pigs landing and its aftermath; Richard Reeves, *President Kennedy: Profile of Power* (New York: Touchstone, 1993); and Nigel Hamilton, *JFK: Reckless Youth* (New York: Random House, 1992), which discusses Kennedy's Addison's Disease. The President's denial of any intention to provide air support for the Cuban invaders comes from "Exclusive Interview with the Attorney General: Robert Kennedy Speaks His Mind" (*U.S. News & World Report*, 28 January 1963, 61–62) and "Setting the Record Straight: What 'U.S. News & World Report' Said About Air Support of the Bay of Pigs" and "Air Cover— What President Kennedy Says" (*U.S. News & World Report*, 4 February 1963, 1). Information on the Great Lakes Training Center and the Naval Historical Center is available at www.ntcyl.navy.mil/ and www.history.navy.mil/nhcl.htm, respectively (accessed January 2002).

Chapter 23. Tilghman Island

My characterization of the reunion of *Seahorse* veterans on Tilghman Island comes from attending that gathering in the fall of 1999. In addition, I drew on "Slade Cutter: Captain, U.S. Navy—A Leader of Men," an unpublished introduction to Bouslog, *Maru Killer,* by Edward L. Beach.

Pamphlets

Cutter, Slade F. "A Story of the Adventures of Henry Clay Cutter in the California Gold Rush." Arlington, Mass.: Arlington Historical Society, 28 November 1927.

Magazines

Cutter, Slade, with Don Eddy. "We Raid the Coast of Japan," *American Magazine*, [n.d.], 26–27, 94–98.

"Exclusive Interview with the Attorney General: Robert Kennedy Speaks His Mind," *U.S. News & World Report,* 28 January 1963, 61–62.

"Setting the Record Straight: What 'U.S. News & World Report' Said About Air Support of the Bay of Pigs" and "Air Cover—What President Kennedy Says," *U.S. News & World Report,* 4 February 1963, 31.

Books

Primary Sources

Kimmett, Larry, and Margaret Regis. *U.S. Submarines in World War II. An Illustrated History.* Kingston, Wash.: Navigator Publishing, 1996.

Love, Robert W., Jr. *History of the U.S. Navy.* Vol. 2, *1942–1991.* Harrisburg, Pa.: Stackpole Books, 1992.

Miller, Nathan. *The U.S. Navy: An Illustrated History.* Annapolis, Md.: U.S. Naval Institute Press and American Heritage Publishing, 1977.

Steinberg, Rafael, and the Editors of Time-Life Books. *Island Fighting.* New York: Time-Life Books, 1978.

Sweetman, Jack. *The U.S. Naval Academy: An Illustrated History,* 2d ed. Annapolis, Md.: U.S. Naval Institute Press, 1995.

Secondary Sources

Adler, Stephanie, and Stephen Wolf, eds. *Fodor's Japan.* New York: Fodor's Travel Publications, 2000.

Brander, Bruce, Mary Ann Harrell, and Hector Holthouse. *Australia*. Washington, D.C.: National Geographic Society, 1968.

Dirks, Tim. Review of *The Caine Mutiny*. Available at www.greatestfilms.org (accessed April 2002).

Dull, Paul S. *A Battle History of the Imperial Japanese Navy (1941–1945)*. Annapolis, Md.: U.S. Naval Institute Press, 1978.

Gailey, Harry A. *The War in the Pacific: From Pearl Harbor to Tokyo Bay*. Novato, Calif.: Presidio Press, 1995.

Georgano, Nick. *The American Automobile: A Centenary 1893–1993*. New York: Smithmark Publishers, 1992.

Hamilton, Nigel. *JFK: Reckless Youth*. New York: Random House, 1992.

Harris, Brayton. *The Navy Times Book of Submarines: A Political, Social and Military History*. New York: Berkley, 1997.

Humble, Richard, and Mark Bergin. *Inside Story: A World War Two Submarine*. New York: Peter Bedrick Books, 1991.

Johnson, Marael, and Andrew Hempstead. *Australia Handbook*. Emeryville, Calif.: Avalon Travel Publishing, 2000.

Kramer, Stanley. *A Mad Mad Mad Mad World: A Life in Hollywood*. New York: Harcourt Brace, 1997.

LaVO, Carl. *Back from the Deep: The Strange Story of the Sister Subs Squalus and Sculpin*. Annapolis, Md.: U.S. Naval Institute Press, 1994.

Mack, Vice Admiral William P., and Lieutenant Commander Royal W. Connell. *Naval Ceremonies, Customs, and Traditions*. Annapolis, Md.: U.S. Naval Institute Press, 1980.

Market House Books, eds. *The Bantam Medical Dictionary*. 2d Revised Ed. New York: Bantam Books, 1994.

Palmer, Tim. *America by Rivers*. Washington, D.C.: Island Press, 1996.

Reeves, Richard. *President Kennedy: Profile of Power*. New York: Touchstone, 1993.

Reeves, Thomas C. *A Question of Character: A Life of John F. Kennedy*. New York: Free Press, 1991.

Ross, Zoe. *Australia. Dorling Kindersley Travel Guides*. New York: Dorling Kindersley, 2000.

Schlesinger, Arthur M., Jr. *A Thousand Days: John F. Kennedy in the White House*. Boston: Houghton Mifflin, 1965.

Stein, R. Conrad. *America the Beautiful: Illinois*. Chicago: Regensteiner Publishing, 1987.

Taylor, Chris, ed. *Japan*. Victoria, Australia: Lonely Planet, 1997.

Van der Vat, Dan. *The Pacific Campaign, World War II. The U.S.-Japanese Naval War 1941–1945*. New York: Simon & Schuster, 1991.

Walker, John, ed. *Halliwell's Film & Video Guide*. Revised and Updated. New York: Harper Perennial, 1999.

ABOUT THE AUTHOR

Carl LaVO is associate editor of the *Bucks County Courier Times* newspaper in Levittown, Pennsylvania. He is the author of *Back from the Deep, The Strange Story of the Sister Subs Squalus and Sculpin* (Naval Institute Press, 1994) and has contributed stories to *Proceedings, Naval History,* and many other periodicals. In 2001 he appeared in the History Channel's four-part series, *Silent Service,* to discuss the story of *Squalus* and *Sculpin,* and in 2002 he was the guest of honor at the last reunion of *Squalus* crew members at the Portsmouth Naval Shipyard in Kittery, Maine. A graduate of the University of Florida with postgraduate studies at Pennsylvania State University, LaVO resides in Bucks County with his wife, Mary Anne, who is a photojournalist. His daughter Genevieve is a professional graphic designer, studio artist, and photographer.

The Naval Institute Press is the book-publishing arm of the U.S. Naval Institute, a private, nonprofit, membership society for sea service professionals and others who share an interest in naval and maritime affairs. Established in 1873 at the U.S. Naval Academy in Annapolis, Maryland, where its offices remain today, the Naval Institute has members worldwide.

Members of the Naval Institute support the education programs of the society and receive the influential monthly magazine *Proceedings* and discounts on fine nautical prints and on ship and aircraft photos. They also have access to the transcripts of the Institute's Oral History Program and get discounted admission to any of the Institute-sponsored seminars offered around the country.

The Naval Institute also publishes *Naval History* magazine. This colorful bimonthly is filled with entertaining and thought-provoking articles, first-person reminiscences, and dramatic art and photography. Members receive a discount on *Naval History* subscriptions.

The Naval Institute's book-publishing program, begun in 1898 with basic guides to naval practices, has broadened its scope to include books of more general interest. Now the Naval Institute Press publishes about one hundred titles each year, ranging from how-to books on boating and navigation to battle histories, biographies, ship and aircraft guides, and novels. Institute members receive significant discounts on the Press's more than eight hundred books in print.

Full-time students are eligible for special half-price membership rates. Life memberships are also available.

For a free catalog describing Naval Institute Press books currently available, and for further information about subscribing to *Naval History* magazine or about joining the U.S. Naval Institute, please write to:

Membership Department
U.S. Naval Institute
291 Wood Road
Annapolis, MD 21402-5034
Telephone: (800) 233-8764
Fax: (410) 269-7940
Web address: www.navalinstitute.org